THE NEW COMPLETE
LHASA APSO

BIS Ch. Licos Kulu La, winner of four all-breed Bests in Show, Kulu La was and still is considered by many authorities the epitome of the breed. He was bred and owned by Grace Licos and handled to his show ring record by Maxine Beam. *Joan Ludwig*

THE NEW COMPLETE
LHASA APSO

Norman & Carolyn Herbel

BOOK HOUSE

New York

Maxwell Macmillan Canada
Toronto

Maxwell Macmillan International
New York   Oxford   Singapore   Sydney

Howell Book House
Macmillan Publishing Company
866 Third Avenue
New York, NY 10022

Maxwell Macmillan Canada, Inc.
1200 Eglinton Avenue East
Suite 200
Don Mills, Ontario M3C 3N1

Macmillan Publishing Company is part of the Maxwell Communication Group of Companies.

Library of Congress Cataloging-in-Publication Data

Herbel, Norman.
    The new complete lhasa apso/Norman and Carolyn Herbel.
        p.   cm.
    Rev. ed. of: The complete lhasa apso. 1979.
    ISBN 0-87605-233-2
    1. Lhasa apsos. I. Herbel, Carolyn. II. Herbel, Norman.
    Complete lhasa apso. III. Title.
    SF429.L5H47   1992
    636.7′2—dc20   91-33286
                        CIP

Macmillan books are available at special discounts for bulk purchases for sales promotions, premiums, fund-raising, or educational use. For details, contact:

                        Special Sales Director
                        Macmillan Publishing Company
                        866 Third Avenue
                        New York, NY 10022

10 9 8 7 6 5 4 3 2 1

Printed in the United States of America

This book is dedicated to the Tibetan people who have developed this breed we know as the Lhasa Apso; to the foundation breeders who imported them from Tibet and pioneered their propagation; to the breeders who have preserved and protected this breed since it was exiled from its country of origin and especially to the breeders of today who are preserving and cultivating our beloved breed so that it can live on in the free world.

BIS Ch. Hamilton Torma with Mrs. Randolph Scott (Mrs. Stillman's daughter), a study in glamour.

Contents

Carolyn Herbel

Norman Herbel

About the Authors

NORMAN AND CAROLYN HERBEL, native-born Kansans now living in Oklahoma, have successfully raised animals most of their lives.

A graduate of the University of Kansas, Mr. Herbel, now retired, was a coach and teacher as well as a breeder of registered Hereford cattle, with particular emphasis on an inbred strain developed by the United States Range and Livestock Research stations.

While the Herbels were attending the University of Kansas in 1957 they acquired their first registered dog, a German Shepherd named Tabu, a name that was to become celebrated in future years as the Herbels' highly successful prefix that would be carried also by champion English Setters, Cairn Terriers, Smooth Fox Terriers and, of course, Lhasa Apsos.

Lhasa Apsos first attracted the Herbels' attention at the 1959 Heart of America Kennel Club show in Kansas City, and they later elected to concentrate on the breed after moving to the Philadelphia, Pennsylvania, area.

No biography about the authors would be complete without including the three children, now adults, who have contributed greatly to the success of Tabu.

The Herbels' daughter, Carmen, was actively involved in Junior Showmanship as well as Conformation. Carmen, who has a Bachelor of Science degree in nursing, is married to Max Spears and together they breed and exhibit several breeds including Tabu Lhasa Apsos.

Kent, the Herbels' son, was involved in Junior Showmanship to some extent, but has contributed most to the Tabu success with his kennel management skills. An expert horseman and cattleman, he is married to his high school sweetheart, Lori. Kent and Lori have two young daughters, Lacey and Kelli, who represent a third generation of avid dog fanciers. Kent and Lori breed Australian Cattle Dogs as well as training herding dogs for ranch work and trials, and are actively involved in the new AKC herding program.

In 1969, Carmen's school chum, Nancy Clarke, came to work in the Herbels' kennel in Pennsylvania. This employment developed into what was to become a lifetime involvement with Lhasa Apsos and a permanent relationship with the Herbel family. When the Herbels returned to Kansas in 1975, Nancy moved with them and is considered a daughter by the Herbels. Nancy is married to Jim Plunkett and now living in Greencastle, Pennsylvania, where she is actively breeding Lhasa Apsos with the Tabu prefix under the guidance of the Herbels.

The authors have both held important positions in the American Lhasa Apso Club. Mr. Herbel is a past president and board member. He has also served as the Futurity chairman, having developed the present format as well as having developed and edited the original magazine-style *The Lhasa Bulletin*, ALAC's official publication. Mr. Herbel presently serves the club as the breed Standard committee chairman and the judges' education coodinator.

Mrs. Herbel has served the club as secretary as well as an unprecedented seven terms as president, and is presently serving the club as treasurer.

Both Norman and Carolyn Herbel are AKC-approved judges of Lhasa Apsos as well as other breeds. Mr. Herbel judges primarily working and herding breeds, while Mrs. Herbel judges Non-Sporting dogs, Toys and Terriers.

The impressive, continuous success of the Tabu Lhasa Apsos is a matter of record. Combining a natural ability with animals and an understanding and appreciation of the special entity that is a Lhasa Apso, the Herbels have owned and bred many of the finest ever seen in competition. Their most far-reaching contribution to the breed, *The Complete Lhasa Apso*, provides a valuable reference for all who are drawn to the Lhasa Apso's distinctive charm. It is a book written for lovers of the breed by lovers of the breed *in* the breed.

What makes the Lhasa Apso special and the expertise the Herbels have gathered over the years are in the pages to follow. Read, enjoy and learn.

Acknowledgments

We WISH to express our heartfelt gratitude to our children: Lori and Kent Herbel for the computer hours they put into the final draft of this book, Nancy Plunkett for the illustrations and Carmen and Max Spears for their help in proofreading.

We are especially thankful to all the fanciers who, over the years, have contributed to our extensive library of Lhasa Apso data.

We are indebted to the American Kennel Club librarians who have dug in the archives to get answers to our questions and have always been responsive to our needs. Also unquestionably helpful was the Library of Congress.

We wish to thank the Register of Merit breeders who generously responded to our request for information and photographs representing their breeding programs.

We sincerely thank Valerie Stringer and Gay Widdrington for the information they provided about England; Elizabeth Luck for her contribution for both England and New Zealand; Frances Sefton for her Australian update; Karin Handrick and Gerti Bracksieck for collecting the European and Scandinavian information; Marianne von Rauschenberger and Carsten Stage for the Danish data; André Cuny for the French update and Jill Laylin for the South African coverage.

Our thanks to the Canadian breeders Arlene Miller, Neil Graves and Ann-Marie Adderly for collecting the breeders' information for their country and always being there to answer our questions.

We are indebted to Dr. Catherine Marley for the "Hubert Notes."

We are grateful to Barbara Trujillo, whose continued search for the truth encouraged us to keep digging through old records.

We appreciate the help from Brenda Schmelzel, ALAC Obedience chairman, who provided us with information for the Obedience chapter from the ALAC records. We are especially thankful to Janine Grinta for unselfishly sharing the many pages of statistical information she compiled, listing all Obedience titlists.

We are indebted to you all for helping us make this book truly *The New Complete Lhasa Apso*.

THE NEW COMPLETE
LHASA APSO

Norbulingka Palace as photographed by Dr. Robert Berndt during his 1986 trip to Tibet.
Courtesy of Dr. Robert Berndt

The Potala—the Dalai Lama's palace prior to the Chinese takeover and the building of modern
Lhasa at the foot of the monastery. *Courtesy of the Office of Tibet*

1

Origin and History of the Lhasa Apso

THE LHASA APSO comes from the mountains and high plateaus of Tibet, a country often called The Roof of the World. The history of the breed is as elusive and mystical as the history of the people with whom it originated. The geographical, political and cultural isolation of the Tibetan people has resulted in only scattered information regarding them reaching the rest of the world.

TIBET

Tibet lies in a remote section of south-central Asia contiguous to India, China, Siberia, Mongolia and Sinkiang. It is a country of high plateaus and mountainous terrain with severe winter weather. In the southern part of the Tibetan plateau the snowy Himalayas rise higher than any other mountain chain in the world. Mount Everest, rising 29,028 feet, is the most famous summit in the Himalayas. The Great Snowy Mountains on the eastern border reach heights of over 25,250 feet. On the north and northwest, the peaks of the Kunlun range rise almost as high. The average elevation of Tibet is 16,000 feet above sea level.

Lhasa, the principal and capital city, is about 12,000 feet above sea level. Its extremes of weather include violent winds with basically low temperatures in the winter and hot, dusty daytimes in the summer. Altitude acclimatization is necessary for the jet-age traveler flying into Tibet. The overland traveler adjusts more easily because of the gradual increase in altitude. In 1976, when an American delegation visited Lhasa, the members were screened for their physical capacity to withstand the rigors of high elevation. Those who were permitted to go were supplied with oxygen masks and required to take rests along the way. Truly, Tibet is the roof of the world.

The city of Lhasa was also the center of the Tibetan religion. The "Potala," palace of the Dalai Lama, rose over 700 feet above the city. The summer palace, the "Norbulingka," was also located in Lhasa. The Tibetans are intensely religious people following the beliefs of Tibetan Buddhism. The Dalai Lama was the spiritual and temporal leader of the country. The present Dalai Lama, the fourteenth, now lives in exile in India.

In 1904, the British extended their influence in Asia and signed a trade treaty with the Tibetans. Thus in the early and middle 1900s there were many English-speaking visitors to Tibet who later wrote their observations. Other Europeans wrote of their visits in their languages. However, Americans generally did not have much access to information regarding Tibet. Only scholars and adventurers were aware of the isolated, mysterious land.

No one knows how many people have lived in Tibet at any one time in history. The twentieth-century figures vary from 6 million down to 2 million and now to 1.7 million under the current Chinese administration. This last figure reflects the 1976 number of pure Tibetans. An additional 300,000 Chinese now live in Tibet.

From 1959, when the fourteenth Dalai Lama fled from Tibet into India, until recent years the Chinese Communist government banned foreign travel to Tibet. On rare occasions since 1975 foreign dignitaries, including Han Suyin, Neville Maxwell, James Schlesinger and Lowell Thomas, have been permitted limited stays in Tibet, and more recently tourist travel has been allowed. Since the 1959 Chinese takeover of Tibet, over 100,000 Tibetans have sought refuge throughout the world.

Before Chinese control, one fifth of the population were monks or lamas who lived in monasteries supported principally by their land ownership incomes and private donations. Many of the monasteries had amassed great wealth in land. The balance of the population included poor farmers, nomads, small shopkeepers, traders, merchants and a few very wealthy landowners.

During the relatively short span of years between 1904 and 1959, the Lhasa Apso as we know it today became popular in other countries of the world. While there has been considerable conjecture as to the origin of the Lhasa Apso, there is not sufficient fact to warrant indulging in discussion of the various theories. All that is known is that it is a small, long-haired companion dog of ancient origin from the country of Tibet.

THE TIBETAN PEOPLE

Since there is so little written history of Tibet available to the Western world, we must develop an understanding of its people and through them the Lhasa Apso.

2

Jokhung Square with the Jokhung Temple in the background, photographed in 1986.
Courtesy of Dr. Robert Berndt

In Tibet, a monk with a treasure in his arms—a Lhasa Apso
Courtesy of André Cuny

3

Tibetans, often called the Hermit People, enjoyed the confinement of the natural barriers of altitude, climate and rugged terrain as protection against foreigners. They feared that outsiders would oppress them. Hence, they rebuffed outside efforts to develop trade relationships.

Initially Tibetans were wary of strangers until they learned that neither their persons nor way of life was threatened. During the initial contact they were politely courteous. Once they found there was no danger to them, they revealed their warm, friendly and happy side.

Difference of class and economic advantages apparent to visitors to Tibet seemed to cause little concern to the Tibetans, because as part of their religion they believed in *Karma*. Karma is the concept of rebirth, and that the good and evil one experiences in this life is determined by the good and evil deeds of prior life and that there will be later lives. The Karma concept did not, however, prevent an individual from trying to improve his present lot. Because of their religion Tibetans accepted their niche in the social and economic system even though the difference between top and bottom was very great.

Tibetans are physically strong, emotionally courageous, independent, merry, courteous, free from self-consciousness but not friendly to strangers.

THE TIBETAN AND HIS ANIMALS

Tibetans and their dogs shared a close affinity. The people loved animals. Their interest in their animals was revealed by the pantheon of their religion before Buddhism. It reflected the human psychology searching for a peaceful interrelationship between themselves, their animals and their god. The Buddhist pantheon also shows each guardian deity associated with a particular animal pictured as its master's messenger. That meant to the Tibetan that he should not only love but also protect animals.

The nomadic people lived by rather crude means. They were usually accompanied by a flock of sheep or small herd of cattle and it is here that the long-haired animals made their importance known. Because of severe cold weather there were many useful purposes served by long-haired animals; not only for the protection of the living animal but also for the domestic value of the hair they grew. The hair of the Sarligues (long-haired cattle) was made into coarse cloth, which served a useful purpose to man as well as protection for the living animal. The people of Tibet prided themselves on the value of a living animal's contributions rather than the destruction of the life of that animal. It was not uncommon to see people rescuing animals from slaughter in order to preserve that life.

In the travels of the nomads, every animal had a useful purpose as well as a life value; however, little thought or planning was employed to improve the physical qualities of their animals. The traveling people took what life had to offer and felt little need to improve their lot.

The small land owners and tenant farmers were more stationary. Their

4

humble dwellings housed both people on an upper level and the family's animals on a lower level. Their animals were a close, integral part of their lives. The small land owners and tenant farmers lived a rather simple but full life. They worked hard and enjoyed their relationship with nature.

Economically, the lower social classes were less capable of developing specific breeds of animals; therefore, it became somewhat of a luxury enjoyed by the nobles, and especially by the clergy. Because of their economic security the clergy not only had the resources but also the time to develop specific breeds of animals. Even some of those financially able to engage in planned breeding programs did not do so, however, since their primary interest was in the direction of spiritual and mental development, rather than physical improvement. This produced a variety of sizes and lack of uniformity in Tibetan animals. Usually humans and animals merely existed and contributed to the success of each other's existence in the harsh environment.

The homes and monasteries were guarded on the outside by large working dogs known primarily as mastiffs. Because of the Tibetans' extreme distrust there were smaller warning dogs found inside the dwelling. Therefore it is believed that the smaller dogs were developed more for the purpose of companionship and protection than for their religious significance.

The Lhasa Apso as we know it today is a product of the Tibetan way of life, for the people themselves have developed the breed in somewhat their own character image.

Mr. C. Suydam Cutting (center) with the Tibetan Commander-in-Chief, Tsarong Dasang Dadul, Shap-pe, and his wife, Mrs. Pema Dolkar Tsarong, the eldest sister of Mrs. Richard Dolma Taring, the author of *Daughter of Tibet,* published by Murray.

Dolma Rinchen (author of *Daughter of Tibet*) and Jigme Taring (Prince of Sikkim), photographed when Canadian Gerald D'Aoust (center) visited them on January 5, 1983.

Courtesy of Gerald D'Aoust

2

The Lhasa Apso
Reaches the West

IN ORDER to completely understand the circumstances under which the Lhasa Apso came to the United States, it is necessary to have a general grasp of the breed's story in England.

In 1901, Miss Marjorie Wild acquired her first Lhasa Apso from the Honorable Mrs. McLaren Morrison, who saw the breed in Darjeeling, India, and brought some with her on her return to England. Thereafter, Miss Wild devoted seventy years to breeding and showing the breed until her death in 1971.

In 1902, a successful application for a separate breed registry was granted by the Kennel Club (England). The breed was then called Lhasa Terrier and was divided into ten-inch and fourteen-inch height classes.

Since Lhasa Terriers (Lhasa Apsos) were shown in sufficient numbers, the Kennel Club was able to issue Challenge Certificates from 1908 until World War I. The War decimated the breed to such an extent that Challenge Certificates were withdrawn.

The comeback of the breed in England dates from the 1928 return of Lieutenant Colonel Eric and the Honorable Mrs. Bailey bringing five descendants, Taktru, Droma, Tsitru, Pema and Litsi, of their original foundation stock (Apso and Sangtru obtained in 1922 from Tsarong Shapē and Demon, a leased bitch) and Lhasa, an eight-year-old gray-and-white male.

In 1930, Miss E. M. Hutchins returned to England from China bringing Hibou, a male, and Shu-ssa, a female, owned by General and Mrs. Douglas

Brownrigg (later Sir Douglas and Lady Brownrigg) and her own male, Lung Fu Ssu, and female, Mei Mei. Mei Mei was killed soon after arrival in England, but Shu-ssa had a litter of five by Hibou, born in quarantine.

After the Brownriggs returned from China in 1931, they went to see the Bailey dogs and commented on the marked difference between their own dogs and the Bailey dogs. The two different kinds were, however, shown together in 1933 at the Ladies' Kennel Association show. Droma and Taktru, which the Baileys had brought from Tibet, were shown by their owner, Mrs. A. C. Dudley. Miss Hutchins showed Lung Fu-ssu and Tang while Mrs. Brownrigg showed Hibou and Yangtze of Taishan, a son of Hibou and Shu-ssa.

In 1934, the English Tibetan Breeds Association ruled that the Chinese dogs owned by Miss Hutchins and Mrs. Brownrigg were not Apsos. The Kennel Club General Committee decided in May of 1934 to allow showing of these dogs under, ''Any other variety, Shih Tzus,'' and to allow Shih Tzus already registered as Apsos to be reregistered as Shih Tzus. In September 1934, it was decided to adopt the name Shih Tzu for the breed. Application was granted by the Kennel Club to change the title of the Apso and Lion Dog Club to Shih Tzu (Tibetan Lion Dog) Club. In 1935, that title was again changed to Shih Tzu Club.

The Kennel Club approved the Apso Standard in 1934. The English Standard was substantially copied in April 1935 for use in the United States, where the breed was known as Lhasa Terrier and was inducted into the Terrier Group.

It is against this background that the following list of imports, derived from extensive research in the American Kennel Club records by the authors, is presented.

Imports (Lhasa Terriers)

May 1, 1935—December 1, 1944

EMPRESS OF KOKONOR (B) (987,979)—Bruce Heathcote. (Br) Miss M. Torrible, Canada. (Wh) Aug. 28, 1933. Cr, little blk on ears. By Chang Daw out of Ching Ming by Taikoo of Kokonor out of Dinkie. Chang Daw by Taikoo of Kokonor out of Dinkie.

TARZAN OF KOKONOR (D) (987,980)—Bruce Heathcote. (Br) Miss M. Torrible, Canada. (Wh) Sept. 5, 1933. Wh blk mkgs. By Taikoo of Kokonor out of Dinkie.

HAMILTON BIDGY (B) (A-50,587)—Mr. and Mrs. C. S. Cutting. Sandy and lt slate. Imported.

HAMILTON SARONG (D) (A-50,588)—Mr. and Mrs. C. S. Cutting. Sandy. Imported.

HAMILTON TSARING (D) (A-50,586)—Mr. and Mrs. C. S. Cutting, Gldn. Imported.

TUNDU (D) (A-57,947)—Arthur S. Vernay. Imported.

KOTA TANG (B) (A-145,260)—Bruce Heathcote. (Br) Madame A. C. Arline, England. (Wh) Sept. 27, 1934. Beige. By Tai-Ping-Llama out of Louisa by Tang out of Shan-hai Kuan by Lung Fu-ssu out of Shu-ssa; Tang by Lung Fu-ssu out of Tai-Tai. Tai-Ping-Llama by Lung Fu-ssu out of Tai-Tai by Hibou out of Shu-ssa.

HAMILTON CHUSUL (D) (A-213,944)—Mr. and Mrs. C. S. Cutting. Sandy.

HAMILTON TSINGTU (B) (A-213,945)—Mr. and Mrs. C. S. Cutting. Sandy.

SHANGHAI (B) (A-326,454)—Mrs. E. J. Barber. (Wh) Mar. 3, 1936. Blk and wh. By Rags out of Betty.

WUFFY OF THE MYND (B) (A-330,952)—Mrs. M. van Beuren. (Br) Mrs. H. Eaden, England. (Wh) May 2, 1938. Fn wh mkgs. By Ching of the Mynd out of Ting Tcheon of the Mynd by Yo Fei out of Tsinan Dragon by Yangtze of Taishan out of Tzu-hsi; Yo Fei by Hibou out of Shu-ssa. Ching of the Mynd by Tang out of Shan-hai Kuan by Lung Fu-ssu out of Shu-ssa; Tang by Lung Fu-ssu out of Tai Tai.

LHASSA (B) (A-351,865)—Harry Catlin. (Br) R. Lynn, China. (Wh) Oct. 1, 1935. Fn and wh. By Monk out of Prim. Monk by Rags out of Peggy.

*APSO (B) (Bred in China, whelped in USA) (A-401,002)—William N. Hatch. (Br) Annette S. Perkins, China. (Wh) Aug. 18, 1936. Br and wh. By Rags out of Tai Ho (A-401,000, Vol. 57).

MING TAI (D) (A-401,001)—William N. Hatch. (Br) Annette S. Perkins, China. (Wh) Dec. 23, 1934. Blk and tn. By Rags out of Peggy.

TAI HO (B) (A-401,000)—William N. Hatch. (Br) Annette S. Perkins, China. (Wh) May 1933. Blk and wh. By Rags out of Peggy.

*SU-LIN (B) (Bred in China, whelped in USA) (A-406,292)—Mrs. Nathan W.

Bard. (Br) Annette S. Perkins, Charleston, W. Va. (Wh) Aug. 18, 1936. Wh and gr. By Rags out of Tai Ho (A-401,000, Vol. 57).

*DING HAO (B) (Bred in China, whelped in USA) (A-419,657)—Ethel S. Kilpatrick. (Br) Annette S. Perkins, China. (Wh) Aug. 18, 1936. Wh and blk. By Rags out of Tai Ho (A-401,000, Vol. 57).

MAI-LING OF BOYDON (B) (A-653,124) Rear Admiral Robert C. Giffen. (Br) Mrs. H. L. Moulton, England. (Wh) Aug. 1, 1939. Blk and wh. By Yangtze of Taishan out of Hsuch Li Chan of Taishan by Yangtze of Taishan out of Toya by Tang out of Shan Hai Kuan; Yangtze of Taishan by Hibou out of Shu-ssa.

*Actually, these are not considered imports because they were whelped in the USA even though they were conceived in another country.

Imports (Lhasa Apsos)
January 1, 1945—December 31, 1955

BINGO (D) A940597 Black and white. December 1937. Mr. and Mrs. Richard S. R. Hubert; Denzil Clarke.

LHASSA (B) A940599 Black and white. November 10, 1940. Monk II A940599 x Patsy★. Mr. and Mrs. Richard S. R. Hubert; R. Hubert.

MONK II (D) A940598 Tan and white. October 10, 1937. Monk I★ x Prim★. Mr. and Mrs. Richard S. R. Hubert; Ralph Lynn.

LAS-SE-GRE (B) R-32451 Black, white and golden. May 7, 1941. Sikkim Johnnie★ x Chong Fey★. Mrs. Dorothy Sabine de Gray; Dr. Joseph C. Flowers.

LINDI LU OF LHAKANG (ENG.) (B) R64026 Sable and white. September 13, 1946. Choo Ling★ x Mee Na of Taishan★. Robert C. Giffen; Mrs. J. Garforth-Bles.

LINYI OF LHAKANG (ENG.) (B) R-64027 White and brown. April 29, 1948. Pu of Oulton x Lindi Lu of Lhakang★. Robert C. Giffen; Mrs. L. G. Garforth-Bles.

LE (TIBET) (D) R-65501 Light sandy. November 1948. Nanchan★ x Lucknow★. Mr. and Mrs. C. S. Cutting; Dalai Lama.

PEHMA (TIBET) (B) R-65502 Light sandy. November 1948. Kuen Lun★ x Gartok★. Mr. and Mrs. C. S. Cutting; Dalai Lama.

YAY SIH OF SHEBO (ENG.) (B) R-65904 Fawn brindle. June 3, 1949. Shebo Schunde of Hungjao★ x Yi of Taishan★. James Madison Doyle; Mrs. A. Fowler.

FARDALE FU-SSI (ENG.) (B) R-71400 Red, brown and white. November 26, 1948. Pu of Oulton★ x Mu Chi of Lhakang★. Dorothy Sabine de Gray; F. R. Dale.

CHUMPA OF FURZYHURST (ENG.) (D) R-90876 White, black markings. April 24, 1951. Dzongpen of Madamswood★ x Zara of Furzyhurst★. Mrs. Elizabeth M. Simpson; Miss J. Hervey Cecil.

FROM THE 1934 CANADIAN KENNEL CLUB STUD BOOK:

″(114902) DINKIE, (Imp.) Female, Lhasa Terrier, Registered under Article 16, Rule 1, Clause J—Raw silk, April 10, 1928, bred in Shanghai, China; imported on Orient Vancouver Seattle Liner 'Heian Maru' May 11, 1931, by Mrs. J. E. Wheeler; 3rd owner, Miss Margaret Torrible; inspected November 13, 1933, by W. H. Pym, Director C.K.C. for British Columbia.

″(114903) TAIKOO OF KOKONOR, (Imp.) Male, Lhasa Terrier, Registered under Article 16, Rule 1, Clause J—Black and white, white mane, July 19, 1930, bred in Shanghai, China; imported on Orient Vancouver Seattle Liner 'Heian Maru' May 11, 1931, by Mrs. J. E. Wheeler; 3rd owner, Miss Margaret Torrible; inspected November 13, 1933, by W. H. Pym, Director C.K.C. for British Columbia.

″(118124) CHING MING, Female, Lhasa Terrier—Smoke and white, November 29, 1931, Mrs. J. E. Wheeler; owner, Miss Margaret Torrible; sire Taikoo of Kokonor (imp.) (114903). Dam Dinkie (imp.) (114902).

"(118125) CHANG DAW, Male, Lhasa Terrier—Black and white, white mane, November 29, 1931, Mrs. J. E. Wheeler; owner, Miss Margaret Torrible; sire Taikoo of Kokonor (imp.) (114903). Dam Dinkie (imp.) (114902).

These entries from the Canadian Kennel Club Stud Book are included because there has been incorrect information circulating for many years stating that the first imports to the United States are Taikoo and Dinkie. Sometimes further elaboration stated that the Cuttings imported and registered these dogs.

This misinformation is due in part to this statement from *The Complete Dog Book*: "The two original dogs brought from Asia to this country were Taikoo, a black-and-white male, and Dinkie, a female the color of raw silk." This statement was removed from the seventeenth edition in 1985 but was included in the history of the breed for at least forty-two years.

Further adding to the confusion of the time, the British publication *Hutchinson's Dog Encyclopedia* published in 1934 a photo with the following caption, "A Famous Canadian Breeder, Miss Margaret Torrible is the owner of the Kokonor Kennels of Victoria B.C., and the only breeder of Tibetan Terriers on the American Continent. She is here seen with two of her famous dogs. The one on the table is an imported animal and a fine specimen of the breed. The other dog is 'Chang Daw', a son of 'Dinkie' by 'Taikoo', and was bred by Miss Torrible."

Also we have seen a copy of the certificate registering Monk II on October 28, 1941, as a Tibetan Terrier with the China Kennel Club.

From the March 1961 English publication, the *Manchu Shih Tzu Society News Letter*, edited by Mrs. S. M. Bode:

SECRETARY'S REPORT

For the year ending 31st December 1960—

Several Shih Tzus were exported during 1960, Mrs. Fowler sending two to Italy, one to Hong Kong, one to the South of France, one to Johannesburg and two to America; Mrs. Newson two to America, and Mrs. Collingwood and Mrs. Forte one each also to America. In the past many Shih Tzus were sent to America with deplorable results, their classification on arrival being changed to Lhasa Apso, consequently being exhibited as Lhasa Apsos and cross-bred with Lhasa Apsos. Vigorous protests were made and a lengthy correspondence with the American Kennel Club on this matter ensued and during one of her visits to America the late Mrs. Phyllis Robson, former Editor of Dog World, personally interceded on our behalf. The only concession made by the American Kennel Club was to the effect that future Shih Tzus imported would not have their classification changed but they continued not to give the breed their rightful status and cross breeding continued. We could not help feeling this was due to influence being brought to bear by the Lhasa Apso group who wished to retain the monopoly of these Oriental dogs and replenish their stock with the aid of Shih Tzus in view of the difficulty of further imports from Tibet. All other foreign Kennel Clubs recognise the status of Shih Tzus. . . .

From a letter dated November 3, 1984, to the authors from Mrs. Gay Widdrington (the former Mrs. Garforth-Bles), Lhakang Shih Tzus Kennel, founded 1939 in England:

Dear Mr. & Mrs. Herbel,

I have been studying with much interest your excellent book *The Complete Lhasa Apso*, particularly your careful recording of the Shih Tzu imports from this country which were re-registered as Lhasa Apsos or Lhasa Terriers by the A.K.C. prior to 1952. I don't think that Shih Tzu people in this country knew the widespread effect these dogs had on early Apso kennels in U.S.A. I have quite a lot of data which would fill in some gaps and some interesting photos—one of Fardale Fu-ssi and puppies by Chiang-fu, son of Las Sa Gre. Also a very good picture of Las Sa Gre standing sideways with a cup.

I bred the Shih Tzu bitch, Mu-chi of Lhakang, dam of Fardale Fu-ssi (who was re-registered as Apso). Mr. F. R. Dale acquired Mu-chi third-hand, due to illness of previous owners. The Shih Tzu Club tried to stop him exporting Fu-ssi to U.S.A. due to the uncertain situation there, however Mrs. Sabine de Grey, who got her, wrote to me and we carried on a friendly correspondence for several years. . . .

I have also an interesting story to tell about a Lhasa Apso line which was introduced unknowingly into Shih Tzu stock here, and has some famous Apso descendents in the U.S.A. and some famous Shih Tzu descendents here. In fact the Apso Best in Show winner at Crufts this year, and the Shih Tzu Best of Breed winner both stem from the same line. It has produced some marvellous red-golds in Shih Tzus.

Mrs. Widdrington's interesting story is as follows:

In 1948 Gen. Telfer-Smollett imported another bitch from Shanghai. This was Ishuh Tzu, grey-brindle with white markings bred by Mrs. Doreen Lennox who called her dogs "Tibetans". Her parents were given as Dandy of Shanghai, gold with black tips, and Chu-Chu of Shanghai, clear fawn. Lady Brownrigg examined Ishuh Tzu in quarantine and deemed her suitable to go on the Shih Tzu register. There was still no clear delineation between the shaggy Chinese and Tibetan breeds in China, nor in America, where the Apso and the Shih Tzu were still considered to be the same breed. In further correspondence with Mrs. Lennox, several years later, it was discovered that Chu-Chu's registered name was Hamilton Maru; she was registered as a Lhasa Apso in America and had won at Westminster. She had been bred by Suydam Cutting, a world traveller who owned the famous Hamilton Farms kennels in New Jersey, and was only four generations from two Apsos given to him about 1930 by the 13th Dalai Lama who lived from 1876–1933, the same one who had presented the last three to arrive in Pekin to Tzu-hsi in 1908, shortly before her death and must have been the same strain. Could they also be related to Leidza, obtained from Palace stock in 1928? The dogs presented to Mr. Cutting, ancestors to Hamilton Maru, were Hamilton Tsaring (golden) and Hamilton Bidgy (sandy-slate). Maru had been owned by Commander Doyle in U.S.A. and had been bred there before going with them to Shanghai, where she was left for a time with Mrs. Lennox. . . .

Maru's sire was Hamilton Kusog (Hamilton Chusul x Hamilton Nakkin), and her dam was Hamilton Kyi Chu (Hamilton Sigmi x Shanghai).

Mrs. Widdrington supplied us with the following details of "Shih Tzus sent to U.S.A. prior to 1952 and re-registered as Lhasa Terriers or Lhasa Apsos. (All parti-colours)":

Kota Tang. Bitch. Bred by Mdme. Arline. Owner: Mr. H. G. Maxson. No further details at present have come to light. Born 27/9/34. Reg. by A.K.C. in 1937. (Lhasa Terrier)

Wuffy of the Mynd. Bitch. Born May 2nd 1938. Bred by Mrs. Harold Eaden. Sire: Ching of the Mynd. Dam: Ting Tcheon of the Mynd. No export pedigree for this bitch is listed in the English Kennel Gazette. (Lhasa Terrier)

Also: Ding-Ding of the Mynd, same information as above for Wuffy of the Mynd.

Yay Sih of Shebo. Bitch. Born June 3rd, 1947. Breeder: Mrs. S. Bode (not Mrs. Fowler as stated). Exported 1949 to (1) Commander James Madison Doyle (2) Became property of Mrs. Jean Robertson, Annapolis. Became an American Champion (Lhasa Apso). Mrs. Fowler was the exporter. K.C. Reg. 753537/49 E.P. D18038 1949 AKC 65904 1949 (Lhasa Terrier)

Mai-Ling of Boydon. Bitch, bl/wh. Born August 1st '39. Sire: Yangtze of Taishan (2nd generation from original imports). Dam: Hseuh-li Chan of Taishan. Exported 1942 to Adml. and Mrs. Giffen, Annapolis. Breeder: Mrs. Moulton. K.C. Reg. 30463/39 E.P. A22270 AKC Reg. 653124 1943 (Lhasa Terrier)

Lindli-lu and Linyi of Lhakang. Born September '46 and April '48, mother and daughter. Bred by Mrs. Widdrington. (Then Mrs. Garforth-Bles.) Exported to U.S.A. by Viscountess Monck, and then transferred to Adml. and Mrs. Giffen, Annapolis. One or both were bred to a Pekingese in the absence of a suitable Shih Tzu sire, and the line was wasted. E.K.C. Reg. 10383/46 & 31613/48 E.P. 18001 & 18002 AKC Reg. R64026 and R64027

Fardale Fu-ssi. Bitch Shih Tzu. (Became an American Champion Lhasa Apso.) Born 26th November 1948. Bred by Mr. F. R. Dale. Exported to U.S.A. 1950. E.K.C. Reg. 48631/50 E.P.D. 18580 1948 AKC Reg. R71400 1950. Sire: Pu of Oulton, bred by Lady Grey Egerton. Chestnut/white. Dam: Mu-chi of Lhakang. Born 13th September 1946. Brindle/wh. Very sturdy and smart, very undershot. (Sire: Ch. Choo-ling, Bl/wh, owned by Lady Brownrigg. Dam: Mee-Na of Taishan, bl/wh (Mrs. Widdrington's foundation bitch—then Mrs. Garforth-Bles). Mee-Na was 3rd generation from the original Chinese imports.) Mu-chi was sold as a pet to Mrs. Caldwell, transferred to Mrs. Marshall. Mr. Dale got her 3rd-hand due to illness. Fardale Fu-ssi became the property of Mrs. Sabine de Gray (Las Sa Gre Knls). . . . Fardale Fu-ssi had 7 puppies by Chiang Fu, son of the bitch Ch. Las Sa Gre. Pups were all well-marked parti-colours.

Mr. Dale also exported a dog, Valiant Buster, born 23rd May, 1951. He went to Mrs. Lloyd Simpson, Pebble Beach, California, in 1952 and may have been put on the newly opened Shih Tzu register. However, he died soon after arrival. He was bred by Miss Reoch.

It is our opinion that during this time in the history of our breed there was no definite distinction between the names used to identify the various breeds from country to country. Further adding to the confusion was the lack of available records that should have remained with the dogs throughout their lives.

Mrs. Cutting with a Lhasa Apso in her arms. Possibly this is the bitch, Tsing Tu, mentioned in Mr. Cutting's book *Fire Ox and Other Years*.

Mr. Fred Huyler with the last two Lhasa Apsos received from Tibet by Hamilton Farm. Note the ideal head structure on these specimens.

16

3

The Founders
of the Breed
in the United States

LEM (HEATHCOTE)

Research in stud books reveals that Taikoo and Dinkie never came to the United States. Their son, Tarzan of Kokonor, and granddaughter, Empress of Kokonor, owned and imported by Bruce Heathcote, Berkeley, California, were the first entries in the AKC stud book, May 1, 1935. Also recorded in the same stud book were the offspring of Tarzan and Empress, a female Lem Ping and a male Lem Pong, bred and owned by Mr. Heathcote. Tarzan and Empress produced in four litters six males and four females; all but two bore the Lem prefix. One of these was Petti Singe, born in 1937, the first of the breed registered as a Lhasa Apso in 1944 when the name was changed from Lhasa Terrier.

Mr. Heathcote also owned the English-bred bitch Kota Tang, which he bred to Lem Pong to produce the bitches Kota Grag and Schu Tzu. Kota Tang was also bred to Lem Koko and produced Chang-Tso-Lin from him.

Mr. Heathcote was active from 1934 to July 1940 when the last Heathcote-bred litter was whelped.

MASQUE (GIFFEN)

Chang-Tso-Lin and Schu Tzu were important as perpetuators of Mr. Heathcote's breeding program because they became the foundation stock for their owner, Rear Admiral Robert C. Giffen of Annapolis, Maryland. Admiral Giffen also owned the English-bred bitches, Mai Ling of Boydon, Lindi Lu of Lhakang and her daughter Linyi of Lhakang.

In 1944, Chang-Tso-Lin was bred to Mai Ling to produce a litter of four, one of which was the dog Pedro, and another the bitch Blackie, who was bred to Chang-Tso-Lin to produce Golden Boy. Golden Boy was bred to Linyi of Lhakang three times to produce six dogs all bearing the Masque suffix. Two, Heng Hao of Masque and Der Ling of Masque, were bred together to produce what appears to be the last litter for Admiral Giffen's Masque breeding program, active from 1942 to 1953.

HAMILTON FARMS

Mr. and Mrs. C. S. Cutting, of Hamilton Farms in Gladstone, New Jersey, were responsible for the Lhasa Apso coming directly from Tibet to the United States. Mr. Cutting was a world traveler and visited Tibet three times, in 1930, 1935 and 1937. A friendly relationship developed via letters with the thirteenth Dalai Lama after the 1930 trip, and although the two never met, gifts, including dogs, were exchanged. Mr. Cutting quotes in his book *The Fire Ox and Other Years* (New York, NY: Scribners, 1940), page 178, "In sending me a pair of Apsos (special breed of Tibetan dogs), the Dalai Lama wrote, 'I am sending you two dogs by way of Kalimpong. Please take great care of them when you receive them.' Dated 7th of the last Tibetan month of the Water Bird Year [1933]." Also on page 221 while describing events of the 1937 trip and before receiving the two from that trip, Mr. Cutting states, "I had received five of these dogs from the late Dalai Lama and started to breed them successfully in New Jersey."

The second entry for the breed, in the March 1936 AKC stud book, three imports were recorded—they were Hamilton Bidgy (B), Hamilton Sarong (D) and Hamilton Tsaring (D). The son of Tsaring and Bidgy, whelped January 10, 1933, Hamilton Tashi (D) was also listed along with a repeat litter whelped July 26, 1935, all bearing the Hamilton prefix: Drepung (D), Khampa (D), Lhunpo (D), Padmeh (D), Rimpochi (B) and Sera (D).

Mr. Cutting returned to Tibet in 1935 with the noted traveler and big game hunter, Arthur Vernay. On this trip Mr. Cutting visited Lhasa for the first time, and because of friendly contacts made on this visit the Tibetan government invited him and Mrs. Cutting to return in 1937.

In the April 1936 AKC stud book is an entry for Tundu, an imported dog, owned by Arthur Vernay.

In an attempt to identify the five Apsos from the late Dalai Lama that Mr. Cutting refers to in his book, we found that the AKC's stud book entries for

Mr. Fred Huyler and Ch. Hamilton Sandupa at the Twin Brooks KC (New Jersey) dog show.

Mr. James Anderson handling Ch. Hamilton Chang Tang at the Morris and Essex KC show, May 23, 1957.

Dorothy and Rudy Benitez with (left to right) Ch. Hamilton Achok, Ch. Hamilton Den Sa and Ch. Hamilton Kung in the grooming facility at Hamilton Farm.

imports did not agree with this number. Three—Bidgy, Tsaring and Sarong—are listed. Because of the date of his birth, we conjecture that it is possible that Hamilton Tashi may have been conceived if not born on the journey to the United States and might have been counted by Mr. Cutting as one of the five he received from the late Dalai Lama. Research of early records reveals that the third litter bred by the Cuttings was sired by Tundu out of Bidgy. This leads us to believe that perhaps Mr. Cutting was counting the Tibetan import Tundu as one of the five he mentioned. Until further information surfaces we will conclude that this is the most likely reason for Mr. Cutting's reference to five when only three Cutting imports are listed in the AKC's records.

In *The Fire Ox and Other Years*, Mr. Cutting described his and Mrs. Cutting's 1937 Tibetan trip and their first visit to the Regent of Tibet, Re-ting Po gya tsap Rimpochi, the supreme ruler of Tibet after the death of the thirteenth Dalai Lama in 1933. From page 221, "At parting, the ruler told my wife he would send her a pair of Apso dogs, which greatly delighted her." On page 241, Mr. Cutting describes their preparation for leaving the city of Lhasa, "The Regent kept his promise, and the last day we received two golden Apsos, the dogs so much admired by the Tibetans." From page 242, en route back to Darjeeling, ". . . there was a great deal of milk for the male and female Apso," and again reference to the pair was made on page 243, "The dogs rode well, especially Tsing Tu, the female, who bounced miraculously on my wife's saddle mile after mile. A mile and a half from every stop they would race ahead chasing marmots, which would squeal at the edge of their holes, waiting till the dogs were on them before ducking in."

These hardy little dogs that Mr. Cutting described were recorded in the February 1938 AKC stud book as Hamilton Tsingtu (B) and Hamilton Chusul (D).

The Hamilton Farms kennels were under the supervision of Fred Huyler, manager, and James Anderson, kennel man. These men skillfully bred and showed the Hamilton Lhasa Apsos.

From July 1935 when the first litter was born at Hamilton Farms (excluding Hamilton Tashi) until the end of 1937, six litters were whelped. Of twenty-three puppies from these litters, seventeen were males; only six were females.

In June 1938 the bitch Lhassa whelped a litter that was bred by the Cuttings out of Hamilton Sigmi (Tundu x Bidgy). This litter was recorded in the November 1939 AKC stud book along with their dam. In June 1940 a litter was whelped, bred by the Cuttings, out of Hamilton Kyichu by Hamilton Kusog that was by Chusul out of Hamilton Nakkin. Nakkin was out of Tundu and Bidgy. Kyichu was bred by Mrs. E. J. Barber of New York City. Kyichu was by Hamilton Sigmi (Tundu x Bidgy) out of Shanghai (Rags x Betty).

The Hamilton bloodlines continued to be bred without introduction of any outside lines until April 1950 when a litter was born at Hamilton Farms out of the last male Lhasa Apso to be imported from Tibet, Le. A female Pehma was imported at the same time, but produced no offspring. After the inclusion of Le in the breeding program, the Hamilton line was closed and remains that way

Ch. Hamilton Tatsienlu at sixteen-and-a-half years of age.

Ch. Le, bred by the thirteenth Dalai Lama, was a foundation stud at Hamilton Farm.

Ch. Pehma, who never had a litter, is shown here with her adopted baby; a little wild rabbit.

even today, more than sixty years later, in about twenty-five kennels dedicated to the preservation of this straight Hamilton line. Without the introduction of any additional bloodlines, the Hamilton line is most unique because it is based on only nine foundation animals—Tsaring, Bidgy, Sarong, Tundu, Chusul, Tsingtu, Lhassa, Kyichu and Le.

During the thirty years Hamilton Farms bred Lhasa Apsos, there were 249 Cutting-bred Lhasa Apsos registered with the AKC. At least forty champions carrying the Hamilton prefix were recorded. This kennel provided the nucleus for a substantial part of the Lhasa Apso population in America.

Mrs. Cutting died in 1961, and in 1962 all the stock was sold to Mrs. Dorothy Cohen of Karma Kennels in Las Vegas, Nevada.

In 1964, Mr. Cutting married Mary Pyne Filley, and in 1972 he died at the age of eighty-three.

WUFFY OF THE MYND

In the July 1939 AKC stud book is an entry for the English-bred bitch Wuffy of the Mynd.

Wuffy's owner, Mrs. Mary A. van Beuren of Newport, Rhode Island, bred her to Hamilton Pedi in 1940 and got a litter of six, three females and three males all bearing the Sunnyfields Farms suffix.

Research indicates that none of these were bred and this is the only influence that Wuffy of the Mynd had on the Lhasa Apso in the United States.

THE DESCENDANTS OF RAGS

According to the recollections of Josette Hubert Williams, daughter of Mr. and Mrs. Richard S. R. Hubert, and from the Hubert's records: "Rags (D) was a Tibetan male owned by Mr. Barber, the owner of a smart ladies' shoe store on Avenue Joffre near the Cathay Theatre in Shanghai, China, from Harbin, Manchuria."

Mrs. Williams further indicates that the bitch Peggy was owned by Annette Perkins, who also had lived in Harbin, Manchuria. Mrs. Perkins's address was identified as both Shanghai, China, and Charleston, West Virginia, in the AKC records.

Monk I was described by Mrs. Williams as "b & w male, born in c. 1935, owned by Ralph Lynn, a dancer in Shanghai, China. Monk I never left China. He was a beautiful dog but not mated much. Monk I was born in Harbin, Manchuria, and bought by Ralph Lynn.

"Prim (B) was a beige female and the property of Ralph Lynn," according to Mrs. William's notes.

Mrs. Williams has considerably more information about Monk II because he was one of the dogs her family brought with them from China when they returned to America. She relates as follows:

> Monk II (D) Beige, black tips on ears & beard. Acquired by Richard S. R. Hubert in Shanghai, China, in 1939 from Ralph Lynn. Very thick coat, quiet dog, perfect with children. Left Shanghai, China, October 1941 on the SS President Coolidge. Was passing through Solomon Islands when Japanese struck at Pearl Harbor. Lived in Pasadena CA, Duluth MN, Montreal, Canada, on way to his final home in Greenwich CT. He was my childhood companion from 1939 until he was killed on Lake Avenue in Greenwich CT in 1950s.

A copy of the certificate registering Monk II on October 28, 1941, as a "Tibetan Terrier" with the China Kennel Club also contains on the letterhead under the bold lettering China Kennel Club, "Shanghai" and "Affiliated with the Kennel Club, London." According to the pedigree on this certificate, Monk I was out of Rags and Peggy and Prim's lineage was unknown.

To add to the confusion of early dogs we found that there were two bitches named "Lhassa." The first one entered in the November 1939 AKC stud book was as a Lhasa Terrier and is the one used by Hamilton Farms. The second one was entered as a Lhasa Apso in the February 1946 AKC stud book and was imported by the Huberts. It is interesting to note that they were both given a Tibetan name although they were both born in China and both were descendants of Rags.

Mrs. Williams has this to say about the Hubert's Lhassa:

> (B) Black & White female born Nov. 11, 1940, in Shanghai, China. Very dainty, quick, bright. Killed in Montreal when 1st litter was one week old. Author's Note: [AKC stud book gives November 10, 1940 as birthdate.]

The Hubert's Lhassa was out of their Monk II (Monk I x Prim) and Patsy, about which Mrs. Williams has this to say:

> Given to RSR Hubert by a woman leaving Shanghai. Good lineage but woman neglected to leave it and could not later be contacted. Patsy was a bright little gold digger.

Mrs. Williams said of the third Hubert import, Bingo:

> Born Dec. 1937 in Peking, China, raised by Mr. Denzil Clarke of British Embassy. Acquired by RSR Hubert October 1941 and brought to Canada with Monk II and Lhassa. Black & White male, longer and thinner than Monk II. Hair silky. Feuded with Monk II and was finally given to Mr. & Mrs. Cecil Gunyon. Killed December 1943 in home near Toronto.

No lineage is available to indicate that this dog is a Rags descendant, but his information is included with the other Hubert imports.

In about 1936, William N. Hatch, Haddonfield, New Jersey, imported a Rags son out of Peggy, Ming Tai, and his older full sister, Tai Ho, in whelp to Rags. Tai Ho had three bitches from this litter, Apso, Su Lin and Ding Hao. Annette Perkins is recorded as the breeder of all five, Ming Tai, Tai Ho and Tai Ho's three daughters, Apso, Su Lin and Ding Hao. Su Lin and Ding Hao were sold, and Mr. Hatch kept Apso along with her dam, Tai Ho, and the male, Ming Tai. Mr. Hatch bred Ming Tai to Tai Ho four times, producing six offspring, three of each sex, one of which was the female Ming Lu, foundation bitch for Frank T. Lloyd, Jr.'s Ming Kennels. A dog, Ming Foo, was sold to Ethel S. Kilpatrick of Hillsborough, California, who also owned Ding Hao.

Mr. Hatch bred Ming Tai to Apso three times to produce five offspring, two bitches and three dogs whose destiny is not so famous.

These seven litters, whelped between 1937 and 1943, seem to be the extent of Mr. Hatch's breeding program.

Rags descendants came to the United States via Mrs. E. J. Barber's bitch, Shanghai, the Perkins-bred animals of Mr. Hatch and later with the Hubert family.

RAHULAH

In August 1948, the American Kennel Club listed as a new champion the Lhasa Apso Rahulah, along with the notation "not registered."

This dog was never registered but sired a litter when Dorothy B. Patterson bred Hamilton Niling to him in 1947. This mating produced a bitch, Tashi, who in turn was bred to Yonton Singhi by Mrs. Patterson and produced a dog, Li Po, and a bitch, Karma. Neither Li Po nor Karma produced any offspring, thus ending any further influence by Rahulah on the breed in the United States.

LOST HORIZON

John A. and Daisy Ellen Frazier's foundation stock was the straight Hamilton littermates Rudok of Tufan and Shatra of Tufan (Hamilton Zinga x Hamilton Kala), bred by Mr. and Mrs. W. C. Koehncke of San Francisco, California.

Whelped in 1946, the Frazier's first litter was out of Rudok and Shatra and produced two bitches, Meditative Mishme and Lhasa Losan. Losan bred back to her father produced Lamasery Bub, the sire of Ch. Tenzing of Lost Horizons, Frazier's Jon of Lost Horizons and Diminutive Delight to name only a few.

The Frazier's bred Jon and Delight together to produce the bitches Ashi of Lost Horizons and Miradel's Fa Le and the dog Tibetan Om-Mani-Padme-Hum.

This intensely inbred line remained straight Hamilton until retired in 1958. During the twelve years of breeding Lhasa Apsos, the Fraziers produced important foundation stock for several successful kennels.

LAS SA GRE

In 1943, the imported bitch, Las Sa Gre, was bred to Ming Foo by her owner at that time, Mrs. Peter Leth-Nissen, to produce a male, Chiang Foo.

Ch. Las Sa Gre's Manchado Dorado (Ch. Fu Al Tirito and Ch. Fu La Diablita) bred by Dorothy Sabine de Gray.

Two of Las Sa Gre's champions with their owner and handler Mrs. Dorothy Sabine de Gray. On the left is Ch. Fu Pacifiquito and on the right is Ch. Fu La Diablita.

In 1946, Las Sa Gre was bred to Juanito Verdejo by her next owner, Mrs. Dorothy Sabine de Gray, to produce the dog Segundo Verdejo, the first Lhasa Apso to earn an Obedience title.

Las Sa Gre was recorded as a champion in March of 1948 along with the notation "not registered" following her name; however, later that year she was listed with a registration number. Juanito was listed as a champion in 1949 with the same "not registered" notation and was never registered. Mrs. de Gray bred Juanito and Las Sa Gre together again in 1947 to produce the brother and sister Caballero Verdejo and Querida Verdejo.

In 1950, Mrs. de Gray acquired the English-born bitch Ch. Fardale Fu Ssi★. The next year Fu Ssi had a litter out of Chiang Foo. This was her only litter, which contained two males, Ch. Fu Al Tirito and Ch. Fu Pacifiquito, and five females, Fu La Castanita, Ch. Fu La Diablita, Ch. Fu La Quartita, Ch. Fu La Simpatica and Ganden Foo.

Tirito and Diablita were bred together and produced the significant sires Ch. Las Sa Gre's Manchado Dorado and Las Sa Gre's Hijo D'Al Tiro.

Tirito was also bred to Castanita to produce the bitch Las Sa Gre's Fu Fu La Sombra and the dog Las Sa Gre's Fu El Rubino, and again to Diablita to produce the bitch Las Sa Gre's Shirmantanc.

Pacifiquito was bred to Quartita to produce the bitch Las Sa Gre's Fu La Audacia, and to Diablita to produce the male Las Sa Gre's Fu Ssi Hijo and the female Las Sa Gre's Azucarita. Pacifiquito was also bred to Sombra to produce Las Sa Gre's La Angelita and Higadito. Whelped in July 1960, this appears to be the last litter for Mrs. de Gray's Las Sa Gre breeding program.

MING

Frank T. Lloyd, Jr., of Merchantville, New Jersey, established his Ming Kennels with the purchase of the bitch Ming Lu (Ming Tai x Tai Ho) from William Hatch. Ming Lu was whelped in 1943 and shown "Listed" by Judge Lloyd at the 1946 Westminster Kennel Club show. Ming Lu was bred in 1946 to Hamilton Dakmar to produce the males Wu Tai and Taiminghyu. She was also bred three times to the Giffen-bred dog Pedro (Chang-Tso-Lin x Mai Ling of Boyden) to produce the three males Ch. Ming Changnopa, Ming Koko and Ming Chetang and two females Ch. Ming Tsarong and Ch. Ming Kyi.

Ming Kyi was bred to Yonton Singhi (Taiminghyu x Honan, litter sister to Ming Lu) to produce Ch. Ming Kara. Tsarong was also bred to Singhi to produce bitches Ming Chik and Ming Nyi and the dog Ch. Ming Sum.

Ming Kyi additionally was bred to Ch. Wu Tai to produce Ch. Ming Tali II, CD★, the foundation sire for Miradel Kennels.

Elbertine E. Campbell handled for Ming Kennels and also bred and co-bred, with Judge Lloyd, Lhasa Apsos under the Ming name, as did Mrs. Campbell, who bought Ming Tsarong.

Ch. Ming Changnopa (Pedro x Ch. Ming Lu) was owned and bred by Judge Frank T. Lloyd. He was the only Lhasa Apso to ever win the Terrier Group in the United States. The Lhasa Apso competed in the Terrier Group here until the beginning of 1956 when he was switched to the Non-Sporting Group.　　　　　　　　　　　*Shafer*

Judge Frank T. Lloyd with one of his Ming Lhasa Apsos.

In 1954, Ch. Americal's Nima was bred to Changnopa by Mr. Campbell to produce Ch. Ming Toy Nola.

At the May 1957 Trenton (New Jersey) Kennel Club show, Ming Kennel exhibited three Lhasa Apsos neither bred nor owned by them. One was the bitch Las Sa Gre's Fu Fu La Sombra, bred by Mrs. Dorothy Sabine de Gray, and the other two bitches, Ming Taicha and Ch. Ming Teri, were littermates by Ming Chetang II (Changnopa x Ch. Ming Rima) out of Sombra and bred by Dr. and Mrs. Philip T. Newman.

In 1958, Judge Lloyd bred Sombra to Changnopa to produce Ming Kokong.

Judge Lloyd died in 1962. Dogs from his Ming Kennel, and their successors, fanned out all over the country, from nearby New Jersey throughout the country and as far west as California.

LYNCHAVEN

Mrs. Anita Lynch acquired straight Hamilton foundation stock from which she bred the first Lynchaven litter in 1947. This litter was by Hamilton Pata out of a bitch bred by the Cuttings, named Aloe of Champlain View (Hamilton Nyang x Hamilton Rugi), and contained a dog, Marshall Bufi, and a bitch, Lynchaven Lotus Flower. Mrs. Lynch repeated this breeding three more times to produce five bitches, including Lynchaven Karma, and one dog, Lynchaven Dorje.

Both Lotus Flower and Karma were bred to Dakmar of Champlain View (Hamilton Dakmar x Hamilton Linga) to produce a dog, Tambo of Ka-Lin, and two bitches, Niki and Lynchaven Nikki.

In 1952, Mrs. Lynch seemed to abandon her early breeding program after she acquired the English-bred bitch Ch. Yay Sih of Shebo, which she bred to Ch. Wu Tai to produce Lynchaven Yay Pitchika, a bitch; to Pata to produce Princes Shebo, a bitch, and Mac D Trix Tang Sunyata, a dog, and three times to Dakmar of Champlain View to produce Lynchaven Gurla, Lynchaven Rin-Cam Re-Ba and Lynchaven Lalla, all bitches.

Yay Patchika was bred to Dakmar of Champlain View to produce Lynchaven Tangla, a bitch, and to Pata to produce Lynchaven Bar-Ba, a bitch, and Lynchaven Mel-Tse, a dog.

In 1959, Lalla was bred to Stittig's Char-Chan Deimar to produce Lalla of Byrd Hill, and most of the subsequent litters bred after this litter contained offspring carrying the Byrd Hill suffix of Jane W. Fischer.

The last litter bred by Anita Lynch was born in 1961, after which it appears that Lynchaven was retired.

4

Lhasa Apsos in the United States in the 1950s

$\mathbf{T}$HERE WAS very little additional activity in the breed during the first half of the 1950s, but during the second half the popularity of the breed increased noticeably.

This increased activity included the founding of the American Lhasa Apso Club in 1959. Concurrent with this increased popularity, the Lhasa Apso was transferred from the Terrier Group, where the breed had been since acceptance by the American Kennel Club, to the Non-Sporting Group, where it remains today.

Several kennels founded during the latter part of the 1950s are still active and many dogs of that time can be found in extended pedigrees of dogs today.

AMERICAL

In 1951, Mrs. Marie Stillman, of Beverly Hills, California, bought her first Lhasa Apsos, Ch. Hamilton Tsang (Ch. Le x Hamilton Gindi) and Hamilton Suchau (Ch. Le x Hamilton Muni) from Hamilton Farms.

These Lhasa Apsos formed the foundation stock for Mrs. Stillman's kennel, named Americal after an American army division in World War II.

Tsang and Suchau produced Ch. Americal's Leng Kong ROM★, foundation sire for Licos Lhasa Apsos, and Americal's Chika Yang.

Mrs. Stillman also acquired the Frazier-bred bitch Tibetan Jaida Lu by Quang Ngai (Lamasery Bub x Shatra of Tufan) out of Meditative Mishme (Rudok of Tufan x Shatra), and that was bred to Tsang to produce the bitches Ch. Americal's Nima and Americal's Myka.

Americal also purchased from Hamilton Farms two females, one that became BIS Ch. Hamilton Torma (Tatsienlu x Hamilton Lachen) and Hamilton Lhamo (Ch. Hamilton Sandupa★ x Hamilton Yogi), and also two males, Ch. Hamilton Kalon (Tatsienlu x Hamilton Tughar) and Ch. Hamilton Chang Tang (Hamilton Maroh x Ch. Hamilton Samada★).

Torma was bred to Tsang in 1953 to produce Ch. Americal's Rika ROM★ and Americal's Kasu. She was also bred in 1955 to Kalon to produce Ch. Americal's Torma Tsing, a bitch. In 1959, her last son was born, Ch. Americal's Torma Lu, sired by Chang Tang.

One of the pioneer breeders, Mrs. Stillman's contribution to the breed will be long remembered through these dogs, as well as Ch. Americal's Lha Lu (Tsang x Lhamo), Ch. Americal's Amo (Chang Tang x Linga), Americal's Sandar of Pamu★ (Chang Tang x Lady Pamu) and Americal's Lhasa ROM★ (Karma Yon Ten x Americal's Sabell) to name only a few.

LICOS

Mrs. Stillman gave Mrs. Grace Licos, a neighbor, two puppies, Americal's Leng Kong in 1952 and Americal's Rika in 1953. Rika was first bred to Ch. Hamilton Kalon and produced Ch. Americal's Licos Linga, and then she was bred in 1956 to her half brother, Leng Kong, to produce the famous breed record holder BIS Ch. Licos Kulu La and his sister Ch. Licos Nimu La. A repeat litter in 1958 produced two bitches, Ch. Licos Karo La and Ch. Licos Nyapso La ROM★★.

Nyapso La was bred in 1959 to Ch. Hamilton Achok★ and produced three males, Ch. Licos Shor Shan La, Licos Khung La (sire of the record holder BIS Ch. Kham of Norbulingka ROM★★) and Ch. Licos Chulung La ROM★, as well as the female Licos Dama La.

In 1960, Karo La was also bred to Achok to produce the male Ch. Licos Chaplia La ROM and the female Licos Simla La.

It was about this time that Mrs. Licos bought a bitch from Hamilton Farms that would become Ch. Hamilton Pluti ROM★ (Sandupa x Ch. Hamilton Den Sa), and when bred to Kulu La produced Ch. Licos Omorfo La ROM★

Other important Licos Lhasa Apsos are Ch. Licos Cheti La (Chaplia La x Nyapso La), the dam of BIS Ch. Tibet of Cornwallis ROM★★★★ and her younger brother Ch. Licos Namni La ROM, as well as Ch. Licos Soji La ROM★, sired by Omorfo La out of Dama's Lu Country Fair (Kulu La x Dama La) and Ch. Licos Kupl La★ (Leng Kong x Pluti).

Mrs. Marie Stillman, Americal, with Ch. Hamilton Chang Tang.

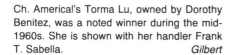

Ch. Americal's Torma Lu, owned by Dorothy Benitez, was a noted winner during the mid-1960s. She is shown with her handler Frank T. Sabella. *Gilbert*

The foundation of Licos' Lhasa Apsos were (from left) Ch. Americal's Leng Kong, Ch. Americal's Rika, Ch. Hamilton Pluti, Ch. Licos Nyapso La, Ch. Hamilton Katha, BIS Ch. Licos Kulu La and Ch. Licos Karo La.

Although this straight Hamilton breeding program qualified years before the inception of the ALAC awards in 1973, it was not until 1978 that the Licos dogs and their breeder were recognized with Register of Merit status. Mrs. Licos retired from breeding Lhasa Apsos in 1975 and died in 1986 after an extended illness.

KARMA

Previously a Poodle breeder, Dorothy Cohen of Las Vegas, Nevada, established Karma Lhasa Apsos in 1956 with the acquisition of Licos Nimu La and Hamilton Karma. Both bitches finished, but it was Ch. Hamilton Karma★ (Hamilton Maroh x Hamilton Docheno) that was to be most important to the future of Mrs. Cohen's breeding program.

Several trips to Hamilton Farms resulted in the acquisition of a few Hamilton dogs and the breeding of Ch. Hamilton Karma★ to Ch. Hamilton Kung★ (Tatsienlu x Hamilton Dobra★), which produced Karma's first litter. This litter contained Group-winning Ch. Karma Getson, Am. & Mx. Ch. Karma Sangpo, Ch. Karma Lobsang and multiple Group-winning Ch. Karma Gyapso.

The last trip to Hamilton Farms in the fall of 1962 resulted in the purchase of all Hamilton Farms' Lhasa Apsos. Thirty-one Lhasa Apsos from the ages of three weeks to thirteen years were shipped to Las Vegas.

Mrs. Cohen was responsible for significant improvements in the Hamilton Farm type. She improved the quality and texture of the coat, as well as the head and bite, while retaining the merits of Hamilton Farms stock.

Mrs. Cohen was known as a strong advocate for the preservation of the "pure Hamilton" Lhasa Apso—a term during that time in Lhasa Apso history that meant a Lhasa Apso that could trace all of its ancestors back to Tibetan imports and did not have any of the Shih Tzus registered as Lhasa Apsos in their background. Mrs. Cohen's binding breeding contracts were famous, but even more famous was the stringent selection that went into finding a purchaser that qualified to sign one of the contracts. Over the years there became enough Karma-bred Lhasa Apsos throughout the country so that she was unable to control their destiny; therefore, they started to appear in mixed pedigrees, and the number of breeders who still breed only "pure Hamilton" are comparatively few.

While numbers of champions bred is not alone significant it is some measure of a breeder's contribution when the quality of these champions is of high caliber.

When Mrs. Cohen announced that, as of September 1974, Karma Lhasa Apsos would no longer actively breed dogs, she published a list of her seventy-one champions. Mrs. Cohen died early in 1977.

STITTIG

The breeding program of Lillian Mae Stittig started with a litter out of Hamilton Peking and Hamilton Pomo, whelped in 1953. In 1955, a litter was

Ch. Hamilton Karma the foundation dam of Karma Lhasa
Apsos was by Hamilton Maroh out of Hamilton Docheno.

Multiple Group winner Ch. Karma Rus Tilopa (Ch. Karma Rus Ti x Ch.
Americal's Lha Lu) was bred by Dorothy Cohen and owned by Maria B. Aspuru.

born out of Peking and Hamilton Durga that contained the bitch Stittig's Moka-Kara Deimar.

In 1956, Stittig's Pao-Tzu Cee (Pu Yao Cheng of Masque x Si San of Masque) was bred to Durga to produce the first litter for this program that was not straight Hamilton.

Pao-Tzu Cee was also bred to Moka-Kara, which produced among many others Clyzett's Butter Lamp, who produced the bitch Green Diamond Decidedly when Mrs. Stittig bred her to Hamilton Kesang.

Stittig-bred Lhasa Apsos bridged the years from 1953 to 1965 and were predominantly Hamilton bloodlines, although an occasional outcross to other lines was not uncommon.

RINPOCHE

Rinpoche Kennel was founded in 1951 when John E. Partanen and his daughter Alice A. Partanen of San Francisco, California, obtained the bitch Chika Rinpoche. Chika was sired by Hamilton Sandur out of Ch. Yay Sih of Shebo and bred by Jean G. Robertson. When bred to Ming Changnopa, Chika produced the male Kham Drukke and the female Karma Rinpoche. She was also bred to Ch. Las Sa Gre's Manchado Dorado to produce the males Dzin-Pa Rinpoche and Ch. Kepa Rinpoche, as well as the female Kai-Sang Tzi-Ren of Miradel.

Karma was bred to Manchado Dorado to produce Rincan of Kelea, the sire of Ch. Colarlie's Shan Bangalor ROM★★ and his sister, Ch. Tashi Rinpoche, that when bred to Kepa produced the female Ron Si Rinpoche.

When Ron Si was bred to Dzin-Pa she produced Ch'ha-Ya-Chi, the dam of Ch. Kinderland's Sang Po ROM★★.

Alice assumed the responsibility of the breeding program in the late 1960s after finishing her education. She was responsible for producing the Group-winning Ch. Kham Te-Ran, CD, a special favorite of hers.

This breeding program ceased activity early in 1970.

CHIG

Robert and Anna Griffing, well-known Boston Terrier breeders, started with Lhasa Apsos in 1954 at Mountainside, New Jersey, when they bought the bitch that became Ch. Ming Toy Nola. This was one of the few kennels to show dogs as early as 1957 in shows held in the New York–New Jersey metropolitan area.

Nola was bred in 1957 to Ch. Ming Changnopa to produce the bitch Ch. Ming Thudi and the dog Ming Changnola. In 1959, Nola was bred to Ch. Hamilton Kung★ to produce the two bitches Ch. Linga-Drog-Po and Promenade Sing A Ling.

Ch. Karma's Rus-Ti (Ch. Karma Dmar-Po x Hamilton Gyo-Tru) was said to be Dorothy Cohen's favorite. He was the sire of at least twelve Karma champions.

Ch. Kham Te-Ran Rinpoche, CD (Ch. Shangri La Sho George x Ron Si Rinpoche), is shown here with his owner-breeder Alice Partanen.

Linga-Drog-Po was bred to Ch. Hamilton Sandupa★ in 1961 to produce the bitch Chig Dkar, and again in 1963 to produce the dogs Ch. Chig Golden Anniversary and Ch. Chig Dob Dob. Dkar was bred to Ch. Hamilton Namsa ROM★ to produce Ch. Chig Rgyal Po.

The Griffings additionally bred and exhibited many Lhasa Apsos, including Ch. Chig Chig (Dob Dob x T'ai Ming Cha) and his son, Ch. Chig Mo, out of Ch. Chig Shatta (Golden Anniversary x Black Beauty) and Ch. Chig Dom (Chig Chig x Pandan Lhamo).

SHANGRI LA

Shangri La Lhasa Apsos was a partnership between the late Ruth Doty and her daughter, Marilyn Sorci. Their foundation stock was comprised of the female Ashi of Lost Horizons and the male Tibetan Om-Mani-Padme-Hum from the Fraziers, Lynchaven Tangla from Anita Lynch and Ch. Hamilton Achok from Hamilton Farms. Later they acquired Ch. Tenzing of Lost Horizons.

Shangri La's first litter was from Ashi bred to Tenzing and the second litter was out of Padme-Hum and Tangla. This second litter produced the dogs Ch. Tara Ho of Shangri La and Ch. Tara Toy of Shangri La and the bitch Tara Tsoo of Shangri La.

Tangla was also bred to Tenzing three times to produce the bitches Ch. Su Lin of Shangri La, Ch. Shangri La Tibetan Butterfly and Shangri La Tibetan Bumble Bee and the dog Ch. Shangri La Tenzing Bhu. When bred to Ch. Hamilton Achok, Tangla produced the dog Ch. Shangri La Rajan of Glenns Pines★.

Tsoo was bred first to Padme-Hum to produce the bitch Shangri La Tara Tina Mia, and next to Achok to produce the dog Shangri La Dari Achok, and finally to Tenzing to produce Ch. Shangri La Sho George.

Achok and Bumble Bee were bred together to produce Ch. Shangri La Chemrezi Caress.

Shangri La was most active from early in 1956 to late in 1959. Although Mrs. Sorci did not stop breeding after 1959, Shangri La was so inactive as to seem retired.

MIRADEL

Miradel Lhasa Apsos were originated in 1954 by Eloris and Lee Liebmann. The foundation sire for Miradel was Ch. Ming Tali II, CD★ and the foundation bitch was the straight Hamilton/Frazier-bred Miradel's Fa Li. These two were bred together three times to produce the first twelve Miradel Lhasa Apsos. Among these were Miradel's Que Tee, a dog, and the bitches Miradel's Chomolungma, Miradel's Nima and Miradel's Kahn Dee, CD.

The next acquisition was the bitch Ch. Fu La Simpatica, that when bred

Ch. Hamilton Achok, owned by Marilyn Sorci of Shangri La Lhasa Apsos, shown in a win under Col. E. E. Ferguson.

Ch. Ming Tali II, bred by judge Frank T. Lloyd and foundation stud for Miradel Kennels, was the sire of at least eleven champions.

An ad published in an early dog magazine describing the size of Miradel Lhasa Apsos.

37

to Ming Tali II produced Ch. Miradel's Ming Fu Dream Girl and Ch. Miradel's Ming Fu Chia, CD★★

The Liebmanns also bought Kai Sang Tzi-Ren of Miradel from the Partanens and bred her to Glenns Pines Chag Po Ri (Las Sa Gre's Hijo D'Al Tiro x Miradel Nima) to produce Kai Sang's Clown of Everglo and Ch. Khan Du Ruffway.

When Ming Tali II was bred to Torlona's Man Cho Ming Dinki (Manchado Dorado x Chomolungma), they produced Ch. Dinki's Miradel Chen Yang, that when bred back to Ming Tali II produced Miradel's Yung Chen of Ruffway★.

During the thirteen years the Liebmanns were active they bred approximately forty-two litters, and Miradel-bred Lhasa Apsos can be found behind most Lhasa Apsos today except those that are straight Hamilton-bred.

CORNWALLIS

Paul Williams started his Cornwallis breeding program in 1956 when he bought the bitch that would become Ch. Miradel's Ming Fu Dream Girl.

Dream Girl was bred to Yonton Singhi (Tai Minghyu x Hon Nan) to produce the bitches Ritah of Cornwallis, Cornwallis Mei Ling Fu and Princess Chu Tsu of Kenwood and the dogs Riches of Cornwallis and Ch. Raggs of Cornwallis. Raggs, when bred back to his mother, sired Cornwallis Ming Ho, the sire of Ruth Deck's first Rondelay Lhasa Apso litter out of Promenade Sing A Ling (Ch. Hamilton Kung x Ch. Ming Toy Nola).

Dream Girl was also bred to Thanksgiving Tabe (Ch. Ming Changnopa x Hamilton Gampo) to produce Rema of Cornwallis, that when bred to Raggs produced Khyber of Cornwallis, a male.

Mr. Williams also bred straight Hamilton lines. He bought a male, Karma Tharpa, and a female that would become Ch. Licos Cheti La. He bred Tharpa to Cheti La to produce three males, BIS Ch. Tibet of Cornwallis ROM★★★★, Ch. Willy of Cornwallis and Pepi of Cornwallis, and one female, Didi of Cornwallis.

Mr. Williams also bought a bitch that would become Ch. Karma Kan Sa ROM★ and bred her to Tharpa to produce BIS Am., Bda., & Can. Ch. Ku Ka Boh of Pickwick. Tharpa was also bred to Ch. Miss Kim of Cornwallis (Seng Tru x Karma Kan Sa) to produce Ch. Mae's Toiling of Cornwallis.

Mr. Williams, who died in 1971, was an asset to Lhasa Apsos by providing breeding stock for many east coast breeders.

GLENNS PINES

Floy and Glenn Bagley originated the Glenns Pines breeding program in 1956 when they bred their foundation bitch, Ch. Miradel's Nima, to Las Sa Gre's Hijo D'Al Tiro to produce the only litter named with the Glenflo prefix

BIS Ch. Ruffway Mashaka (Ch. Everglo's Spark of Gold ROM x Ch. Ruffway Kara Shing ROM), owned, bred and handled by Georgia Palmer.

Ch. Ruffway T'Ang Chu ROM (Ch. Reiniet's Roial Chanticleer x Ch. Ruffway Kham Chung), owned and bred by Georgia Palmer.

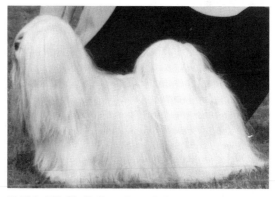

Multiple BIS Ch. Ruffway Patra Pololing, bred by Georgia Palmer, Ruffway, and Pat Boyd, Patra, was owned by Victor Cohen, Victory, and William and Betty Bowman, Tiko. *Alverson*

and including the bitch Ch. Glenflo's Girja. Tiro and Nima were bred together two more times to produce the bitches Glenns Pines Merry Xmas and Glenns Pines Jingle Bell and the dog Glenns Pines Chag Po Ri.

Of the more notable Lhasa Apsos produced by the Bagleys were Ch. Glenns Pines Flash of Gold, a dog, and Ch. Glenns Pines Ringka, a bitch, both out of Ch. Shangri La Rajan of Glenns Pines★ and Nima; Ch. Joli Grumpa of Glenns Pines, a dog, out of Rajan and Joli Ja Kali of Glenns Pines (Rajan x Merry Xmas); Ch. Glenns Pines Nanda Devi out of Rajan and Tongsa of Glenns Pines (Shangri La Dari Achok x Miradel's Ama Dablam).

Although the Bagleys bred few dogs, about ten litters during fourteen years of activity, the Glenns Pines name is behind many dogs today.

RUFFWAY

F. R. and Georgia Palmer of Addison, Illinois, originally bred Rough Collies under the Ruffway prefix. In 1956, they started their Lhasa Apso breeding program under the same name with the acquisition of two puppies that became Ch. Miradel's Ming Fu Tzu and Ch. Glenflo's Girja. Together, they produced the first Ruffway-bred Lhasa Apso, a litter of one female that became Ch. Ruffway's Solitaire. Bred together two more times, Fu Tzu and Girja produced two bitches, Ruffway New Year's Eve and Ruffway Hun-Nee-Bun, and a dog, Ruffway Auld Lang Syne.The Palmers then obtained the bitch that became Ch. Miradel's Dinah Might, that when bred to Rincan of Kelea produced the bitches Foo Ling of Saddlewood★ and Ruffway Tee-En-Tee, and then to Country Fair's Kushikhan (Taylor's Chado of Miradel x Country Fair's Dasi Mae) to produce Ch. Ruffway Tsong Kappa★, a male, and Ruffway Kata, a bitch.

In the early 1960s, Mrs. Palmer acquired the straight Hamilton-bred bitch Stittig's Moka Kara Deimar about the time that Mrs. Gloria Fowler, Everglo, was establishing her straight Hamilton bloodline. Through an exchange of stock, Moka Kara was bred to the west coast dog Ch. Licos Chulung La ROM★, and produced Ch. Kyima of Everglo ROM★ and Dakini of Everglo. Mrs. Palmer also bred Moka Kara to Cubbi Kyeri to produce Ruffway Khambu ROM★, the dam of Ch. Ruffway Nor Pa and Ch. Ruffway Chogal, both out of Frosty Knight, that was at that time a young dog and on loan from Mrs. Fowler.

Unlike Everglo, Ruffway did not breed only straight Hamilton but also bred Khambu to Sparky to produce Ch. Orlane Meling of Ruffway, the dam of BIS Ch. Little Firs Shel Ari of Chiz ROM★★ by Ch. Ruffway Marpa ROM★. Marpa and his litter brothers, BIS Ch. Ruffway Mashaka ROM and Ch. Ruffway Norru were by Sparky out of Ch. Ruffway Kara Shing ROM (Chogal x Ch. Kai Sang's Clown of Everglo).

It is this foundation that has provided Ruffway with the continued success during the more than thirty-five years of involvement in Lhasa Apsos.

Additional winning and producing Ruffway-bred dogs of importance are Group-winning Ch. Ruffway Mashala Chu ROM★★★; Group-winning Ch. Ruff-

Ch. Lui-Gi's So-Nan (Al Tabu of Lhasarab and Ch. Lui-Gi's Melodi), owned and bred by Mrs. Albertram McFadden.

Ch. Colarlie's Shan Bangalor ROM at fourteen months, owned by Ruth Smith. He ultimately sired seventeen champions.

Group winner Ch. Colarlie's Dokki, CD (Ch. Colarlie's Shan Bangalor ROM x Miradel's Ming Fu Chia, CD), owned and bred by Ruth Smith. He was the first black Lhasa Apso to become a Group winner.

way T'Ang Chu ROM★★; BIS Am. & Can. Ch. Ruffway Patra Pololing and his full sister Ch. Ruffway Patra Tashi Tu ROM★★ and their dam, Ch. Ruffway Tashi★★★.

Ruffway Lhasa Apsos received the ALAC ROM breeders' award in 1976.

LUI GI

Mrs. Albertram McFadden, Lui Gi, of Las Vegas, Nevada, bred Blue Mist of Lost Horizons (Frazier's Jon of Lost Horizons x Lhasa Losan) in 1956 to the English import Ch. Chumpa of Furzyhurst. His sire, Dzongpen of Madamswood, was a Tibetan import and his dam, Zara of Furzyhurst, was a combination of Ladkok and Lamleh. This litter produced the females Ch. Lui Gi's Melodi and Ch. Lui Gi's Zerdechal and the male Ch. Lui Gi's Amiral. Zerdechal was bred to Ch. Hamilton Jimpa and produced Ch. Lui Gi's Shigatzoo.

A few months later Mrs. McFadden bred another Frazier-bred bitch, Darjeeling of Lost Horizons (Quang Ngai x Lhasa Losan), to the Frazier-bred dog Seng Kye (Jon x Diminutive Delight) to produce females Lui Gi's Altune Sis, Lui Gi's Tsin Tsan, Lui Gi's Bal Petee-Yi and Lui Gi's Sirna-Shik and one dog, Lui Gi's Aslan. This was the foundation of Lui Gi that became famous for their excellent stock.

Unfortunately, Mrs. Mc Fadden found it difficult to accept that Shih Tzus had been reregistered as Lhasa Apsos when they came here from England. She spent considerable time and money trying to correct what she considered to be a blight on the breed. She really believed in her crusade, but her methods for correcting the problem were frequently not conducive to success.

KYI CHU

Mrs. Ruth Smith, originally a Collie breeder, bred Lhasa Apsos under the name of Colarlie and later, Kyi Chu. She got her first Lhasa Apso in 1956 for her daughter, Terry. This was the eleven-month-old Miradel's Ming Fu Chia, CD★★ whose sire was Ch. Ming Tali II, CD★ and whose dam was Ch. Fu La Simpatica. Chia became Mrs. Smith's foundation bitch, producing seven champions, four with the Colarlie prefix and three with the Kyi Chu prefix.

Mrs. Smith acquired from his breeders, Frances and Ron Vendetti, the puppy that was to become her foundation sire, Ch. Colarlie's Shan Bangalor ROM★★.

Chia had three litters by Shan Bangalor to produce six champions, among them Group-winning Ch. Colarlie's Dokki, CD, the first black Lhasa Apso to win a Group and the sire of Ch. Kyi Chu Impa Satan ROM★ out of Ch. Karma Ami Chiri, and Ch. Colarlie's Miss Shanda ROM★★, the dam of multiple BIS Ch. Kyi Chu Friar Tuck ROM★ and Ch. Kyi Chu Kira, CD, ROM★★.

Kira was the dam of the Best in Show–winning bitch Am. & Can. Ch.

Ch. Panda Bear Sing of Kyi Chu (Ch. Colarlie's Shan Bangalor ROM x Colarlie's Pitti Sing), was bred by Ruth Smith and owned by Patricia and Tom Chenoweth.

Three puppies that made good—(from left) Ch. Kyi Chu Friar Tuck (eight months), Ch. Kyi Chu Impa Satan (nine months) and Ch. Kyi Chu Whimsi of Sharbet (fourteen months). All finished their championships in 1965.

Ch. Kyi Chu Shufi (Ch. Kyi Chu Kum Nuk x Ch. Kyi Chu Kira, CD) bred and owned by Ruth Smith, Kyi Chu.

Kyi Chu Shara ROM★ and her litter brother Group-winning Ch. Kyi Chu Whimsi of Sharbet, both sired by Ch. Karma Kanjur, CD (Hamilton Maroh x Ch. Karma Gyapso). Kira was also the dam of Ch. Kyi Chu Kissami ROM★ out of Impa Satan, that when bred to Ch. Kyi Chu Kum Nuk ROM★ (Ch. Gyal Kham Nag of San Jo ROM★ x Kyi Chu Dalamar Nor) produced Ch. Kyi Chu Inshalla, the dam of Ch. Kyi Chu Chaos, whose sire was multiple BIS multiple Ch. Chen Korum Ti ROM★★.

Mrs. Smith's breeding program stressed the basic soundness of the dog and its ability to move well as proof of that fact. Her emphasis upon proper size and temperament that would socialize easily made them keynotes of her breeding program.

Many Kyi Chu–bred Lhasa Apsos were ROM and star producers, and many had Obedience titles.

COUNTRY FAIR

Harley W. and Eleanore Poore obtained from Mrs. J. L. Weltz the bitch Miradel's Chomolungma and her two daughters, Country Fair's Susanna and Country Fair's Dasi Mae, both by Ch. Las Sa Gre's Manchado Dorado and bred by Mrs. Weltz.

The Poores bred Chomolungma back to her father, Ming Tali II, in 1957 to produce their first litter containing Wee Tshechokung, a female.

Chomolungma was bred a year later to the Ming Tali II son Ch. San Yu Ti of Abbotsford. This litter produced among others the dog Country Fair's Golden Charm, CD, who was used as a sire by the Poores.

Susanna was also bred to San Yu Ti and produced Country Fair's Sir Panther, that also sired for the Poores.

Dasi Mae was bred to Taylor's Chado of Miradel (Manchado Dorado x Miradel's Khan Dee) to produce Ch. Country Fair's Kushikhan.

Sir Panther was bred to Miradel's Cho Jo Blossom (Las Sa Gre's Hi Jo D'Al Tiro x Chomolungma) to produce, among others, Ch. Country Fair T-Su, a female.

It was from this basic foundation that the Poores developed the program that produced at least sixty-three litters in the fifteen years they bred Lhasa Apsos. The Poores' breeding program was unique because they apparently did not breed for the show ring. Only two champions named with the Country Fair prefix are recorded.

Many Lhasa Apsos with or without the Country Fair prefix and bred by the Poores can be found to be foundation stock for other kennels.

CHEN

Chen Lhasa Apsos began in 1959 when Tom and Patricia Chenoweth got Colarlie's Pitti-Sing (Ch. Taylor's Ming of Miradel x Miradel's Ming Fu Chia,

BIS Am., Bda., Col. Ch. Chen Korum Ti ROM won the 1971, 1972 and 1975 Western ALAC Specialties and the 1972 Eastern ALAC Specialty. He is shown with handler Robert Sharp.

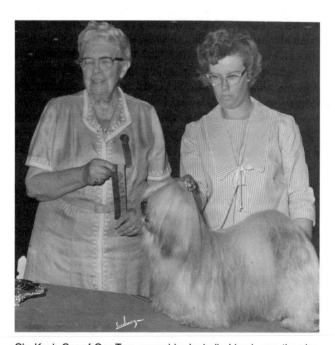

Ch. Kash Gar of Gar Ten, owned by Isabelle Lloyd, was the sire of some sixteen champions. He is shown here scoring a win under the legendary Mrs. L. W. Bonney, handler Nancy Tinker.

Ludwig

CD★★). Bred to Ch. Colarlie's Shan Bangalor ROM★★, she produced their first homebred champion, Ch. Shenji Sing of Kyi Chu. Sing was bred to Ch. Shar Ming of Bangalor★ (Shan Bangalor x Kathy's Miradel Copi of Ming) to produce the first champion to carry the Chen name, Ch. Shenji's Miss Kachika of Chen ROM★.

In 1964, a seven-week-old puppy that became Ch. Kyi Chu Kara Nor ROM★★ was added to the breeding program, and when bred to Ch. Licos Omorfo La ROM★ (BIS Ch. Licos Kulu La x Ch. Hamilton Pluti ROM★) produced Ch. Chen Makalu Nor of Dzungar. Additionally, Licos Gia La (Chulung La x Pluti) was obtained, and when bred to Makalu produced Ch. Chen Nyun Ti ROM★★. This provided the foundation stock for the straight Hamilton line that Chen developed which produced the dominant-producing Nyun Ti sons, Group-winning Am. & Can. Ch. Chen Krisna Nor ROM★★ and Ch. Pan Chen Tonka Sonan ROM★.

BIS Am., Bda. & Col. Ch. Chen Korum Ti ROM★★, although not a straight Hamilton-bred, was a dominant producer and successful show dog for the Chenoweths.

Chen Lhasa Apsos was one of the charter recipients of the ALAC ROM breeders' award in 1973 when it was awarded for the first time.

In November 1984, the Chen Kennel in Saratoga, California, burned. Many dogs and a lifetime of records were lost. The Chenoweths, with the determination to look to the future, have regrouped and are again breeding the famous Chen Lhasa Apsos, albeit on a smaller scale. The youngster Chen Jami Memory of a Titan is the result of the thirty-year-old straight Hamilton line developed by Chen.

GAR TEN

Mrs. Isabelle Loyd, Gar Ten Lhasa Apsos, acquired Lou Lan of Gar Ten (Hamilton Kala x Hamilton Sakya) from her breeders Richard and Mary Louise Janes in 1958. In 1959, Lou Lan was bred to Ch. Karma Getson to produce Tengin of Gar Ten.

Tengin was bred to Hamilton Shi Pon in 1961 and produced the female Ch. Baba Tarim of Gar Ten and Ch. Kashgar of Gar Ten★, sire of sixteen champions and the leading sire for the Gar Ten breeding program.

Next Mrs. Loyd acquired the bitch Kara Loyd of Gar Ten (Ch. Yan Sen of Gar Ten x Majon's Candra). Yan Sen was by Ch. Koko of Gar Ten (Ch. Hamilton Achok★ x Lou Lan) out of Tengin. Candra's sire was Ch. Hamilton Jimpa★ and her dam was Kyi Chu Jasmine (Shan Bangalor x Ming Fu Chia). Kara was bred twice in 1966, first to Ch. Licos Chulung La ROM★ to produce the bitch Ch. Chu Chu La of Gar Ten, and next to Kashgar to produce the dog Ch. Kambu Bombo of Gar Ten and the bitch Ch. Kasha of Gar Ten.

Mrs. Loyd continued to use this base to breed the Gar Ten dogs until her retirement in the late 1970s.

NORBULINGKA

Mrs. Phyllis Marcy commenced activity when she obtained her first Lhasa Apso in 1957 from Marilyn Sorci, Shangri La. He was Shangri La Tenzing Bhu and he readily finished his championship.

Norbulingka's foundation stock, however, was a male, Licos Khung La (Ch. Hamilton Achok★ x Ch. Licos Nyapso La ROM★★) and a female, Karma Kosala (Ch. Hamilton Sandupa★ x Am. & Mex. Ch. Karma Sangpo). These two, when bred together, produced in 1961 Mrs. Marcy's first homebred champions, the breed record holder BIS Ch. Kham of Norbulingka ROM★★ and his littermate Ch. Kyetsang of Norbulingka.

Of the twenty champions that Kham produced, the one most influential to Norbulingka's breeding program was Ch. Lingkhor Bhu of Norbulingka ROM★, whose dam was Can. Ch. Lui Gi's Tonka of Lingkhor (Alta Bu of Lhasa Rab x Hamilton Lhanji), that sired Am. & Can. Ch. Minda's Tsong of Bhu ROM out of Minda Linga (Ch. Licos Namni La ROM x Karma A Li Kambu). Tsong of Bhu sired the champions Ch. Norbulingka's Prosciutto out of Lady W's Ibis of Karriad (Ch. Mor Knoll Chok's Grand Slam ROM★ x Ch. Lady W's Becky Sharpe), Ch. Norbulingka Anna Bel out of Ch. Lady W's Sunshine Gal (Ch. Potala Keke's Golden Gatsby ROM★ x Ch. Lady W's Miss Sadie Woo ROM) and Ch. Norbulingka's Crazy Daisy ROM out of Norbulingka's Suki (Tsong of Bhu x Ch. Tshewla Happy Budha). Daisy produced three Norbulingka champions, one of which was the Group winner Ch. Norbulingka's Khyber, by BIS Am. Can. Ch. Bihar's Revenger of Sammi Raja★. When Khyber was bred to Char Ru's Sha Na Na II (Char Ru's Root 'N Toot 'N Dakota x Ch. Char Ru's Sha Na Na ROM★), he produced Ch. Norbulingka's Ms Anna-Mation.

Prosciutto is the sire of Ch. Norbulingka's Boston T Parti, also out of Sha Na Na II, a bitch Mrs. Marcy obtained from Char Ru Lhasa Apsos.

Mrs. Marcy was one of the charter recipients of the ALAC ROM breeders' award in 1973.

RONDELAY

Ruth Deck, Rondelay, originally bred Standard Poodles before becoming interested in Lhasa Apsos. After seeing a picture of a Lhasa Apso, she purchased a bitch in the early 1950s that was not registerable.

Mrs. Deck next purchased from the Griffings a bitch, Promenade Sing A Ling (Ch. Hamilton Kung★ x Ch. Ming Toy Nola) born in 1959. Next the male Cornwallis Ming Ho (Ch. Raggs of Cornwallis x Ch. Miradel's Ming Fu Dream

Ch. Norbulingka's Crazy Daisy, bred by L. Clarke and co-bred and owned by Phyllis Marcy, Norbulingka. *Gilbert*

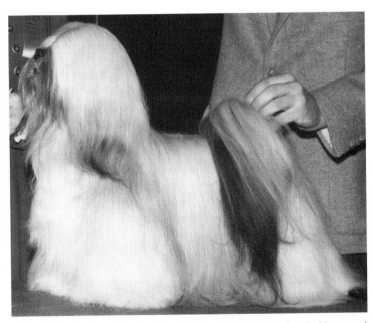

Ch. Norbulingka Prosciutto, bred by Barbara Buckland and Phyllis Marcy and owned by Walter Nordin and Phyllis Marcy. *Kernan*

Girl) joined Rondelay, and when bred to Sing A Ling produced Mrs. Deck's first registered litter of Lhasa Apsos, which was whelped in 1961. In this litter was Rondelay Seng Tru, that when bred to Ch. Chig Golden Anniversary produced Ch. Baijai's Phutuu. Sing A Ling was also bred to America's Lhasa ROM★ to produce Ch. Rondelay Zhu Danga.

Mrs. Deck's next acquisition was the bitch Hamilton Tsing Phuti, that when bred to Ming Changnola produced Rondelay Hara Chakbo. When Chakbo was bred to Drax Shahnaz (Shan Bangalor x Ch. Ramblersholt Shahnaz), he produced Ch. Rondelay De Chu Ming Quitian and Ch. Rondelay Dalai.

Another important purchase was that of the champion bitch Dhuphy's Sesame (Shan Bangalor x Kyi Chu Pandi). Bred to Zhu Danga, she produced Ch. Rondelay Lhamo Kutra, the dam of Ch. Rondelay Shay Na Poon Um, Ch. Rondelay Vee Fib Ri La Shun and Rondelay Kyi-Lin Senge, all sired by Ch. Sengri Tashaling. Tashaling was by Ch. Everglo's Charlie Brown ROM★ out of Ch. Hilador Winsome Kurma La (Ch. Licos Kupl La x Ch. Licos Takpa Shiri La).

Kyi-Lyn Senge was bred to Rondelay Samada Sprite (Tip Seng Tasha x Sharpette's Black Sprite) to produce Ch. Rondelay Raja of Rjay.

A breeder of Lhasa Apsos since 1961, Mrs. Deck has not made the show ring the primary reason for breeding Lhasa Apsos. Most Rondelay-bred Lhasa Apsos can be found as happy pets, many in the homes of celebrities.

ZIJUH

Mrs. Bea Loob, Zijuh Lhasa Apsos, bought her first in 1959. Very soon, however, she realized it was not of the quality of Marie Stillman's dogs. When Mrs. Loob sought to buy an Americal Lhasa Apso, Mrs. Stillman did not have one available, but she helped Mrs. Loob to acquire a female from Hamilton Farms Kennel. That was Ch. Hamilton Shim Tru★, that when bred to Ch. Karma Kushog produced Ch. Zijuh Tsam★ and Ch. Zijuh Kata. She was also bred to Frosty Knight to produce Ch. Zijuh El Torro and to Hamilton Toradga to produce Ch. Zijuh Seng Tru ROM★★.

Mrs. Loob's next purchase was another female, Donna Cardella's Tsng. (Ch. Karma Lobsang x Karma Dakini), that when bred to Tsam produced Ch. Zijuh Thori and Ch. Zijuh Jinda★.

The first male Mrs. Loob purchased came from Gloria Fowler, Everglo. Named Ch. Everglo's Zijuh Tomba by Mrs. Loob, he sired a litter from Ch. Zijuh Teri★ (Ch. Licos Zaskar La x Jinda), from which came champions Zijuh Chi Gi, Cha La and Tomon O Mai Tai. Teri was also bred to Ch. Kashgar of Gar Ten★ to produce Ch. Zijuh Jooley.

Shim Tru did not like the show ring, but with considerable effort Mrs. Loob showed her to her championship. She vowed, however, that she would not go through such an effort again, so when Tomba indicated a distaste for the show ring, she gave him and Jinda to Sharon Rouse-Bryant, who had come looking for stud service. Mrs. Rouse-Bryant put considerable effort into his training and eventually after a year handled Tomba to his championship. Jinda showed herself and readily earned her title.

SAN JO

Marianne Nixon obtained her first Lhasa Apso in 1953, but it was not until she bred her first litter in 1960 that she coined the San Jo prefix. This first litter was out of Ch. Jomo Dkar-po of Abbotsford (Can. Ch. Miradel's Que Tee x Can. Ch. Ping) that Mrs. Nixon purchased as a puppy from the Canadian breeder Mrs. James Roberts, Abbotsford. The sire of this litter was Jomo's half brother Ch. San Yu Ti of Abbotsford (Ch. Ming Tali II, CD x Can. Ch. Ping), and it was this litter that produced San Jo's first homebred champion and multiple Group-winning foundation sire, Ch. Gyal Kham-nag of San Jo ROM★.

Mrs. Nixon met Ruth Smith, Kyi Chu, in 1966 when Kyi Chu Dalama Nor (Ch. Ruffway Kamet x Ch. Karma Ami Chiri) was sent to be bred to Kham-nag. Because of this meeting Mrs. Nixon obtained the half sister and brother that were both out of Ch. Kyi Chu Kira, CD, ROM★★ and were to become Am. & Can. Ch. Kyi Chu Kissami ROM★, sired by Ch. Kyi Chu Impa Satan ROM★ (Ch. Colarlie's Dokki, CD x Ami Chiri), and Ch. Kyi Chu Manshifa of San Jo ROM, sired by Ch. Kyi Chu Kum Nuk ROM★ (Kham-nag x Dalama Nor).

Kham-nag was bred to Kissami and produced BIS Ch. San Jo's Torgi and his litter sister San Jo's Bandi of Gartok ROM★.

Equally important to the success of San Jo is Mrs. Nixon's daughter, Leslie Ann Engen, who in 1972 when just a teenager, finished Ch. San Jo's Tonsen Me of Sheridan, by San Jo's Senge Me (Kum Nuk x San Jo's Dessa) out of Tonka Me of Sheridan (T-Sus PeeWee x Mandy). It was Tonsen Me that, when bred to the Manshifa x Kissami daughter Ch. San Jo's Lena ROM, produced Canadian BIS Am. & Can. Ch. San Jo's Raaga Looki Mei ROM★.

When Ch. King's Brandi Kyi of San Jo was bred to Ch. San Jo's Sorta Sooty, the record-holding bitch BIS Ch. San Jo's Hussel Bussel ROM★★ resulted.

Ch. Zoroshah Morific of San Jo (Ch. Everglo Sir Tom ROM x Everglo Tangerine) bred to the Tonsen Me daughter San Jo's Pandora produced the Group winner Ch. San Jo's Shenanigan ROM★★. Morific was also bred to the Manshifa daughter Ch. San Jo's Tamara of Rob-Tell ROM to produce Ch. San Jo's Kian Kandi Kan ROM★★, the dam of BIS S. J. W. Waffle Stomper ROM★★ sired by Looki Mei.

When Shenanigan was bred to the Looki Mei daughter Group-winning Ch. San Jo's Tabatha ROM★, he sired BIS Ch. San Jo's Shindig ROM★.

Mrs. Nixon developed a breeding program guided by her interpretation of the Lhasa Apso standard and bred primarily to perpetuate her own breeding stock. Therefore, San Jo stock was rarely seen outside the Pacific Northwest and had little effect elsewhere in the country until the last decade when the San Jo bloodline was released by Mrs. Nixon through numerous co-ownerships. Now the line is being successfully used by kennels throughout the United States and Canada.

San Jo received the ALAC ROM breeders' award in 1977.

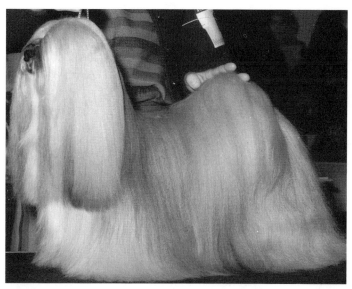

BIS Ch. San Jo's Shindig ROM*, owned by Victor Cohen, Victory, sired at least seven champions and was bred by Marianne Nixon, San Jo, and Windy Everest. *Lindemaier*

Ch. San Jo's Rusty Nail ROM**, the sire of at least twenty-two champions, was bred by Marianne Nixon and Leslie Ann Engen, San Jo. *Lindemaier*

BIS Am. Can. Ch. Arborhill's Rapso Dieh was by BIS Ch. Everglo's Spark of Gold ROM x Ch. Arborhill's Lee Sah. He was owned by Janet Whitman.

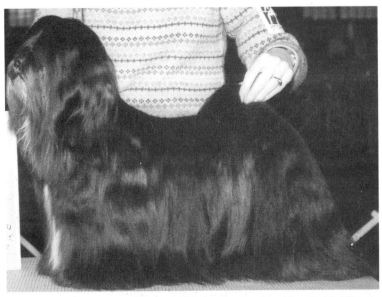

Ch. BarCon's The Critic's Choice ROM*, bred, owned and handled by Connie and Barry Tompkins. *Ashbey*

5

The Breed Gains in Popularity in the 1960s

ARBORHILL

Sharon Binkowski, Arborhill Kennels, is the breeder of the brothers BIS Ch. Arborhill's Rapso Dieh ROM★★ and Group winner Ch. Arborhill's Bhran Dieh ROM★★ and BIS Ch. Arborhill's Rah Kieh ROM★, by Rapso Dieh and out of Ch. Arborhill's Lhana ROM★ (Kham x Ch. Arborhill's Karoling Karolyn ROM★).

Although Mrs. Binkowski bred Lhasa Apsos only about ten years, her Arborhill bloodlines can be found behind many successful Lhasa Apso breeding programs today.

BARCON

BarCon was originated when Barry and Connie Tompkins purchased a four-month-old particolor Lhasa Apso in 1969. ''Gus'' was to be a family pet, but after visiting a dog show he doubled as a show dog and became Ch. BarCon's Arveragus (Ch. Lakeland's Ta Hsing of Miradel x Kara Koram).

BarCon's foundation bitch, BarCon's Madam Eglantyne, by Ch. Keke's Petruchio (Tibet x BIS Ch. Kyi Shara ROM★) out of Keke's Little Ginger (Ch.

Mr. Kay of Cornwallis x Ch. Keke's T'Chin Ting T'Chin ROM), was bred to Spark of Gold to produce Ch. BarCon's Double Trouble and her famous record-breaking brother, multiple BIS Ch. BarCon's the Avenger ROM★★.

Double Trouble produced Ch. BarCon's Stage Door Jonny, sired by Group-winning Ch. Potala Keke's Tomba Tu ROM★, and Ch. BarCon's Wheeler Dealer, sired by Tibet.

Ch. BarCon's Rave Review ROM★ was by the Avenger bred to his daughter, Ch. Bihar's Act Tu of BarCon (litter sister to Ch. Bihar's Revenger of Sammi Raja★), a bitch the Tompkins considered correct in every way but size. Rave Review when bred to Ch. Kian's Rah Hide (Ch. San Jo's Wellington Kandy Man ROM★ x Ch. Kian's Hide 'N Go Peep★), a total outcross, produced five BarCon champions including Group-winning Ch. BarCon's The Critic's Choice ROM★ and Ch. BarCon's Opening Night.

Always working as a family unit, the Tompkins enjoyed their dogs and the sport and found success qualifying for the ALAC Register of Merit award in 1985 with only nine litters in twenty years as breeders.

CHIZ ARI

Madeline Durholz and her daughter, Joanne Baker, started Chiz Ari Lhasa Apsos with the purchase of their first dog, Chiz Ari Kheley, CD, in 1969.

The next acquisition for Chiz Ari was Pongo's Tashi Thu, who provided experience in the conformation ring and introduced Joanne to junior handling.

Chiz Ari's foundation bitch, Kinderland's Winne of Chiz ROM★ by Ch. On Ba Jes Su Khan (Zer Khan x Zim Zim) out of Crest O Lake Ming Lee (Ch. Maraja Dolpho Karmo x Crest O Lake Miss Muffet) was co-owned with Ellen Lonigro.

In 1973, Chiz Ari purchased a five-month-old male that was to become multiple BIS Ch. Little Fir's Shel Ari of Chiz ROM★★ (Marpa x Ch. Orlane Meling of Ruffway), having been piloted to two of his Best in Show wins by seventeen-year-old Joanne.

When bred to Shel Ari, Winne produced Ch. Chiz Ari Ko Khyi, and when bred to Ch. Pan Chen Tonka Sonan ROM★, she produced three champions, among them the top producing bitch Ch. Chiz Ari Sehilot ROM★★★★★ and Ch. Chiz Ari Alisa of Kijer, the dam of Ch. Chiz Ari Billie's Follie Doll by Chiz Ari Maverik and Ch. Chiz Ari Maggie's Kara Stan by Shel Ari of Chiz.

Sehilot, sold on a breeder's terms contract, was co-owned with Wellington and when bred to Shel Ari of Chiz produced six champions carrying the Chiz Ari and Wellington names, among them BIS Chiz Ari Wellington Shofar ROM★★.

Chiz Ari qualified to receive the ALAC Register of Merit award in 1980.

During the 1970s and early 1980s, Chiz Ari carried on a successful breeding program, and although the kennel has been inactive in recent years, there are

Multiple BIS Ch. Little Fir's Shel Ari of Chiz ROM** shown here winning Best in Show under judge Dr. Bernard Esporite and handled by co-owner Joanne Baker. Also in photo is owner Madeline Chizever-Durholz.   *Alverson*

Ch. Darno Gemini Morningstar, bred and owned by Norma and Darrell Mileham, Darno, and handled here by Mrs. Mileham.   *Booth*

plans for Miss Baker to activate the Chiz Ari breeding and showing program in the near future.

DARNO

Norma and Darrell Mileham, Darno Lhasa Apsos, became interested in the breed while searching for an Obedience prospect. Mrs. Mileham became acquainted with Lillian Stittig and obtained her first two Lhasa Apsos from her, Darno Kesang Tru-A, a grandson of Ch. Hamilton Tatsienlu★, in 1964 and a great-granddaughter of Ch. Le in 1965. The female, Stittig's Lucknow Deimar, produced the Mileham's first homebred champion, Ch. Darno Be Mieh of Maraja, when bred to Ch. Karma Pempa. Additionally, a bitch, Darno Su Lin of Maraja, was obtained from Jane Bunse, Maraja, and a Sparky son, Ch. Sakya Maximillian of Orlane, was obtained from Dorothy Kendall, Orlane. This is the foundation stock that established the Darno line.

Mrs. Mileham shows the Darno Lhasa Apsos as well as clients' dogs, as she became a handler in 1974.

Some Lhasa Apsos bred by the Milehams that helped qualify Darno to receive the ALAC ROM breeders' award in 1983: Darno Brocade Billie ROM and her three champion sons, Ch. Darno Pretty Boi Floyd out of Ch. Luty Just Dandy of Darno, Ch. Darno Ramrod out of Darno Omega of Wynsippi and Ch. Darno Ragtime out of Ch. Tru Be's Mr. Hard To Come By; Darno Su Lin of Maraja, the dam of Ch. Darno Lama and Ch. Darno Kazak of Vijan, both by Ch. Morgantown's Golden Boy; Darno Nirvana, the dam of Ch. Darno Tumbling Jill by Ch. Sakya Maximillian of Orlane and Ch. Darno Windwick Tootsie by Pretty Boi Floyd. Tumbling Jill produced Ch. Darno Gemini Morningstar by Pretty Boi Floyd and Ch. Darno The Rose by Ramrod. Pretty Boi Floyd is also the sire of Ch. Darno Amazingly Gracie out of Ruffway Peper of Darno.

DRAX

The late Mrs. Winifred Drake's Drax Kennels was established in the early 1960s and ultimately combined American and English bloodlines in a breeding program that was awarded an ALAC ROM breeders' award in 1976. Drax ceased activity upon Mrs. Drake's death in the mid-1980s.

DZONG

Dzong Lhasa Apsos was owned by Mrs. Beverly Garrison and was the home of Ch. Colarlie's Miss Shanda ROM★★. Dzong was awarded the ALAC ROM breeders' award in 1974. Dzong has been inactive since 1976.

56

Ch. Everglo Ku Su (Everglo Marmelade x Everglo Ara) was bred by Gloria Fowler, Everglo, and was owned by Winifred Graye and Carolyn Blondel when he became a champion.

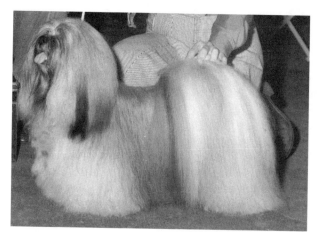

A Group winner from the classes, Ch. Everglo ArKay Paper Lion was bred by Gloria Fowler, Everglo, and was owned and handled by Bill and Becki Kraus, ArKay. *Alverson*

Ch. Everglo Somethin (Everglo Rempa ROM* x Everglo Abra) was bred and owned by Gloria Fowler, Everglo, and co-owned by Mrs. Fowler and Catherine Marley when he became a champion.

EVERGLO

Mrs. Gloria Fowler, who uses the name Everglo for her kennel, has basically had two different breeding programs.

She started her first program when she obtained the Rinpoche-bred bitch Kai Sang's Tzi-Ren of Miradel from the Liebmanns, Miradel, along with her son Ch. Kai Sang's Clown of Everglo.

In 1960, she bred Tzi-Ren to Ruffway Auld Lang Syne to produce Everglo's first Lhasa Apso, Cinderella of Everglo.

Another bitch acquired by Mrs. Fowler was Ruffway Hun-Nee-Bun, that when bred to Clown produced Tibetan Cookie of Everglo. When Cookie was bred back to her father, she produced BIS Ch. Everglo's Spark of Gold ROM★★★★.

Because of the controversy during this time period, and Mrs. Fowler's decision to disperse all of her original stock, Spark of Gold was sold as a puppy along with his young half sister, the future Ch. Kai Sang's Flame of Everglo ROM★, as foundation stock for Dorothy Kendall, Orlane.

In 1963, Mrs. Fowler started over with the acquisition of straight Hamilton stock, namely, Hamilton Norden★ (Ch. Hamilton Sandupa★ x Ch. Hamilton Den Sa), a bitch from Hamilton Farms, and the future Ch. Kyima of Everglo ROM★, by Hamilton Yi Tru (Sandupa x Den Sa) out of Stittig's Moka Kara Dei Mar (Ch. Hamilton Peking x Hamilton Durga), from her breeder, Georgia Palmer, Ruffway.

Mrs. Fowler first bred Norden to Ch. Licos Chulung La ROM★, which produced the male Cubbi Kyeri of Everglo, that when bred to Kyima produced Kambu of Everglo ROM.

Mrs. Fowler purchased BIS Ch. Karma Frosty Knight O Everglo ROM★ as a puppy. When bred to Kambu, he sired the brothers Ch. Everglo Zijuh Tomba ROM★★ and Ch. Everglo Charlie Brown ROM★.

Kyima was also bred to Frosty Knight to produce among others, the bitch Dandi Golden Gypsy of Everglo ROM★. Kyima was then bred to Ch. Licos Omorfo La ROM★ to produce the three bitches Everglo Buttercup ROM★, Everglo Mai Ling Tsung ROM★ and Everglo Bright Star.

Buttercup, when bred to Karma Sha-Do of Everglo (Ch. Karma Lobsang x Karma Zim-Po), produced among others the males Ch. Everglo Aro and Everglo Rempa ROM★ and the female Ch. Everglo Ma La Bu★. When Buttercup was bred to Chulung La, she produced Ch. Dixie's Beau of Everglo ROM★.

Everglo Encore Ember, sired by Karma Heki (Karma Takster x Hamilton Amdo) out of Ferns Flame of Tibet (Cubbi Kyeri x Kambu), produced Ch. Everglo Flair ROM★ when bred to Rempa and Everglo Red Regent ROM★ when bred to Sha-Do.

Mrs. Fowler bred from this base, keeping what she liked and putting emphasis on the breeding program through the females. The success of Everglo is due in part to the numbers bred from which to choose, and most of today's stock traces back to these original dogs as Mrs. Fowler believes in line breeding.

The show records on Everglo dogs are primarily those made by purchasers

Ch. Likalas Tyg Gyr Tu of Hylan, bred by Midge Hylton and Gerry Gordy and owned by James and Lila Kaiser, Likala, completed his championship in 1977. *Mik-Ron*

Shown here is Ch. Chen Hylan Jampal as a class dog winning BOW, handled by John Hylton, Hylan, and Ch. Hylan Tisa of Tacin as a puppy winning RWB, handled by Midge Hylton, Hylan, in 1973. *Bennett Associates*

because Mrs. Fowler has not made showing a priority. A tribute to Mrs. Fowler's breeding program is that most modern pedigrees contain Everglo dogs.

Although Everglo qualified for the ALAC ROM breeders' award before its inception, it was not until 1985 that Mrs. Fowler applied for and received ROM status.

HYLAN

Hylan Lhasa Apsos was established when John and Midge Hylton, successful Shetland Sheepdog fanciers, applied their show and breeding expertise to Lhasa Apsos, obtaining their first in 1968. This was the puppy bitch that became Ch. Pandan Panchen (Nyun Ti x Pandan Nan-Gi) and later the young male that became Ch. Potala Pandan Apollo ROM★ (Tibet x Ch. Karma Kansa ROM★), Hylan's original foundation stock.

When Apollo was bred to Panchen, they produced Ch. Pandan Hylan Korba of Karo La, Ch. Hylan Che Ba and Hylan Pan Po ROM★. Che Ba was bred to Nyun Ti and produced Ch. Hylan Ti Ko Can and Group-winning Ch. Hylan Tse-Tsan. When Pan Po was bred to Ch. Chen Nor Hapi Resolution (Seng Tru x Kara Nor), she produced Ch. Likalas Tyg Gyr Tu of Hylan; when bred to Ch. Chen Hylan Jampal (Chen Angus Nor x Chen Tom Tru), she produced Ch. Hylan Tisa of Tacin and Ch. Tacin Coco Bear of Pawprints and when bred to Krisna Nor, she produced Ch. Hylan Knjira and Hylan Hol Lei. When Tyg Gyr was bred to Hol Lei, they produced Ch. Hylan Nakai of Kyu-Ru, who when bred to Hylan Tessa of Kyu-Ru (Maru's Palamine x Maru's Scarlet of Everglo) produced Ch. Hylan Tallisyn and Hylan Chanda.

The Hyltons were awarded the ALAC ROM breeders' award in 1979.

Mr. Hylton handled the Hylan Lhasa Apsos until he became too ill to do so, at which time Pat Keen started handling for the Hyltons. Mr. Hylton died in 1983.

JOYMARC

Winifred and Eugene Graye, Joymarc, originated Joymarc Lhasa Apsos in 1966 with the purchase of a show dog from Mrs. Albertram McFadden, Lui Gi. He did not prove good enough so Mrs. McFadden replaced him with what was to become the Joymarc foundation bitch, Lui Gi's Blossom Tyme (Lui Gi's Saint Michael x Lui Gi's Tibby). Although never shown and not a producer herself, she can be found behind most Joymarc champions, usually several times.

Joymarc's first champion and foundation sire was Am. & Can. Ch. Verles Jigme Tru, imported at five months from the English kennel Verles of Mrs. Hesketh-Williams by the Grayes in 1969. He was a champion in two countries by age fourteen months. His only champion is the Grayes' first homebred champion, Ch. Joymarc's Karraghan Gold Dust, who is out of the Blossom Tyme

BIS Ch. Arkay Tsuro The Energizer (Ch. Everglo Ku Su x Ch. ArKay Lai Dieh Jane) was bred by Bill and Becki Kraus and owned by the Kraus' and Roger and Susan Hild, Tsuro. The winner of five Bests in Show, The Energizer was exclusively handled throughout his career by Bill Kraus.
Photo by Phoebe

Group Winning Ch. Hylan Tse-Tsan, was bred by John and Midge Hylton, Hylan, and owned by Tony Ross and John Hylton.
Kloeber

Multiple Group winning Am. Can. Ch. Joymarc's Terra Cotta, bred by Daisy Medford and Winifred Graye, was owned and handled by Bill and Becki Kraus, ArKay. *Alverson*

daughter, Joymarc's Topsi. Jigme Tru can be found behind most Joymarc champions, usually two or three times.

Another sire that was important to Joymarc was On Ba Lho Bho O' Joymarc (Tomba x Zim Zim), the sire of six Joymarc champions, among which are the multiple Group-winning bitch Am. & Can. Ch. Joymarc's Terra Cotta out of Joymarc's Casaba and Ch. Joymarc's Blama Claudia out of Joymarc's Baby Jane. Claudia is the dam of Ch. Joymarc's Foxy Lady, that when bred to Ch. Joymarc's Pretty Boy Floyd (Ch. Joymarc's Banacheck x Ch. Joymarc's Miss Mischief) produced three champions, Ch. Joymarc's Lady Killer, Ch. Sharil's Painted Lady and Ch. Joymarc's Lady Flash. Foxy Lady is by Can. Ch. Ocon Joymarc Daredevil, also the sire of Ch. Sharil Joymarc Patent Pending out of Everglo Joymarc Mary Mary.

Joymarc qualified for the ALAC ROM breeders' award in 1982, but it was not awarded until 1989.

KINDERLAND

Ellen Lonigro, Kinderland kennels, was originally a German Shepherd breeder, and acquired the bitch Clyzett's Butter Lamp in 1962.

Her first champion was Ch. Jigmie of Carycliff (Ch. Hamilton Kung x Hamilton Mar Dree), who finished his championship in 1962, but when he died prematurely Mrs. Lonigro purchased Ch. Larrmar De-Tsen ROM★ (BIS Ch. Licos Kulu La x Ch. Shangri La Tibetan Butterfly CD), who became her foundation sire. De-Tsen and Butter Lamp were bred together twice in 1963, resulting in the first homebred Kinderland champion, the female Ch. Kinderland's Ne-Mieh.

In 1965, a puppy was purchased that became Ch. Kinderland's Sang Po ROM★★ and the foundation bitch for Kinderland. When De-Tsen and Sang Po were bred together, they produced two champions as well as Kinderland's Buddha, that when bred to her grandsire, Kham, produced Ch. Kinderland's Mi Terra ROM★.

Sang Po was also bred to BIS Ch. Tibet of Cornwallis ROM★★★★ to produce multiple BIS Am. & Bda. Ch. Kinderland's Tonka ROM★.

Mrs. Lonigro obtained the Spark of Gold son Ch. Ruffway Marpa ROM★, that produced five Kinderland champions when bred to Sang Po.

When Marpa was bred to the Kham granddaughter Dally Kim Su (Ch. Mighty of Norbulingka★ x Jackson's Melody Su), they produced Ch. Kinderland's Pat Rica, that when bred to Ch. Ruffway T'Ang Chu ROM★★ produced multiple BIS Ch. Kinderland's Kishri Ruff.

In 1973, Mi Terra was bred to Ch. Zijuh Seng Tru ROM★★. From this mating came the puppy bitch Ch. Kinderland's Chok's Seneca, a puppy that would prove to have an everlasting impact on the future of Kinderland.

Mrs. Lonigro and Susan Giles formed a co-ownership on Seneca that was to overlap to all of her descendants, and the partnership of Kinderland Ta Sen was born.

Ch. Kinderland's Sang-Po ROM and her owner Ellen Lonigro. Sang is the dam of at least nine champions. She is daughter of BIS Ch. Kham of Norbulingka ROM and Ch. Ha-Ya-Chi.

Ch. Ruffway Marpa ROM, owned and handled by Ellen Lonigro, sire of twelve champions.

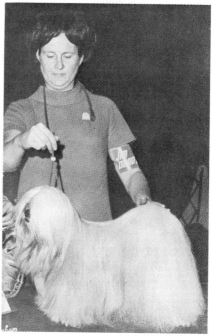

Ch. Ruffway Norru and his owner Ellen Lonigro. He was bred by Georgia Palmer and is a son of BIS Ch. Everglo Spark of Gold ROM and Ch. Ruffway Kara Shing ROM.

KNOLWOOD

Marion Knowlton obtained her first Lhasa Apsos in 1968 when she and her daughter each chose for a pet a puppy from a newspaper ad. In search of another Lhasa Apso as beautiful as the first she saw, Mrs. Knowlton contacted Diana Dansereau, Dandi, and obtained Ch. Dandi's Golden Sheba (Ch. Crest O Lake Kin Go ROM x Dandi Golden Gypsy of Everglo ROM★) on a co-ownership. Sheba became Mrs. Knowlton's first champion in 1972.

Mrs. Knowlton and Mrs. Dansereau bred Sheba to Ch. Geradene's Namu Tso (Ch. Licos Namni La ROM x Ch. Licos Naminka La), and her daughter Tai Alice of Kar La became a champion in the fall of 1973.

In the years that followed, Mrs. Knowlton combined Hamilton with Orlane, which produced many champions, among them multiple BIS Ch. Tom Lee Manchu of Knolwood ROM★★ (Inimitable x Ch. Ruleo's Peppermint Patti) that produced at least twenty-one champions. Among them, sixteen carry the Knolwood kennel name, one of which is Ch. Knolwood's Tom Tru, the sire of Ch. Knolwood's Josh My Gosh, whose dam is the Tom Lee daughter Ch. Knolwood's Golden Tassel out of Ch. Samara's Knolwood Kharisma (Ch. Amberhurst Samhain x Samara's Amiable Amy). Mrs. Knowlton considers Tom the cornerstone of her breeding program.

Mrs. Knowlton considers the other dominant male at Knolwood to be Ch. Innsbrook's Patrician O Sulan ROM★. This dog sired at least twenty champions, including Ch. Knolwood's Apso Seng Kye out of Ch. Knolwood's Tsanatisha (Ch. Kinderland's Ta Sen Dakini x Ch. Dunklehaven Red Cleauver); Ch. Knolwood's Gypsy Rose Lee out of Ch. Knolwood's Su-Je Kematso (Ch. Honeydew Me N' Bobi McGee x Knolwood's Zara Linga); Ch. Knolwood's Crown of Glori out of Amberhurst Farrah of Samara (Ch. Amberhurst Samhain x Samara's Amiable Amy) and Ch. Knolwood's Mei-Leigh-Lee out of Ch. Hope-Full's Heloise of Knolwood (Inimitable x Ch. Hope-Full's Heirloom ROM★). Additionally, he produced BIS Ch. Sulan's Gregorian Chant ROM★ out of Knolwood's American Spirit (BIS Ch. Joi-San's Happieh Go Luckieh x Ch. Dunklehaven Red Cleauver) and the litter sisters BIS Ch. Samara's Timekeeper Patti and Ch. Samara's Suger Is Sweet out of Samara's Sweet Shalom ROM (Ch. Brush's Simon of Samara x Dunklehaven Honey Bear ROM★).

Mrs. Knowlton was awarded the ALAC Register of Merit breeder's award in 1987.

KRISNA

Wendy Harper, Krisna, purchased her first show-quality Lhasa Apso from Patricia Chenoweth, Chen, in 1967. She was Ch. Chen Kamala Nor (Nyun Ti x Chen Himalayan Hanah Nor ROM★).

The following year, Mrs. Harper obtained a co-ownership with Mrs. Chen-

Multiple Best In Show Ch. Tom Lee Manchu of Knolwood ROM** was bred by Marion Knowlton, Knolwood. *Missy Photo*

Ch. Knolwood's Josh My Gosh sired by Ch. Knolwood's Tom Tru Tu, Marion Knowlton, Knolwood. *Bonnie*

Ch. Krisna Fancy Pants bred by Wendy Harper, Barbara Dwelly and Phyllis Hebrard and owned by Wendy Harper and Donna Peterson. *Callea*

Am. Can. Ch. Krisna Kam-Tora of Sunji bred by Robertha Matranga, Sunji, and owned by Wendy Harper, Krisna.

65

oweth on the male puppy that would become multiple Group-winning Am. & Can. Ch. Chen Krisna Nor ROM★★ and the namesake for Mrs. Harper's breeding program.

Krisna Nor was bred to Kamala Nor and sired Krisna Kam-Tu, that when bred to multiple BIS Am., Can. & Col. Ch. Chen Korum Ti ROM★★ produced Am. & Can. Ch. Krisna Kam-Tora of Sunji, and when bred back to Krisna Nor produced Ch. Krisna Talika.

Kamala Nor was also bred to BIS Ch. Tibet of Cornwallis ROM★★★★ and produced the bitch Krisna Kusuma. Bred back to Krisna Nor, Kusuma produced multiple Group-winning Ch. Krisna Likala Kar-Dan, that when bred to Kam-Tora produced Ch. Krisna Kara-Sin.

After Mrs. Harper lost Kam-Tora, she purchased the bitch that was to become multiple Group-winning Ch. Stonelea Bangles, by Ch. Orlane's Double Treat (Ch. Kinderland Ta Sen Dakini ROM★ x Orlane's Brandy Mine★) out of Sho Tru Pem Ms Behavin (Ch. Sakya Hallelujah x Bara's Kisstabel of Pam). Mrs. Harper made a dramatic change in the Krisna Lhasa Apsos when she introduced this totally new style. Mrs. Harper continued with this line by breeding Bangles to Ch. Sho Tru Hylan Stetson (Ch. Orlane Impudent of Windwick x Sho Tru's Kiss Ma Grits ROM★★), which produced Ch. Krisna Fancy Pants and Sho Tru Krisna Flo-Jo Hylan.

Mrs. Harper also co-owns Ch. Sho Tru Hylan Rocks Anne and Ch. Sho Tru Hylan Rock A Bye Baby, by Ch. Orlane's Scirocco ROM★ out of Sho Tru's Kiss Ma Grits ROM★★ (Intrepid x Sho Tru Tabriz of Orlane). These litter sisters became the top-winning brace in the history of the breed.

Mrs. Harper qualified for the ALAC Register of Merit breeders' award in 1989.

LORI SHAN

In 1968, Lorraine Shannon obtained her first Lhasa Apso, and although Mai Ling was not a successful show dog, it was because of this dog that Mrs. Shannon became involved in breeding and showing Lhasa Apsos.

The first Lori Shan winner was Lori Shan Goldie Lhama, but the first champion was the straight Hamilton-bred Ch. Frosty Chulung of Shang T'ou (Ch. Karma Kublai Khan x Zijuh Pak Jan). This dog produced three champions, including Ch. Lori Shan Labert Junior ROM out of Mai Toi of Shan T-ou (Ch. Karma Kublai Khan x Kerry On Muy Muy of Everglo). Labert Junior produced six Lori Shan champions, three out of the foundation bitch Stone's Ku Ki of Gar Ten ROM (Kalimar Raybir Gar Ten x Garba of Gar Ten). Of these, Ch. Regal Reginald of Lori Shan ROM, when bred to Little Bit of Lori Shan ROM★, by Sharbo Kohoutek (Tomba x Ch. Everglo Flair ROM★) out of Chamdo's Terai of Lori Shan (Chamdo's Makara x Ch. Tsela of Abbotsford ROM★), produced four champions, including Ch. Lori Shan Mona Lisa★, the dam of Mexican BIS

Little sisters, Group winner, BISS Ch. Sho Tru Hylan Rocks Anne and Ch. Sho Tru Hylan Rock A Bye Baby together are the top winning brace of all time. Bred and handled by Pat Keen, they are co-owned by Wendy Harper, Pat Keen and Midge Hylton. *Missy*

Ch. Lori Shan Puttin' On The Ritz, bred and owned by Lorraine Shannon and the dam of three Lori Shan champions.

Ch. Lori Shan Mona Lisa*, bred and owned by Lorraine Shannon, Lori Shan, the dam of five Lori Shan champions.

Group winner Ch. Marlo Somethin Else, bred and owned by Lynn Lowy, Marlo.
Photo by Ludwig

Am., Can. & Mex. Ch. Lori Shan Creative Chaos, Ch. Lori Shan Puttin' On The Ritz, Ch. Lori Shan Celebration and Ch. Lori Shan Snowbound's Flurry, all sired by Ch. Lori Shan Snowbound, by Labert Junior and Lyngso Terra (Am., Can. & Mex. Ch. On-Ba Jo-Bo ROM★ x Lyngso Am-Ri-Ta).

In 1987, Mrs. Shannon introduced Orlane bloodlines into what had been a predominantly Hamilton breeding program when she obtained Ch. Lori Shan Hylan Gold Nugget, bred by Midge Hylton, Hylan, and Don Ross, Madoros. Sired by Ch. Orlane's Impudent of Windwick★ out of Ch. Madoros Misty Magic (Inimitable x Madoros Misty Pebbles), Nugget was bred to Puttin' On The Ritz to produce Ch. Lori Shan Hylan Gold Cody, to Lori Shan Miss Junior Miss to produce Ch. Lori Shan Tuffers and to Lori Shan Sable Coat to produce Ch. Lori Shan Unforgettable.

Mrs. Shannon also bred Puttin' On The Ritz to Ch. Orlane's Double Treat to produce Ch. Lori Shan My Ladies Mercedes and Ch. Lori Shan Crystal Pistol.

Lori Shan qualified for the ALAC ROM award in 1981.

MARLO

Lynn Lowy, Marlo, acquired her first Lhasa Apso in 1969 when she visited some friends who had a Lhasa Apso pet, fell in love and promptly went out and bought the first one she found, a male named Simba, who remained her favorite for sixteen years.

A year after acquiring Simba, Mrs. Lowy got her first Hamilton Lhasa Apso, Ch. Cordova Tom-Tru (Karma Kacho x Ch. Karma Sakyi). He finished his championship quickly and Mrs. Lowy acquired another Hamilton dog, Ch. Dolsa Krisna Khorog. The two dogs did not get along and Khorog was sold. There was a long period of buying and selling dogs, looking for the foundation stock with which to start the Marlo breeding program.

The first of the foundation stock was the bitch Marlo's Tara of Dolsa ROM (Ch. Zijuh Don-Na Tsamten ROM★ x Cameo's Densa Dobra), who is behind all the Marlo Lhasa Apsos. The first foundation sire was Tara's half brother, Group-winning Ch. Marlo's Icecream Man O'Rimmon, who was sired by Ch. Rimmon Ripsnorter (Ch. Daktazl Tsung x Ch. Potala Keke's Pumpkin).

Tara produced Ch. Marlo's Melanie, by Ch. Dolsa Yojimbo ROM★, and Ch. Marlo Kyi Chu Artful Dodger and Ch. Marlo's Flim Flam Man, both by Ch. San Jo Shenanigan ROM★★. Flim Flam Man sired Ch. Marlo's I Love Lucy ROM★ from Marlo's Cleopatra (BIS Ch. Yojimbo Orion x Tara), thus doubling up on Tara. Lucy, when bred to Ch. San Jo Soshome Up ROM★, produced five champions, among them the brothers BIS Am., Can., Mex., Int., Dutch., Lux., & Fin. Ch. Marlo Rocky Road and Canadian BIS Am. & Can. Ch. Marlo Pride and Joy.

Another Marlo foundation bitch is Ch. Marlo's One of a Kind ROM, by Am & Can. Ch. Pawprints Pied Piper ROM★ out of Marlo's Icecream Sundae.

Ch. Marlo's One Of A Kind ROM*, bred and owned by Lynn Lowy, Marlo.   *Bonnie*

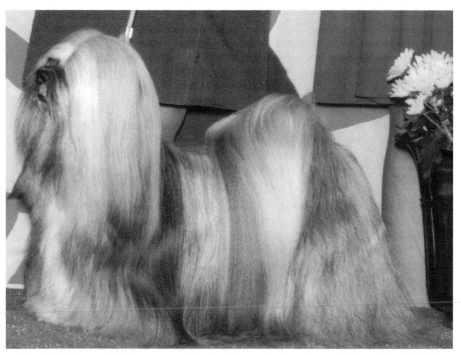

Ch. Marlo Unexpected Pleasure was bred and owned by Lynn Lowy, Marlo.   *Fox & Cook*

One of a Kind was bred to Ch. Suntory Four On The Floor (Ch. Suntory Silver Shadow x Suntory Anemone) and produced four champions, among them the Group-winning bitch Ch. Marlo Somethin Else.

The next step in the Marlo breeding program was to breed Lucy's children to One of a Kind's children, which resulted in many Marlo champions. Marlo qualified to receive the ALAC ROM breeders' award in 1984.

MILAREPA

Mary Smart Carter, Milarepa, established her kennel in 1969 when she obtained Ch. Milbryan Kim Ly Shim, by Ch. Ruffway Nor Pa out of Milbryan Merry Muffin; Carter's Tara of Everglo ROM★★, by Ch. Everglo Aro out of Sma Ra Kyimo of Everglo, and the bitch Licos Kargan La, by Ch. Licos Shag La out of Ch. Licos Namcha La.

Tara produced seven Milarepa champions, among them were BIS Ch. Tulku's Yeti of Milarepa and Group-winning Am., Can. & Bda. Ch. Tibs Tribulation of Milarepa, both by BIS Ch. Tibet of Cornwallis ROM★★★★. She produced three champions by Ch. Everglo Charlie Brown ROM★—Ch. Ainu Milarepa Tsung, Ch. Carla Milarepa Tsung and Am. & Can. Ch. Milarepa Cloister's Unicorn—Ch. Farview Murfo of Milarepa by Ch. Licos Omorfo La ROM★ and Ch. Milarepa Kim Ly Shim by Ch. Milbryan Kim Ly Shim, who also sired Ch. Tulku's Shades of Magic from Kargan La. Kargan La also produced Isis Milarepa Tsung when bred to Tribulation.

Mrs. Carter committed herself to breeding only pure Hamilton when she realized that there would never be any additional stock from the city of Lhasa or all of Tibet because of the Chinese occupation.

Mrs. Carter's Milarepa breeding program was awarded the ALAC ROM award in 1982.

MILBRYAN

Mrs. Mildred Bryant bred mostly Hamilton through Ch. Licos Shor Shan La (Ch. Hamilton Achok★ x Ch. Licos Nyapso La ROM★★), Ch. Milbryan Karma Vegas (Ch. Karma Getson x Hamilton Gyo Tru), Ch. Milbryan Licos Gayla La (Ch. Americal's Leng Kong ROM★ x Dama's Lu Country Fair ROM★★) and Ch. Ruffway Nor Pa (BIS Ch. Karma Frosty Knight O Everglo ROM★ x Ruffway Khambu ROM★).

ORLANE

Mrs. Dorothy Joan Kendall, Orlane kennels, bought her first Lhasa Apsos in 1963 from Gloria Fowler, Everglo. This foundation stock consisted of a three-month-old puppy that would become the famous sire BIS Ch. Everglo Spark of Gold ROM★★★★ and his diminutive half sister that would become Ch. Kai Sang's Flame of Everglo ROM★. Both sired by Ch. Kai Sang's Clown of Everglo, Spark of Gold's dam was Tibetan Cookie of Everglo and Flame's dam was Hamilton Norden ROM★.

When Orlane moved east in 1978, the breeding program changed from the predominately one sire (Spark of Gold) line. The use of BIS Windsong's Gusto of Innsbrook ROM★ as an outcross on heavily linebred Spark of Gold bitches produced the half brothers Ch. Orlane's Inimitable ROM★★★ and American and English. BIS Am. & Eng. Ch. Orlane's Intrepid ROM★★.

Inimitable's dam is the Spark of Gold daughter Yorktown's Sassy Satin, whose dam is Orlane's Golden Chrisma (Ruffway's Sharpa of Orlane x Orlane's Yser Loma). Intrepid's dam is Ch. Orlane's Brandywyne★, who is out of the Spark of Gold son BIS Ch. BarCon's The Avenger ROM★★ and Orlane's Mi Ti Jenny Lee Ch. Orlane's Gold Chipper x Orlane's Yum Yum of Venture).

Mrs. Kendall continued to use the old lines while bringing in Gusto of Innsbrook for his show ring glamour; The Avenger for his soundness; Inimitable for the style for which Orlane is so well known and culminating all these traits through Intrepid.

A line that is still primarily based on Spark of Gold, the Orlane breeding program has successfully progressed through the many generations since the original foundation, and has strongly influenced many other winning kennels in the United States. Orlane has also had a global impact with stock in England, Finland, Denmark, Japan and many other foreign countries.

Mrs. Kendall earned the ALAC Register of Merit breeders' award in 1979.

PANDAN

Pandan Lhasa Apsos was a family affair. The Martins, C.R. (Bob), Onnie and their daughters, Ann, Jane and Lynn, were a big part of the Lhasa Apso scene during their involvement with the breed.

Pandan's first champion was Ch. Pandan Lhamo, CD (Ch. Karma Kanjur x Kelea's Pin-Up Girl), that when bred to Tsan's Chosul produced Ch. Pandan's Po Nya.

Pandan's foundation dam was Ch. Nan Tando of Pandan, CD, ROM★, that when bred to the foundation sire Ch. Zijuh Seng Tru ROM★★ produced Ch. Choshe Ke Tu of Pandan, Ch. Pandan Kambu, Ch. Pandan Rea Po Ce ROM, Ch. Pandan Ka Tanda Tu and Pandan Nan-Gi.

When Rea Po was bred to Ch. Potala Pandan's Apollo ROM★, she produced Ch. Likala's Kar Ba of Pandan, Ch. Pandan Kitsi and Ch. Pandan Tsar Ba Tjim.

Pandan was a charter recipient of the ALAC ROM breeders' award when it was first awarded in 1973.

An AKC judge as well as a Lhasa Apso breeder, Mrs. Martin retired from both activities in 1977.

In 1983, the Martin's oldest daughter, Ann, obtained a bitch, Tabu's Rodeo Cowgirl (Ch. Tabu's Music Man x Tabu's Third Time's The Charm), that had Ch. Pandan Choshe Tsen in her background. The Pandan name was taken out of retirement when Cowgirl was bred to Tabu's CL LTD Edition Kyilee and produced, among others, Ch. Tabu's On The Road of Pandan and Tabu's On The Go of Pandan.

PAWPRINTS

Robert and Nancy Damberg purchased their first Lhasa Apso in 1969, more for a pet than a show dog, but he did become multiple Group-winning Am. & Can. Ch. Josie's Boy, by Ch. Hi Lillies Happi Harrah out of San Jo's Sugar Baby.

The real beginning of the Pawprints breeding program came, however, with the purchase of two bitches from Mr. and Mrs. James Roberts, Abbotsford—Am. & Can. Ch. Tsela of Abbotsford ROM★, by American's Nehru out of Ch. Panga of Abbotsford, and Sushi of Abbotsford, by Sinbad of Abbotsford ROM★ out of Goldilex of Abbotsford. Sushi finished with three five-point majors before she was a year old and won a Group shortly thereafter.

The next year brought a litter out of Am. & Can. Ch. Teako of Abbotsford and Tsela, which produced Ch. Tibet Tu of Pawprints, the Damberg's first homebred champion and the sire of Ch. Pawprints Sezhes Sombuddy. Also, the foundation sire that was to become Am. & Can. Ch. Kyma of Abbotsford ROM★★ was acquired. Kyma sired eighteen champions, including Ch. Pawprints Bandit of TehrKhan out of Jizon Pama II and Ch. Pawprints Pied Piper ROM out of Pawprints Kyalee.

Early in 1974, the Roberts expressed a desire that the Dambergs take a number of the Abbotsford dogs, and so it was that the few dogs at Pawprints became a full-fledged Lhasa Apso kennel. Especially to be noted among the dogs to come from Abbotsford to Pawprints was Sinbad of Abbotsford and his brilliant red sister, Kansa of Abbotsford; American's Nehru (Tsela's sire and a gift of friendship from the Stillmans to the Roberts); and very importantly the English import, Brackenbury Kandron, a small male with a fantastic attitude.

When Tsela was bred to Sinbad, she produced Ch. Pawprints Tsela Tsamo ROM; when bred to Ch. Dolsa Ringmaster, she produced Ch. Pawprints Coming Up Roses and Ch. Pawprints Ready to Ruffit and when bred to Kyma, she produced Pawprints Shigatse ROM, who when bred to Ch. Syung's Chico The Cocane Kid produced Ch. Pawprints GLD and Ch. Pawprints Meggers. Shigatse bred to Pawprints Shadrac produced the Group-winning Am & Can. Ch. Pawprints Weekend Warrior, sire of four champions, among them Ch. Pawprints Steals The Thunder out of Pawprints Bonvivant, Ch. Pawprints Spoonful Of

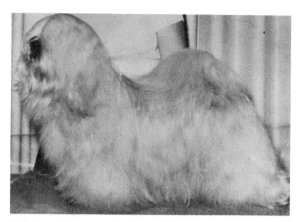

BIS Ch. Everglo's Spark of Gold ROM****, by Ch. Kai Sang's Clown of Everglo x Tibetan Cookie of Everglo, is the sire of forty-four champions. He was owned by Dorothy Kendall, Orlane.

Ch. Orlane's Dulmo ROM**, a son of BIS Ch. Everglo's Spark of Gold ROM**** and Ch. Orlane's Chitra of Ruffway ROM**, shown here at ten years of age, was the sire of twenty-four champions. Dulmo was owned by Lary Smith, Yat Sen and bred by Dorothy Kendall, Orlane.

Multiple BIS Am. Can. Ch. Orlane's Be Sparky of Al Mar ROM*, a son of Ch. Orlane's Dieh Bieh* and Orlane's Holly Berry, was bred by Dorothy Kendall and was owned by Marjorie Lewis, Al Mar. He was the sire of fourteen champions.

Sugar out of Kyalee and Ch. Pawprints Konstant Kamotion out of Ch. Phambu Pawprints Red Buttons. Shadrac and Shigatse are also the parents of Pawprints Zorro ROM★, sire of seven champions, among them Chs. Pawprints Sunrise Serenade, Performing Arts, Oreo Cookie and Dt Strutter, all out of the English-bred bitch Dewell Tracy Belle ROM★.

Pawprints was awarded the ALAC breeders' ROM award in 1983.

POTALA

Mrs. Keke Blumberg-Kahn used the names Keke's, Potala's and Potala Keke's to prefix the Lhasa Apsos bred at her Potala kennel.

Mrs. Blumberg-Kahn purchased her first Lhasa Apso, a bitch that was later to become Ch. Keke's T'Chin T'Chin (Ch. Hamilton Namsa ROM★ x Smedley's Seeou Ying), from her breeders, William and Janet Smedley. T'Chin was bred to BIS Ch. Kham of Norbulingka ROM★★ to produce Ch. Keke's T'Chin Ting T'Chin ROM, who when bred to BIS Ch. Tibet of Cornwallis ROM★★★★ produced Ch. Keke's Bamboo ROM★★.

Bamboo was bred to Ch. Zijuh Seng Tru ROM★★ to produce the litter sisters BIS Ch. Potala Keke's Yum Yum ROM★ and Ch. Potala Keke's Zin Zin ROM★. Zin Zin, when bred to BIS Ch. Chen Korum Ti ROM★★, produced BIS Ch. Potala Keke's Zintora. Yum Yum was bred to Ch. Everglo Zijuh Tomba ROM★★ to produce Chs. Potala Keke's Tomba Tu ROM★★, Potala Keke's Kal E Ko, Potala Keke's Superman, Potala Keke's Kelana ROM and Potala Keke's Nayana. Yum Yum was also bred to Ch. Daktazl Tsung to produce Ch. Potala Keke's Andromeda ROM★.

Tomba Tu was bred back to his granddam, Bamboo, to produce Ch. Potala Keke's Mistique.

Potala also housed BIS Ch. Kyi Chu Shara ROM★, the dam of these Potala champions: Keke's Ha-Le and Karnes Khambo by Kham, Keke's Petruchio and Keke's Zorro by Tibet and Potala Keke's Ebony and Potala Sundance Kid by Ch. Kinderland's Bhu Sun.

Potala was a charter recipient of the ALAC ROM breeders' award in 1973 when it was first awarded.

Mrs. Blumberg-Kahn retired from breeding Lhasa Apsos in 1980 and has since pursued an active judging career.

QUA-LA-TI

Nancy Coglianese obtained her first Lhasa Apso in 1969, a pet bitch from a pet shop. In an effort to breed her, Mrs. Coglianese found Berano Kennels, and she discovered dog shows.

In 1973, she obtained a nine-month-old puppy that would become BIS Ch. Tiffany's Qua-La-Ti ROM★, by BIS Ch. BarCon's The Avenger ROM★★ out

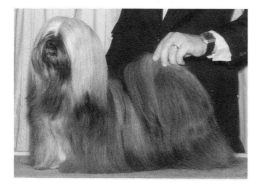

Ch. Tabu's On The Road of Pandan, bred by Ann Martin Esperance and Carolyn Herbel, he is owned by Zachary and Debbie Stadelman and Carolyn Herbel.   *Photo by Rinehart*

Can. BIS Am. Can. Ch. Pawprints Coming Up Roses winner of the 1982 Canadian National Specialty, breeder-owner handled by Nan Damberg, Pawprints.

Multiple BIS Ch. Potala Keke's Candy Bar, bred by S. Kletter and owned by Janet and Marvin Whitman, Ja Ma, and Keke Blumberg (Kahn), Potala.   *Alverson*

BIS Ch. Sharbo Zijuh Zer Khan ROM was a son of Ch. Everglo Zijuh Tomba and Ch. Zijuh India.

of Ch. Tiffany's Wendi-La★. He sired fifteen champions, was a true show dog and became the namesake for Mrs. Coglianese's kennel.

Additionally, Mrs. Coglianese purchased the foundation bitch Ch. Tiffany's Yolanda La-Tsu ROM★ (The Avenger x Ch. Tiffany's Tami-La), who produced BIS Ch. Qua-La-Ti's Makara ROM★ out of Ch. Ruffway T'Ang Chu ROM★★, multiple Group winner Ch. Qua-La-Ti's Barjea out of Makara and multiple Group winner Ch. Qua-La-Ti's Kahlua and Cream and Ch. Qua-La-Ti's Show Stopper, both out of Qua-La-Ti.

Another foundation bitch for Mrs. Coglianese was Ch. Haji's Liberated Lady Ki-Sulo ROM★★ (Ch. Shyr Lyz Shama Shama x Shaffner's Lahti-Da). When bred to Qua-La-Ti, she produced seven champions: Qua-La-Ti's Max-Min's Mol-Le-Oui, Norbulingka Cleo, Dee Dee of Barjea, Ermine of Knolwood, Good as Gold Rockee, Magic Motion and Love Talk Barjea.

Qua-La-Ti Lhasa Apsos qualified for the ALAC ROM breeders' award in 1982, but appears to have been inactive for several years.

RGYAL

Hugh and Brenda O'Donnell bought Ch. Chig Rgyal Po (Ch. Hamilton Namsa ROM★★ x Chig Dkar) from his breeder, Mrs. Anna Griffing, Chig, and showed him to his championship in 1969.

They then obtained Kinderland's Ginger Rgyal II ROM★ (Marpa x Sang Po) and bred her to Po, which produced Ch. Rgyal Khetsa Po ROM★, who was co-owned with Barbara Wood, and when bred to Ch. Potala Keke's Tomba Tu ROM★ produced the two males Ch. Rgyal Zig of Lejo and Ch. Rgyal Bu Tomper.

Ginger was also bred to Ch. Mor Knoll's Alex A Hente and produced Ch. Rgyal's Kisco Kid of Volents, Ch. Rgyal Busy Bee Bee and Ch. Mor Knoll Darlin of Rgyal ROM★.

Darlin, co-owned with Liz Morgan, Mor Knoll, produced five champions, three when bred to Ch. Potala Keke's Golden Gatsby ROM★, one of which was Ch. Mor Knoll Rgyal Tiffany ROM★.

Rgyal Lhasa Apsos qualified for the ALAC ROM breeders' award in 1978 and seems to have been inactive since 1980.

SHARBO

Although Sharon Rouse-Bryant first met the breed in 1953 when she cared for her mother's Lhasa Apso, it was not until 1965 that she acquired one of her own, the female puppy Lao Tai-Tai.

It was in search of a mate for Tai that Mrs. Rouse-Bryant found and later acquired from Bea Loob, Zijuh, the eighteen-month-old male that became multiple Group-winning Ch. Everglo Zijuh Tomba ROM★★.

During the effort to finish Tomba, Mrs. Rouse-Bryant learned that Tai was not a suitable foundation bitch and arranged to get a straight Hamilton-bred bitch. She was Ch. Zijuh Jinda, a one-star producer. When bred to Ch. Chen Nyun Ti ROM★★, Jinda produced Ch. Sharbo Zijuh Tsa, Sharbo's first homebred champion, and Ch. Sharbo Zijuh Spanggur. Jinda was also bred to Tomba and produced Ch. Sharbo Zijuh Kamaru★ and the BIS winner Ch. Sharbo Zijuh Zer Khan ROM★.

Sharbo's third litter was Tomba to Tsa Chu, which produced three champions, including BIS Ch. Sharbo Topguy, the only black Lhasa Apso to date to win an all-breed BIS in the United States.

Mrs. Rouse-Bryant purchased another straight Hamilton foundation bitch that was from Gloria Fowler, Everglo, who became Ch. Everglo Flair ROM★ (Everglo Rempa ROM★ x Everglo Encore Ember), and when bred to Zer Khan produced Chs. Sharbo Mondo Khan of Ramurka, Sharbo Ai Khan Tu of Ramurka and Everglo Ra Hu Khan of Sharbo. Flair was also bred to Tomba to produce Chs. Sharbo Me Shanda Ba and Sharbo Thuji Ba of Marpori.

SHARP

Robert Sharp bred Lhasa Apsos under the names of Sharbet, Sharp's, Agra and Sharpette, and although the breeders of many champions, is best known for the many Lhasa Apsos he handled to their titles for others.

Mr. Sharp handled BIS Am., Can., Bda. & Mex. Ch. Kyi Chu Friar Tuck ROM★ to his breed record. He also handled BIS Am., Bda. & Col. Ch. Chen Korum Ti ROM★★ to his eight BIS wins, as well as accumulating enough wins to make him the number one Non-Sporting Dog (*Kennel Review* System) for 1972 and winning the Ken-L Award for 1972 by having won the most Non-Sporting Groups, that being forty-two.

Mr. Sharp handled BIS Am. & Bda. Ch. Kinderland's Tonka ROM★ to her record-making BIS and Group tally, as well as her son Ch. Tabu's King of Hearts ROM★★★ to his multiple Group wins, and his son BIS Am. & Can. Ch. Rimar's J.G. King Richard to BIS, Group and BOB wins.

The Korum Ti son Ch. Potala Keke's Zintora was shown to his BIS by Mr. Sharp. He also handled the Group-winning Ch. Kyi Chu Tukki Dar, a Friar Tuck son.

Some Lhasa Apso champions that carry Mr. Sharp's prefixes are: Sharpette's Gaylord, Sharpette's Number One Son, Sharpette's Maya Maya, Sharpette's Bobette, Sharpette's Galahad, Agra's Imprecious, Sharpette's Hasty Pudding, Sharp's Bee Gee ROM★, Sharpette's Lady Godiva and Kyi Chu Whimsi of Sharbet.

To list any of the numerous champions Robert Sharp has finished for other breeders would risk missing some of importance; however, it is safe to say that this number is well into the hundreds.

SHYR LYZ

Shirley and Ward Scott, Shyr Lyz, obtained their first Lhasa Apso in 1966. A six-month-old puppy, she would become Ch. Drax Ka Ba Kol Ba (Drax Sen Ge Cun Wa x Drax Kikuli Nar Mo), and although she was not a champion producer, it was her granddaughter Am., & Can. Bda. Ch. Shyr Lyz Misa Cun-Tia Kai-Lei ROM★★ that was the producer. With nine champions to her credit, six were by Ch. Ruffway T'Ang Chu ROM★★, among them multiple Group-winning Ch. Shyr Lyz Shama Shama ROM★, Ch. Shyr Lyz Fabalous Flirt ROM★ and Ch. Shyr Lyz Flamboyant Flair ROM★. Misa Cun-Tia's other three champions were Ch. Shyr Lyz Red Baron of Rgyal, Ch. Shyr Lyz Shakira of Knolwood and Ch. Shyr Lyz Chatti Kathi, all sired by Ch. Rin Po Che III★.

Ch. Josette's Mai Li Shir La ROM★ (Ch. Licos Singi La x Ch. Cher-ryshores Cha Cha La) was acquired about a year after Kol Ba and also finished quickly. She produced Chs. Shyr Lyz Ko Shan, Mieh Bah Bieh Tu and Shi-Zang Flower of Joy, sired by Ch. Cherryshores Bah Bieh Boi ROM★★★, and Ch. Shyr Lyz De Ly Lah of Rito's, sired by Ch. Pan Chen Tonka Sonan ROM★.

When Flirt was bred to Ch. Shyr Lyz Copper Caper of Ming Toy, she produced Ch. Shyr Lyz Tha Sha T'Ang, Ch. Shyr Lyz El-Lagarto and Ch. Shyr Lyz Sassi Red Hots, and when she was bred to Shama Shama, she produced Ch. Shyr Lyz That Magic Moment and Ch. Shyr Lyz Shan Mar.

Shyr Lyz Lhasa Apsos qualified to receive the ALAC ROM breeders' award in 1977.

SULAN

Suzette Michele became a co-owner of Ch. Kinderland's Kandy (Ch. Willy of Cornwallis x Ch. Jo Khang of Naishapur★) after watching her shown to her championship.

Kandy was bred to Ch. Kinderland's Timpa to produce Sulan's Peco Co-Pa, a winner at ten months. Shortly after this win, Miss Michele spent several years getting a grooming business started and did not show her dogs.

When she returned to showing, she acquired Am., & Can. Ch. Al-Mar's Ala-Kazam ROM★ (BIS Ch. Orlane's Be Sparky of Al-Mar ROM★ x Dar Roc's Ama Lilli Dewdrop), who was the sire of Group-winning Ch. Sulan's Charlie Chan Jo Mar out of Sandman's Dreamer of Knolwood.

The next acquisition was the ten-week-old male that would become Ch. Innsbrook's Patrician O'Sulan ROM★★. Patrician sired over twenty champions, with the most significant to Sulan being BIS Ch. Sulan's Gregorian Chant ROM★ and Ch. Sulan's Tapestry Weaver, both out of Knolwood's American Spirit. Ch. Sulan's Seanna, out of the Ala-Kazam daughter Hair-Um's Ding A Ling, and Ch. Sulan's Cayenne, out of Jeniffer Juniper of Sulan ROM. Jeniffer was also

Ch. Sharpette's Gaylord (BIS Ch. Kyi Chu Friar Tuck ROM x Ch. Karma Ja Lu) was BOB at the Western ALAC Specialty in 1973 and was handled by his owner, Murray Teitelbaum to this good win, The breeder was Lucy C. Joyce.

Can. BIS Am. Can. Ch. Suntory Affirmative Action ROM was bred and owned by Raul and Cassandra de la Rosa, Suntory. *Lethbridge*

Am. Ch. Gyantse of Abbotsford, bred by James Roberts and owned by Raul and Cassandra de la Rosa, Suntory. *Robert*

bred to Gregorian Chant to produce Chs. Sulan's Franciscan and Sulan's Victorian Sonnett ROM★.

Seanna was bred to Gregorian Chant to produce Ch. Sulan's Westminster Abbie and Ch. Sulan's Cookie Monster Jo Mar. Miss Michele purchased the male Ch. Wellington's Comeuppence (Soshome Up x Sehilot), and when he was bred to Tapestry Weaver, they produced the record-breaking male BIS Ch. Sulan's Master Blend, that when bred to Seanna produced Ch. Sulan's Master Charge O'Morgan, and when bred to Sulan's Broadway Melody produced Ch. Sulan's Precision Blend.

Master Blend was also bred to the Gregorian Chant daughter Jo Mar's Gregorian Allelluia out of Sulan's April Fool of Jo Mar and produced Ch. Sulan's Lovebug of Morgan and Ch. Sulan's Mi Max Appeal.

Sulan qualified to receive the ALAC ROM breeders' award in 1985.

SUNTORY

Cassandra and Raul de la Rosa purchased their first Lhasa Apso in 1969. She was Taji Khan (Ch. Joli's Poo Ling x Crestwood Golden Glow) and the dam of the de la Rosas' first litter, sired by Group-winning Ch. Choshe Ke Tu of Pandan and named with the Taji prefix.

Taji was the dam of their second litter sired by Ch. Potala Pandan's Apollo ROM★, which produced the foundation bitch Suntory Roshi Nor Po ROM and was the first litter to carry the Suntory name.

The second foundation bitch was straight Hamilton-bred and was purchased from Patricia Chenoweth, Chen, in 1971. This bitch was to become Ch. Chen Krisna Tsoma Nor ROM★ (Krisna Nor x Chen Soma Lo), the dam of five champions, all sired by Ch. Kyma of Abbotsford ROM★★—four bitches, Ch. Suntory Sonata ROM, Ch. Suntory Arabesque★, Ch. Suntory Selena ROM and Ch. Suntory Adina ROM, and one male, Ch. Suntory Samurai Nor.

Samurai was bred to Roshi to produce the bitches Suntory Anemone ROM and Andromeda. When Andromeda was bred to Ch. Sa Mar of Abbotsford★, she produced Can. BIS Am. & Can. Ch. Suntory Affirmative Action ROM. Bred to Adina, he sired Ch. Suntory Stocking Stuffer. Samurai was also bred to Suntory San Souci to produce Ch. Suntory Silver Shadow. When Silver Shadow was bred to his half sisters, Anenome produced Chs. Suntory Four On The Floor and Padparascha and Andromeda produced Ch. Suntory Spellbinder.

San Souci was also bred to Pawprints Jinda to produce Ch. Suntory Semira, that when bred to Stocking Stuffer produced Ch. Suntory Superfudge, that was bred to Anemone to produce Ch. Suntory's Executive Action.

Suntory received as a gift, after Mrs. Roberts's death, from the Roberts family the puppy that would grow up to be Group-winning Ch. Gyantse of Abbotsford, by Affirmative Action out of his half sister Ch. Dolpho of Abbotsford. When Gyantse was bred to Adina, he produced champions Suntory Celeste and Cherubim, with the latter bred back to Affirmative Action to produce

Ch. Suntory Barbo Penelope. When Celeste was bred to Executive Action, they produced Ch. Suntory Never Amber.

Suntory Lhasa Apsos earned the ALAC ROM breeders' award in 1980.

TABU

Although the authors' involvement with the Lhasa Apso began as early as 1965 with handling for others, it was not until 1967 that the Herbels' first Lhasa Apso was obtained and Tabu Lhasa Apsos was established.

This acquisition was the fourteen-month-old straight Hamilton male that would become BIS Ch. Tibet of Cornwallis ROM★★★★. The following year a female stud fee puppy out of Tibet and Ch. Kinderland's Sang Po ROM★★ was acquired and later became the breed record holder, multiple BIS Am. & Bda. Ch. Kinderland's Tonka ROM★.

Six months later, a straight Hamilton female puppy was purchased that would become Ch. Gindy of Norbulingka ROM★★★.

Tabu has always bred two bloodlines. One is straight Hamilton, which simply means that *all* dogs in the pedigree can be traced back to Hamilton Farms' nine foundation dogs, and the other line simply cannot make this claim, although with the use of straight Hamilton sires this second line is predominantly Hamilton as well.

Tonka was the first of the four foundation females for the second line, and when bred to the straight Hamilton male, Ch. Zijuh Seng Tru ROM★★ produced the Group winner Ch. Tabu's King of Hearts ROM★★★ and his sister Ch. Tabu's Kiss Me Kate. When Kate was bred to her grandsire, Tibet, she produced the Group winner Ch. Tabu's Gold Galaxy.

The second foundation female for the second line was the leased bitch Ch. Taglha Muni ROM, a Tibet daughter whose dam was Am. & Can. Ch. Kimrik's Jeh Sah Cah. When bred to the straight Hamilton male Ch. Pan Chen Tonka Sonan ROM★, Jeh Sah Cah produced Ch. Tabu's Make Mine Minx ROM (dam of champions Tabu's Bronze Bonanza, Bric A Brac and Beau Raintree); Ch. Tabu's Miss Chimney Sweep; Tabu's Mini Magic (dam of Am. & Can. Ch. Tabu's Idle Time and Ch. Tabu's Indian Summer) and Tabu's Mr. Bo Jangles. Tibet was the sire of both Minx's and Magic's litters.

The third foundation female for the second line was Ch. Chok's Darfe, a stud fee puppy and a Tibet daughter out of Ch. Kinderland's Mi Terra ROM★. Darfe was bred to the straight Hamilton male Ch. Tabu's Jazz Man ROM★ to produce Ch. Tabu's Stars and Stripes.

The fourth foundation female was Ch. Tabu's Cinnamon Stick, also a stud fee puppy and a Tibet daughter out of Chi Chou Lee Bagel (Karma Shin Jed II x Jed's Sharika Chen), who when bred to King produced Ch. Tabu's Queen of Hearts ROM, who when bred to Stars and Stripes produced champions Tabu's Hearts Are Trump, Heart Throb, Heart Strings of Gramar ROM and the two South African champions Heart to Heart of Gramar and Heart of Gold O Gramar.

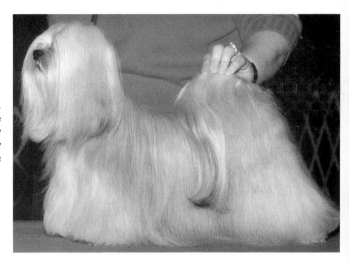

Tabu's CL Hit It Off (Tabu's CL Singin The Blues x Tabu's Coffee With Cream) bred and owned by Carolyn Herbel and handled by Carmen Spears, Tabu. *Petrulis*

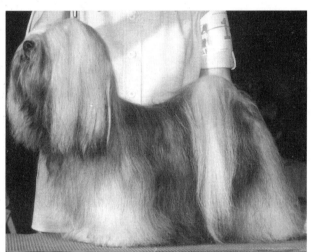

Ch. Tabu's Magic Magic of Tiara ROM, bred by Carolyn Herbel, Tabu, and Becky Johnson, Tiara, and owned by Mrs. Johnson.

Meyer

Ch. Tabu Mint Condition, bred, owned and handled by Nancy Plunkett, Tabu. *Kernan*

Lhasa Apsos have been held in high esteem by Tibetan holy men for centuries. Even in modern times the breed is the special pet of Tibetan Buddhists. Here is the *Tara Tulku*, head of the Buddhist Tantric College, Dalhousie, India, with his Lhasa.

Kristen Wannisky and her Lhasa pals, Ki Ki Ling of K Wannisky, CD and Tabu's No No Nanette.

Int. Ch. Cinderella van de Lancelot (right) with a Bearded Collie friend.

Three generations of obedience Lhasas, owned by Melodye Haverly. They are (from left) Mee-Tu of Charmel, UD, Canadian CDX; Charmel's Ming-Tu, CDX Canadian CD and Charmel's Ding A Ling.

Irresistible is the word that best describes this litter of golden Lhasa babies.

Tabu's Beau Raintree at just under six months.

Ch. Rimar's Rumplestilskin.

Ch. Tabu's Idle Time.

Ch. Tabu's Make Mine Minx.

Ch. Chen Korum Ti, one of the breed's top winners.

Int. Ch. Annapurna U'Hyoko (France).

Hamilton Maroh in a playful mood at Hamilton Farms.

Europasieger (European champion) Dolsa Red Alert.

Ch. Daktazl Tsung.

Ch. Yojimbo Orion (Ch. Dolsa Yojimbo ex Blackbay Sass A Fhrass), owned and bred by Elaine Spaeth, was the breed's standout winner during 1977 and into 1978. "Ryan's" record includes 14 Bests in Show, tieing the breed record, the 1977 Western ALAC Specialty and numerous Group 1sts and other placements. He is the first Lhasa to win the Group at Westminster, this historic achievement taking place in 1977 under judge C. L. Savage. He was also the winner of the Ken-L Award in 1977 for winning the most Non-Sporting Groups in the United States that year. This outstanding campaigner has been handled throughout his brilliant career by John R. Thyssen.

Gindy was the first of three foundation bitches for the straight Hamilton line, and when bred to Tibet produced in several litters Chs. Tabu's Rhapsody in Red; Raquel; Rags To Riches; Double or Nuthin; Dresden Doll; Appleseed Annie; Group-winning Fame And Fortune and Firebird ROM. When Gindy was bred to Tonka Sonan, she produced Chs. Tabu's Jazz Man ROM★ and Jinger With A J.

The second foundation bitch was Goldmere Dharma, by Ch. Karma Mi Ser out of Goldmere Dzasa. When bred to Jazz Man, she produced Ch. Tabu's Unsinkable Molly Brown and Tabu's White Lace And Promises. Dharma was also bred to Rags To Riches and produced Ch. Tabu's Very Short Tale and Tabu's Very Much A Lady ROM★. When Molly Brown was bred to Fame And Fortune, Ch. Tabu's Fancy Face resulted.

The third foundation bitch was Maru's Julie of Laran ROM, a Tibet daughter out of Maru's Ka Bu Ki Narobe, that when bred to Jazz Man produced champions Tabu's Music Man and Music Country Style.

It was at this time in the program that the future American and South African Ch. Chiyoko Nobody Doesit Better was aquired. He was out of Julie's litter sister Ch. Chiyoko's Nik Ki of Laran and sired by Am., Bda., & Can. Ch. Shen Pa Ni Khim ROM★.

When Jazz Man was bred to Firebird, the result was Ch. Tabu's Strawberries N' Cream, and when bred to Nobody Doesit Better produced Tabu's Coffee With Cream. The latter was the dam of Ch. Tabu's A Partikin out of the Music Man son Hi-Life's Kavalier O Wil-O-Wik out of Ch. Bit O Gold Buffae of Canton.

When Lady was bred to Everglo Red Regent ROM★, she produced Group-winning Ch. Tabu's Cover Story ROM★, Ch. Tabu's Cover Up, Tabu's Cover Alls and Tabu's Cover Girl, the dam of Tabu's Prince Matchabelli ROM★ by Nobody Doesit Better. When Lady was bred to BIS Am., & Mex. Ch. Everglo Sundance ROM, she produced Chs. Tabu's Magic Magic of Tiara ROM and Magic Piper of Tiara, co-bred with Becky Johnson, Tiara. When Piper was bred to White Lace and Promises, the result was Tabu's Third Time's The Charm, that when bred to Nobody Doesit Better produced Ch. Tabu's First In Line ROM, Tabu's First Fling, Tabu's First Lady and Tabu's CL First Class.

Fancy Face when bred to Nobody Doesit Better produced Ch. Tabu's Azure Gamble of Kyilee, and when bred to Piper produced Tabu's CL LTD Edition Kyilee, the sire of Ch. Tabu's On The Road Of Pandan.

Cover Story was bred to Music Country Style to produce Ch. Tabu's Southern Delight, the dam of Ch. Tabu's Mint Condition, whose sire is another Tabu acquisition, Ch. Tai Chi Vouvray, by Ch. Likalas Tyg-Gyr Tu of Hylan out of Chen Kris-Shana Nor.

Tabu was awarded the ALAC ROM breeders' award in 1976.

In 1981, the decision was made to close the Tabu straight Hamilton line by excluding the use of any animals that do not trace back to a carefully selected base foundation, therefore developing a concentrated gene pool that will produce with dominance and predictability.

TAGLHA

Wilson and Jane Browning got a pet Lhasa Apso, Chinghiz, in the 1960s before they bought the bitch that would become Ch. Kimricks Jeh Sa Cah (Ch. Arborhill's Wah Cha Mieh x Madame Misty Su Lee) and the dam of their first litter by BIS Ch. Tibet of Cornwallis ROM★★★. This litter produced Ch. Taglha Dum Cho and Ch. Taglha Muni ROM.

The second foundation bitch was Ch. Kinderland's Tonka Tu. She produced Ch. Taglha Sinsa of Kinderland, sired by BIS Ch. BarCon's The Avenger ROM★★, and Ch. Taglha Bee Uti of Kinderland, sired by Tibet.

Dum Cho when bred to Korum Ti produced Ch. Taglha Pokhara of Nottoway ROM, and when bred to Group-winning Ch. Tabu's King of Hearts ROM★★★ produced BIS Ch. Talgha Kambu ROM★, Ch. Taglha Kusu ROM★ and Ch. Taglha Puckyi.

Kusu when bred to Ch. Everglo Eager Beaver produced Ch. Taglha Kubo and Ch. Taglha Kusuma, and when she was bred to Ch. Mor Knoll Chok's Grand Slam ROM★ produced Ch. Taglha Mi Tambu ROM★ and Ch. Taglha Lin Tu.

When Tambu was bred to Kambu, Chs. Mi Taglha Pebbles Rambu, Taglha Mi Sok Tsu, Mi Taglha Tulip and Mi Taglha Tomm-Bu resulted, and when Kusuma was bred to Kambu she produced Ch. Taglha Valentine.

Taghla Lhasa Apsos qualified for the ALAC ROM breeders's award in 1979.

TN HI

Mrs. Joyce Hadden got her first Lhasa Apso in 1966 from Ron Tyler, Luty. This male, sired by Ch. Keepsake★ (Canada) out of Welch's Cindee, was to become Ch. Tn Hi Di-Ly-Hri, Mrs. Hadden's first champion.

Drax Spring Shon-Po (Drax Kamba Dzong x Drax Den-Sa of Everglo), Mrs. Hadden's foundation bitch, was bred to Di-Ly-Hri and produced Tn Hi Glo-Ri Tchen ROM.

When Tn Hi Pan Dha Ba Ba was bred to Baijai's Brunhilde Binamni by Frank Holder, Baijai, Mrs. Hadden acquired Ch. Tn Hi Bud Dhi Boi, and when bred to Glo-Ri produced Ch. Tn Hi Pahti Shyshy.

Mrs. Hadden obtained the male Ch. Ocon Karba Seng, who was bred to Pahti Shyshy to produce Tn Hi Me'N My Shadow.

Another male that Mrs. Hadden acquired was Ch. Cameo's Khor-Ke San of Honeydew, that when bred to Shadow produced multiple Group winner Ch. Tn Hi Zeus The Dethroner ROM★, the sire of more than nine champions. They include Chs. Tn Hi Sonata's Wings of Love, Pixie's Poppy, Piping Hot and Brick The Big Bang, all out of Ch. Tn Hi Pixie Minx ROM★, sired by Ch. Tn Hi Lammi Po Kah out of Tn Hi Me She.

Ch. Tn Hi Brick The Big Bang was bred and owned by Joyce Hadden, Tn Hi. He is shown here in a Best of Breed win under John Devlin, handler Greg Strong.   *Kernan*

From left, multiple Group winner Ch. Tn Hi Zeus The Dethroner ROM* with handler Pat Martello and his daughter, Ch. Tn Hi Pixie's Poppy with Joyce Hadden, Tn Hi, the breeder and owner of both Zeus and Poppy, Ch. Tn Hi Napolean Brandy, bred by Mrs. Hadden and John Lyons, owned by Debra Edelman and shown here with Robert Munch.

85

Khor-Ke San was also bred to Pixie Minx to produce Ch. Tn Hi Hot Toddy, and to Tn Hi I'm A Pixie Tu to produce Ch. Tn Hi Napoleon Brandy and Lady Jaz Min.

Mrs. Hadden's Tn Hi Lhasa Apsos qualified for the ALAC ROM breeders' award in 1986.

TSUNG

Miss Maria Aspuru, Tsung, had primarily a show kennel. Miss Aspuru rarely sold or let any of the Tsung dogs leave her kennel or ownership.

Tsung was the home of BIS Ch. Drax Ne Ma Me ROM, BIS Ch. Karma Frosty Knight O Everglo ROM★, BIS Ch. Shar Bo Zijuh Zer Khan ROM★, Group-winning Ch. Tabu's Chubby Checkers ROM, Ch. Everglo's Charlie Brown ROM, Group-winning Ch. Kwan Ting Tsung, Group-winning Ch. Banji Bang Bang Tsung and Group-winning Ch. Daktazl Tsung, to name only a few of the more famous Tsung dogs.

Tsung qualified to be an ALAC ROM breeder in 1976.

6

American Breeders of the 1970s and 1980s

ANBARA

Anbara Lhasa Apsos was established in 1971 by Barbara Wood when she was given her first Lhasa Apso, Buttons, who became the dam of Miss Wood's first titlist, Rgyal Bo-Jangles, CD. Later, as a hobby breeder, she produced many champions—mostly breeder/owner-handled.

Group-winning Ch. Anbara's Abra-Ka-Dabra ROM (BIS Ch. Rimar Rumpelstiltskin ROM★ x Ch. Rgyal Khetsa-Po ROM★) is the basis of Miss Wood's breeding program. Abra-Ka-Dabra was the dam of four champions, including multiple BIS Ch. Anbara's Hobgoblin, by multiple Group-winning Ch. Tabu's King of Hearts ROM★★★. Goblin is the sire of several champions, including Ch. Anbara Rimar's Footloose Fox ROM★★★. Footloose Fox's first litter, by multiple BIS Ch. S.J.W. Waffle Stomper ROM★, included Group-winning Ch. Anbara Rimar Cobby Cuddler and BIS Ch. Anbara Rimar Mary Puppins, the latter being Miss Wood's favorite. Subsequent litters produced brothers Ch. Anbara Rimar's Hot Ticket and Hot Tip by Ch. San Jo Shenanigan ROM★★, and Ch. Anbara Rimar Raisin' A Ruckus ROM by Ch. San Jo Rusty Nail ROM★★.

BIS Ch. Anbara Rimar's Grin N' Bear It ROM★ (Ch. Anbara Justa Teddy Bear x Ch. Rimar's The Frivolous Fox ROM★), a grandson of Abra-Ka-Dabra, when bred to BIS Ch. San Jo's Hussel Bussel ROM★★ produced the brothers Ch. San Jo's Out Of The Blue ROM★★ and Rusty Nail.

Anbara qualified to receive the ALAC Register of Merit award in 1981.

ART-EST

Art and Esther De Falcis decided in 1978 to breed and show Lhasa Apsos. They acquired a brood bitch, Gene's Flaming Mame (Paso De Rojo El Tojo x Shandy of Brunning), which they bred to BIS Ch. Qua La Ti's Makara ROM★ (T'Ang Chu x Ch. Tiffany's Yolanda La Tsu ROM★) to produce the foundation bitch Ch. Art-Est She Ma ROM★★.

She Ma's first litter was by Ch. Tabu's King of Hearts ROM★★★ and produced four Art-Est champions, Art-Est Chin-Te Shih-Ko, Gene's Han Som of Art-Est, Gene's Victor of Art-Est and Art-Est King of the Road.

She Ma's second litter was within the same lines sired by BIS Ch. Anbara's Hobgoblin (King x Ch. Anbara's Abra-Ka-Dabra ROM★). This mating produced two champions, including Ch. Art-Est Genteel Gizmo, the foundation sire for Art-Est.

She Ma's third litter was sired by Ch. Mor Knoll Chok's Grand Slam ROM★ (Intrepid x Joppa Bu Mo) and produced Group-winning Ch. Art-Est Most Valuable Player, who is the dam of Ch. Art-Est Gorgeous Georgia Red by Gizmo.

Art-Est added new blood to its program through the acquisition of Ch. Kinderland Ta Sen Nite Satin (Ch. Westgate's Give 'Em Hell Harry x Isis), which was bred to Gizmo. Also by breeding Ch. Kinderland Ta Sen Candy Tuft (Play It Again Sam x Isis) in partnership with Kinderland Ta Sen Lhasa Apsos, it produced Ch. Kinderland Ta Sen Art-Est Kyi and Ch. Kinderland Ta Sen Art-Est Chu II, both sired by Ch. Ruffway Mashala Chu ROM★★★.

The De Falcises became ALAC Register of Merit breeders in 1988.

BARJEA

Barbara and Dale Peterson acquired their first Lhasa Apso as a pet in 1973, and six months later they purchased the bitch Sunji Teddy Bear Nya (Sun Bde Gee x Ch. Pandan Po-Nya), who would become the dam of the Petersons' first champion, Ch. Barjea Joshua, sired by a breed record holder, multiple BIS Ch. Yojimbo Orion.

The Petersons also acquired Ch. Qua-La-Ti's Kushu Tsu (Qually x Carnival Sungold), who when bred to Joshua's litter sister, Barjea Tanya, produced Ch. Barjea's Little Guy, the second Barjea homebred champion.

In April 1983, the Petersons bought Ch. Norbulingka Qua-La-Ti Sandman ROM★ (Qually x Norbulingka Sangralu), and in September 1983 they purchased the puppy that was to become Ch. San Jo Zhantor Sugarplum ROM★ (Soshome Up x Songbird). Sandman is the sire of three Barjea-bred champions, Ch. Norbu-lingka's Trina of Barjea, whose dam is Barjea's Blaze (Ch. Tabu's Very Short Tale x Barjea Tanya); Ch. Barjea's Snooty Lady, whose dam is Qua-La-Ti's Mrs. Kri Ter, and champions Barjea's Rhett Butler and Barjea's Scarlett O'Hara, whose dam is Sugarplum.

Multiple BIS Am. Can. Ch. Anbara's Hobgoblin was bred by Barbara Wood and was handled by Jean Lade for owners William and Betty Bowman. *Ashbey*

A Group winner from the classes, Ch. Art-Est Most Valuable Player, was bred and is owned by Esther De Falcis, Art-Est. *Klein*

Ch. Barjea's Scarlett O'Hara, bred and owned by Barbara and Dale Peterson, Barjea. *Missy*

Sugarplum was also bred to San Jo sires to produce five champions carrying both the Barjea and San Jo prefix: Whip To Th' Top, Smart N' Snappi, Mr. President, Sugar N' Spice and Rise 'N Shine.

Barjea became eligible to receive the ALAC ROM breeders' award in 1989.

BIHAR

Bihar was originated in 1966 by Carol Strong when she obtained an Afghan Hound, but it was in 1970 that a Lhasa Apso came to Bihar to be leash-trained as a favor to her breeders-owners, Marlene Annunziata and Ann Hoffman. This Lhasa Apso stayed and became Am. & Can. Ch. Khabachen Kasha's Thetis★, the first champion and foundation bitch for Bihar Lhasa Apsos. Her sire was BIS Ch. Chen Korum Ti ROM★★ out of Ch. Kasha's Tsonya of Tal Hi ROM★ (Ch. Keke's Petruchio x Can. Ch. Keke's Little Ginger).

Thetis was first bred to Ch. BarCon's Stage Door Jonny and produced eleven puppies, several of which became foundation stock for others. It was Thetis's second litter at Bihar that produced BIS Am. & Can. Ch. Sun Trader of Bihar by Am. & Can. Ch. Orlane's Sun Toy of Geodan (The Avenger x Orlane's Miss Nichola).

Thetis was co-owned by Joseph Colantonio when she was bred to The Avenger. That litter produced BIS Am., Can. &. Bda. Ch. Bihar's Revenger of Sammi Raja★, Ch. Bihar's Act Tu of BarCon and Am. & Can. Ch. Bihar's Galadriel of Kwala. Revenger and Galadriel bred together produced Ch. Kwala 'N Bihar's Sundarijal. Revenger was also bred to Ch. Vanity's Chrysanthemum, by Ch. BarCon's Kings Ran-Som (The Avenger x Ch. Dolsa Solo) out of Khabachen Fortune Cookie (Jonny x Thetis), to produce Ch. Bihar 'N Kwala Katie Kan.

When Bihar's Promises Promises (Revenger x Potpourri's Cun-Ba Bumo) was bred to Ch. Norbulingka Khyber (Revenger x Ch. Norbulingka Crazy Daisy ROM), she produced Ch. Bihar Attitude Adjustment.

Bihar Lhasa Apsos was awarded the ALAC ROM breeders' award in 1989.

CHAR RU

Char Ru was originated by Ruth Hayden and Carolyn Paulson, a mother-daughter team. They obtained their foundation bitch, Hayden's Princess Ming Mami ROM (Maria's Golden Lhasa x Babe of Everglo Twinkle), as a show prospect, but she proved to be more valuable as a producer. Two breedings to Ch. Bara's Bigwig (Ch. Bara's Glowing Ember of Yat-Sen x Bara's Rapunzel) produced the bitches Ch. Char Ru's Sha-Na-Na ROM★, Char Ru's Saucy Sioux, Ch. Char Ru's Glance My Way, Char Ru's Its A Bingo and the male Ch. Char Ru's Happiness Is. These five are the foundation for the Char Ru line.

Am. Can. Ch. Bihar Attitude Adjustment, bred by Elsie Basler, Potpourri, and Carol Strong, Bihar, and owned by Marie Niemeyer and Helen Vroman. *BK*

Ch. Char Ru's Roulette, bred by Ruth Hayden, and owned by Ruth Hayden and Carolyn Paulson, Char Ru.
Olan Mills

Multiple Group winner Am. Can. Ch. Char Ru's Mystery Guest, bred by Ruth Hayden and Carolyn Paulson, Char Ru, and owned by Joseph and Sylvia DiBenedetto, Remus.
John Ashbey

91

Sha-Na-Na was Char Ru's first homebred champion, having finished in 1977. Ch. Char Ru's Roulette (Ch. Bara's Wags to Witches ROM★ x Its A Bingo) was bred to Happiness Is and produced multiple BIS Ch. Char Ru's Happy Gambler and Ch. Char Ru's Double or Nothing ROM★★.

In 1989, there were three Char Ru Lhasa Apsos in the top ten listings. They were Ch. Char Ru's Read 'Em and Weep, Ch. Char Ru's Living Legend O'Taka and Ch. Char Ru's Mystery Guest, all sons of Double or Nothing by Ch. Tatli Su's Flying Tiger (Ch. Tatli Su Star Ship Enterprise x Knolwood's Shanay Adams).

Jackie Rose's Bara sires were the basis for the success of Char Ru breeding. Char Ru's linebreeding on Sparky is unique only because of the two Sparky sons Ch. Orlane's Dolmo ROM★★ and Ch. Arborhill's Bhran-Dieh ROM, on which Char Ru placed emphasis.

Char Ru received the ALAC ROM breeders' award in 1984.

DOLSA

Dolsa was founded in 1970 by Jean Kausch-Fergus when she finally, after several unsuccessful acquisitions, obtained a bitch from Helen Davies, Chamdo, that became Ch. Chamdo's Tsering Dolma, out of Ch. Chamdo's Sir Lancelot (Kashgar x Ch. Tsi Pa Me of Abbotsford) and Americal's Moma (Kashgar x Americal's Serpo), and Dolsa's first foundation bitch. When Dolma was bred to Ch. Karma Bandito of Maru, she produced Ch. Dolsa Maru Topaz, and when bred to Ch. Zijuh Don Na Tsamten ROM★ produced Ch. Dolsa Merry Gold, who produced Ch. Yarlin Dolsa All Systems Go by Pawprints Jinda.

Mrs. Kaush-Fergus obtained as a second foundation bitch the straight Hamilton-bred bitch Cordova Sin Sa ROM★★★★, the dam of thirteen champions carrying the Dolsa prefix.

Dolsa was a combination of Hamilton and Abbotsford, with the Hamilton from Americal, Licos, Chen, Karma and Zijuh, and the Abbotsford from Chamdo and Pawprints.

Mrs. Kaush-Fergus kept no more than four adults at one time and had no more than two litters per year. This afforded many other breeders the opportunity to obtain proven Dolsa stock for their foundations.

Ch. Dolsa Yojimbo ROM★ (Ch. Chen Krisna Nor ROM★ x Sin Sa) was the sire of the multiple BIS Ch. Yojimbo Orion ROM. Am. & Can. Ch. Dolsa Ringmaster ROM★ (Kyma x Sin Sa) had a dominant effect on many breeding programs. Sin Sa spent her last years with Lynette Clooney and is the namesake for that kennel, having produced these three champion offspring with both names: Ch. Dolsa Sin Sa Chia Pao, Ch. Dolsa Sin Sa Miqsee and Ch. Dolsa Sin Sa Skar Ma, all sired by Ch. Dixie's Beau of Everglo ROM★ (Chulung La x Everglo Buttercup ROM★).

Dolsa qualified to receive the ALAC ROM breeders' award in 1978.

Ch. Dolsa Yojimbo (Am. Can. Ch. Chen Krisna Nor ROM x Cordova Sin Sa ROM) was owned by Elaine Spaeth, Yojimbo, and bred by Jean Kausch, Dolsa. He sired the multiple BIS Ch. Yojimbo Orion.

Ch. Dolsa I've Been Spotted (Hi Lan's T'Ai Chi Chih x Ch. Rimzhi's Collectors Item) bred and owned by Jean Kausch Fergus, Dolsa and co-owned by Stella Kman, Kman Lhasa Apsos.

Group winner Am. Can. Ch. Dolsa Ringmaster ROM*, bred and owned by Jean Kausch-Fergus, Dolsa. *Missy*

93

Ch. Dorjon J-Toi's Penny Lane, bred by Dorothy Sweeney, Dorjon, and owned by John Windish and Jack Haserick, J-Toi. *Ashbey*

Ch. Almon's JB of Nyima ROM, bred by Marjorie Lewis and Priscilla David and owned by Mary Schroeder, Fleetfire, is the foundation matron for Fleetfire Lhasa Apsos.

DORJON

In the early seventies while showing and breeding German Shepherd Dogs, Dorothy Sweeney bought a Lhasa Apso puppy from Liz Morgan as a gift for her daughter. She fell in love with the breed, and in 1975 bought a puppy that would become Ch. Mor Knoll Rgyal Tiffany ROM★ out of Ch. Potala Keke's Golden Gatsby ROM★ and Ch. Mor Knoll Darlin of Rgyal ROM★ (Ch. Mor Knoll's Alex A Hente ROM x Kinderland's Ginger Rgyal II ROM★), as a foundation bitch for Dorjon.

In February 1978, Tiffany had her first litter, which produced Ch. Dorjon's Mor Knoll Gia of Tao-Yin, BIS Ch. Cymbi's Tashi Singay of Dorjon and Ch. Dorjon's Champagne Edition ROM★. Champagne Edition became the Sweeney's foundation sire and produced at least thirteen Dorjon champions.

Tiffany's second litter was by Ch. Orlane's Inimitable ROM★★★, from which Ch. Dorjon's Nicole of Emerel★ was kept, co-owned with Ellen Hines, and when bred to Champagne Edition produced Chs. Dorjon's Honeygold of Ja-Sai, Dorjon's Champagne Gala, Dorjon Barker's Zip Code and Dorjon's I'm J-Toi's Penny Lane.

In 1976, Ch. Rgyal Busy Bee Bee was obtained, and after becoming a champion was bred to Shyr Lyz Razamataz of Rgyal. From this litter came a small red bitch, Dorjon's Katie Did ROM★, co-owned with Ellen Hines, that produced five champions all sired by Champagne Edition.

Dorjon received the ALAC ROM breeders' award in 1984.

EXCEL

Patricia Fitton bred and showed Doberman Pinschers, and purchased a Lhasa Apso for her children in 1971. This acquisition was Sue-Kim's Little Lady, by Ch. Chen Tawney Leo of Sharpette (Nyun Ti x Kara Nor) out of Donna's Wingwards Mozique (Friar Tuck x Tina's Raggy Doll of Wingward). When Little Lady was bred to Majoma's Mighty Mac, she produced Ch. Kandi Su's Golden Dawn and S & K's Short Change. Little Lady was also bred to Ch. Volent's Kon Tiki Ti and produced Kon Tiki's Golden Girl, who when bred to Mighty Mac produced Am. & Can. Ch. Choo Choo Charlie.

When Short Change was bred to Ch. Rgyal's Kisco Kid of Volents, she produced Ch. Excel's Sir Hugo and Excel's My Happiness, and when bred to Ch. Majoma's Tombstone Timothy, she produced Ch. Excel's Cin-Dee-Lou. My Happiness was bred to Timothy and produced Ch. Excel's Luv Mi Tu, and to Ch. Rhojondy's Spring Fling to produce Excel's Summer Breeze, the dam of Ch. Excel's Blackstone's Domino, whose sire is Ch. Excel Tau Mi Hawk of Tra-Mar.

When Golden Dawn was bred to Cozmik Raz★, she produced Ch. Excel's You Needed Me ROM★. When You Needed Me was bred to Tau Mi Hawk, she produced Ch. Excel's Christopher Robin, Ch. Excel's Elites Make It Big and Ch. Excel's Mum's The Word, and when bred to Ch. Tra-Mar's Defender, she produced Ch. Excel's Misti Acres Tassie and Ch. Excel's Solid Gold.

Excel Lhasa Apsos qualified for the ALAC Register of Merit breeders' awarded in 1989.

FLEETFIRE

Fleetfire, founded in 1980, is a partnership between Mary Schroeder and Debby Rothman. The foundation stock, obtained from Jerry Berman Schwartz was a dog, Ch. Nyima's A Little Nachas (Ch. Nyima's Knick's DeBusschere★ x Ch. Shana of Halmar), and a bitch, Ch. Almont's JB of Nyima ROM★★, also sired by DeBusschere out of Almont's Dew Drop.

Fleetfire's first litter was whelped in 1980 when Nachas and JB were bred together to produce Group-winning Ch. Fleetfire Hot Tam Alie and his sister Ch. Fleetfire Zshoi Zher. A repeat mating produced Ch. Fleetfire Replay.

In 1982, Fleetfire bred JB to BIS Ch. Rimar Rumpelstiltskin ROM★ and produced Ch. Fleetfire Zhel Lee Bhel Lee ROM★.

Fleetfire then acquired Ch. Niall's Fleetfire O'Blu Patina, sired by Ch. Anbara's Ruffian out of Niall's Hsin Dih Bear ROM. Blu, when bred to JB, produced Ch. Fleetfire Red Zin Ger and Ch. Fleetfire Par Ting Shot. When Blu and Zhel Lee Bhel Lee were bred together, they produced Ch. Fleetfire Fash On Red and Ch. Fleetfire Put On Your Red Shus.

Zhel Lee Bhel Lee was also bred to her half brother, Par Ting Shot, to produce Ch. Fleetfire Tela Taecht-Anna and Ch. Fleetfire Red Fern, and to Hot Tam Alie to produce Ch. Fleetfire Shiver Me Timbers.

Mrs. Schroeder received the ALAC ROM breeders' award in 1987 and Mrs. Rothman received the award in 1989.

GARDENWAY

The Gardenway Lhasa Apsos of Robert Cooper began in 1974 with the purchase of a puppy bitch named Hair-Um's Tina of Gardenway, by Hair-Um's Fireball out of Everglo's Shady Lady of Hair-Um. Although never shown, she was good enough to be bred so a young male, Shiraz's Big Gy of Gardenway, was purchased for that breeding only. The breeding was not a success, although the education gained was quite beneficial to the future of Gardenway.

An acquaintance with Ron Tyler and Sam Lufkin resulted in the purchase of a puppy bitch that became Ch. Luty Copper Penny Gardenway (Ch. Luty Reddy Freddy x Luty Zsa Zsa), Mr. Copper's first champion. When bred to Ch. Luty Pistol, she produced Ch. Gardenway's Penny Candy.

Also purchased from Luty was Copper Penny's sire, Reddy Freddy (Ch.

Ch. Fleetfire Red Rover Red Rover CD, bred by Margaret Andress and Mary Schroeder and owned by Mary Schroeder, Debby Rothman and Joyce Dzinciolski, was sired by Ch. Nyima's Hot Stuff ToNite out of Fleetfire No Zhel Lee.

Cott/Daigle/Francis

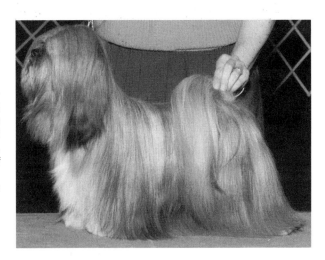

Ch. Luty Copper Penny Gardenway, bred by R. D. Tyler and O. L. Lufkin and owned by Robert Cooper, Gardenway. *Booth*

Multiple Group winner Ch. Orlane's Insignia ROM*, bred by Linda Smith, Orlane, and owned and handled by Robert Cooper, Gardenway.

Meyer Photo by Sharon

Orlane's Buddy of Luty x Ch. John's Hazel of Luty), which became Mr. Cooper's second champion, and a puppy bitch that became Ch. Luty Easy Come Easy Go ROM (Ch. Schuman's Little John x Luty Anna). These four were the foundation stock for Gardenway.

Tina was bred to Ch. Luty Pistol and produced Ch. Gardenway's Friendly Casper, and to Freddy and produced Ch. Gardenway's Surprize Package, who produced Ch. Gardenway's Sound Decision and Ch. Gardenway's Mai Tai, both by Ch. Je-An's Checkmate.

Freddy, in addition to Surprize, sired Ch. Gardenway's Brookfield Square and Am. & Can. Ch. Gardenway's Honey Delite when bred to Easy.

When Easy was bred to Ch. Hell's A Blazen Billy The Kid, an all-champion litter of three resulted, Ch. Gardenway's Rock A Fella, Ch. Gardenway's Precious Moment and Ch. Gardenway's Holiday Magic.

Although not bred by Mr. Cooper, the most successful show dog and a Gardenway favorite was the dog obtained from Dorothy Kendall that would become Group-winning Ch. Orlane's Insignia ROM★, the sire of six champions to date.

Gardenway was awarded the ALAC ROM breeders' award in 1987.

HALE ALII

Valiene Weathers-Heckart, Hale Alii, bought her first Lhasa Apso in 1974 from Peggy Huffman, Tara Huff, when they both lived in Hawaii.

This acquisition, although intended to be only a pet, started an association between the two breeders that proved to be very beneficial, because together they were able to overcome the complications created by the import laws of the island and the limited numbers of the breed that make it so difficult for single breeders to develop successful breeding programs in Hawaii.

Together Mrs. Weathers-Heckart and Mrs. Huffman imported Ch. Kuchi's Tara of Wynsippi★★ (Rah-Kieh x Orlane's Ming Su of Wynsippi), their foundation bitch. From her litter by Ch. Ruffway T'Ang Chu ROM★★ were three champions, one of which was the bitch Hale Alii Kupono, who at the age of two was sent to the mainland to be shown and eventually bred. Her championship was completed quickly and she came back to quarantine in Hawaii bred to BIS Ch. Windsong's Gusto of Innsbrook ROM★★, a mating that produced two champions, Ch. Hale Alii Sunshine Luv and Ch. Hale Alii Dragonslayer ROM★.

Bred to Ch. Tabu's Triple Threat, Tara produced Ch. Hale Alii Maggie May, and bred to the Australian Best in Show winner and champion Hale Alii Bit of Gusto (Gusto of Innsbrook x Kupono), she produced Ch. Hale Alii One Fine Feller and Ch. Hale Alii Marlena Mistique.

Additionally, Mrs. Weathers-Heckart imported as a puppy Group-winning Ch. Tru-Be's Special Edition, sired by Ch. Orlane's Inimitable ROM★★★ out of Car-bun's Lady Be Mine and the sire of Ch. Hale Alii Sweet Okole ROM when bred to Tara. Sweet Okole was bred to Bit of Gusto and produced champions Hale Alii G Wata Grouch, Tropical Storm and Triagin of Mara.

Hale Alii received the ALAC ROM breeders' award in 1984.

HALTBAR

Haltbar is the prefix of Barbara Richman-Hack, and was carried by Lhasa Apsos as early as 1975 when Haltbar Laizee Daizee (Ch. On Ba Yasha Khan of Sharbo x Galewyn's Lucrecia McEvil) was bred to Ch. Everglo Zijuh Tomba ROM★★ to produce Haltbar Dynamite. Mrs. Richman-Hack bred Innsbrook Electra Cute to Yasha Khan in 1977 to produce Haltbar Electra-Fy.

Mrs. Richman-Hack obtained additional foundation stock from Shyr Lyz, and because of the Scotts' retirement was able to get the Group-winning Ch. Shyr Lyz Shama Shama ROM★ (T'Ang Chu x Misa Cun-Tia), that when bred to Ch. Shyr Lyz De-ly-la of Ritos produced Ch. Haltbar Rhett Butler ROM, that in turn when bred to Electra-Fy produced Haltbar Short Circuit, the dam of champions.

Additionally, Mrs. Richman-Hack acquired the bitches Ch. Shyr Lyz Fabalous Flirt ROM★, Ch. Shyr Lyz Flamboyant Flair ROM★ and a co-ownership on Ch. Shyr Lyz Sassi Red Hots that collectively produced champions Haltbar Kris Kringle, Pat-N Leather and Dynastys Ninja.

Some next generation breedings produced Ch. Haltbar Brika's Banjo Beau by Kris Kringle and Ch. Haltbar One Of The Good Guys out of Pat-N Leather.

Haltbar Lhasa Apsos received the ALAC ROM breeders' award in 1985.

HOPE-FULL

Jeanne Hope founded the Hope-Full breeding program in 1971 with the acquisition of two daughters of BIS Ch. Potala Keke's Yum Yum ROM★, Ch. Potala Keke's Kelana ROM, by Ch. Everglo Zijuh Tomba ROM★★, and Ch. Potala Keke's Andromeda ROM★, by Group-winning Ch. Daktazl Tsung.

Kelana produced Ch. Jopan's Jubilee of Potala and Ch. Potala Jopalan Camelot when bred to Ch. Tabu's Double Or Nuthin, and Ch. Hope-Full's Honykom of Potala when bred to Ch. Tabu's King of Hearts ROM★★★.

Andromeda was bred to Ch. Ruffway T'Ang Chu ROM★★ to produce Ch. Hope-Full's Horatio.

These litters were predominately Hamilton with emphasis on Frosty Knight, Seng Tru and Tibet.

In 1978, Mrs. Hope outcrossed her established line by breeding Andromeda to Ch. Orlane's Inimitable ROM★★★, which produced Ch. Hope-Full's Headliner and Ch. Hope-Full's Happy Go Lucky. Andromeda was also bred to BIS Ch. Orlane's Intrepid ROM★★ to produce Ch. Hope-Full's Heirloom ROM★, that when bred to Inimitable produced champions Hope-Full's Heloise of Knolwood, Hope-Full's Helious of Knolwood and Hope-Full's Heidi of Knolwood, and when bred to Horatio produced Ch. Hope-Full's Happy Holiday.

With the judicious blending of Hamilton and Orlane and in spite of very limited breeding, Mrs. Hope qualified for an ALAC ROM breeders' award in 1983.

JA MA

Ja Ma Lhasa Apsos began in 1972 by Janet and Marvin Whitman when they obtained a black puppy bitch that became Ch. Ven-Ti's Mai Tai (Ch. Martin's King Kong Puff x Sharpette's Chi Chi Maria).

The foundation sire at Ja Ma was multiple BIS Ch. Arborhill's Rapso Dieh ROM★★, obtained as an adult and already a BIS winner, from Sharon Binkowski, Arborhill.

The foundation bitches for Ja Ma were Ch. Joval's Midnight Lace ROM★ (Ch. Potala Chiang x Ch. Tabu's Rhapsody In Red) and Ch. Lifelong's Stolen Hours ROM★ (Ch. Kyi Chu Whimsi of Sharbet x Ch. Lifelong's Joy).

Midnight Lace, predominantly Hamilton-bred, produced five Ja Ma champions, all by Rapso Dieh including BIS Ch. Ja Ma's Rah Bieh of Karlan.

Stolen Hours when bred to Ch. Mor Knoll's Alex A Hente produced Ch. Donicia's Tai Suki Lu ROM★, and when bred to Rapso Dieh produced Ch. Ja Ma's Rhe-Bhel-Yen of Jabu ROM and Ch. Ja Ma's Bohemian Rapso Dieh ROM. She was also bred to Ch. Shyr Lyz Mieh Ba Bieh Tu and produced Ch. Ja Ma's Nickelodeon of Seng-Lu and Am., Can.& Bda. Ch. Ja Ma's Renegade★, and to Ch. Martin's King Kong Puff to produce Ch. Ja Ma's Me Tu O Kai Bi.

Another bitch that produced well for the Whitmans was Ch. Ja Ma's Scarlet of Dolsa Syung ROM★ (I'm Steppen Out x Ch. Dolsa California Girl), that when bred to Ch. Kai La Sha Rahu-La O' Ja Ma produced Ch. Ja Ma's Infra Red and Ch. Ja Ma's Flor-Es-Cent, and when bred to Bohemian Rapso Dieh produced Ch. Ja Ma's A Little Night Music and Ch. Ja Ma's Scarlet Ribbons.

Ja Ma received the ALAC ROM breeders' award in 1979.

JOYSLYN

Joyslyn's Lhasa Apsos, owned by Lynn and Joyce Johanson, had its beginnings when the Johansons purchased a bitch in 1972 as a belated wedding gift to themselves. Completely captivated by the Lhasa Apso personality, a month later they purchased a second bitch, Joyslyn's Miss Buffy Jo (Raggedy Andy of Jerr Lee x Glenfall's Golden Cricket), a Sparky granddaughter, who became their foundation bitch. Buffy produced Ch. Joyslyn's Raggedy Rebel and multiple Group-winning Am. & Can. Ch. Joyslyn's Piece of the Rock ROM★, both by BIS Am. & Can. Ch. Arborhill's Rah Kieh ROM★. Piece of the Rock was

Ch. Hope-Full's Headliner, bred and owned by Jeanne Hope, Hope-Full.
Klein

Ch. Orlane's Ja Ma All The Rage (Ch. Orlane's Allstar x Ch. Orlane's Sparkler), bred by Linda Kendall Smith and owned by Janet Whitman, Ja Ma and Mrs. Smith, Orlane. *Tatham*

Am. Can. Ch. Ja Ma's Bohemian Rapso Dieh ROM, bred by Marvin and Janet Whitman, Ja Ma, and Edna and Monroe Kornfeld, Lifelong, and owned by the Whitmans. *Ashbey*

Joyslyn's first champion and his accomplishments contributed a great deal to the Johanson's early success, having produced several Joyslyn champions, three out of Ch. Sinka's Sirronna Khan ROM (Ch. Yat-Sen's Khana x Friday's Gift of Gold), namely Chs. Joyslyn's Clown Prince, Joyslyn's Promise ROM★ and Joyslyn's Rachmaninoff.

Joyslyn Lhasa Apsos earned the ALAC ROM breeders' award in 1985.

JUELL

Juell Lhasa Apsos began in 1979 when the gift of a Lhasa Apso puppy, Julie's Frosted Bonus Baby, introduced Julie K. Elliott to the breed. Assisted by her two children, Monette and Michael Thiele, their first show dog was Ch. Shyr Lyz Shan Mar (Ch. Shyr Lyz Shama Shama ROM★ x Ch. Shyr Lyz Fabalous Flirt ROM★). Acquired as a puppy, he was successful in the ring and at stud and was Monette's partner in a successful junior handling campaign. Monette was also very successful with Shan Mar's daughter, Ch. Amberwood's Alcheringa, bred by Val Ferrias.

The next acquisition was the puppy bitch that would become Ch. Orlane's Golden Girl ROM★ (Intrepid x Ch. Orlane's Whimsy of Innsbrook★), who produced Ch. Juell's Pride And Prejudice when bred to Ch. Saxonsprings Alamo ROM★, and Chs. Orlane Juell Angel Dust, Orlane Juell Hot Shot and Juell's Dancing In The Dark when bred to Ch. Orlane's Shot In The Dark ROM.

Ch. Light Up's Golden Graffiti ROM★★ (Intrepid x Light Up's Soda's My Pop) was acquired from Cynthia Klimas, Light Up, and when bred to Ch. Orlane's Insignia ROM★ produced Juell's first homebred champion, Ch. Juell's Calligraphy and Ch. Gardenway's Love Ly Juell. Graffiti was also bred to Pride And Prejudice to produce Chs. Juell's Lord of the Rings, Orange Blossom Special and Weekend Warrior, and to Inimitable to produce Chs. Juell's Double Indemnity and Sparkling Topaz.

Juell Lhasa Apsos qualified for the ALAC ROM breeders' award in 1988.

KALEKO

Debbie Burke's first champion and namesake for her kennel was purchased as a puppy in 1970 from Keke Blumberg-Kahn and became Ch. Potala Keke's Kal E Ko (Tomba x BIS Ch. Potala Keke's Yum Yum ROM★). Kal E Ko was bred to Orlane's Teddy of Norbulingka and produced Kaleko's Drop of Gold who, when bred to BIS Ch. Potala Keke's Candy Bar, produced Mrs. Burke's first homebred champion, Ch. Kaleko's Almond Joy.

In 1972, Mrs. Burke obtained a bitch from her mother, Dot Primm, who became Ch. Kalypri Kaleko's Kimsha Tu (Ch. Potala Kinderland's Goliath ROM★ x Carlee's Chuli). Kimsha produced Ch. Kaleko's Gyn Rhumi when

Multiple Group winner Am. Can. Ch. Joyslyn's Piece of the Rock ROM* was bred and owned by Lynn and Joyce Johanson, Joyslyn.

Ch. Joyslyn's Rachmaninoff, bred and owned by Lynn and Joyce Johanson, Joyslyn.

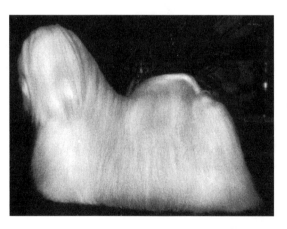

Am. World Ch. Juell Lord of The Rings, bred by Julie Elliott, Juell, and owned by Anke Rudd DeWijis, Holland.

Am. Can. Ch. Juell's Orange Blossom Special, owned and bred by Julie Elliott, Juell. *Alex Smith*

Ch. Kaleko's Gyn Rhumi, bred and owned by Debbie Burke, Kaleko, and shown here at age eleven months.

Group winner Ch. Kaleko's Sophisticated Lady ROM, bred, owned, and handled by Debbie Burke, Kaleko. *Petrulis*

Group winner Ch. San Jo Kian Kandi Kan ROM**, bred by Marianne Nixon, San Jo and Ann and Kirk Lanterman, Kian, and owned by Paul and Lois Voigt, Wellington, and Leslie Ann Engen, San Jo.

bred to BIS Ch. Orlane's Be Sparky of Al-Mar ROM, and Ch. Kaleko's Foxy Lady when bred to Orlane's Teddy of Norbulingka.

Kimsha's last litter was by On Stage Ruff 'N Ready (BIS Am. & Can. Ch. Rimar's Rumpelstiltskin x Ch. Mor Knoll's Breezin Bi). This litter produced the bitch Kaleko's Kristiana of Kamala, who in turn was bred to Ch. Andor's Red Baron to produce Kaleko's Lillian and Group-winning Ch. Kaleko's Sophisticated Lady ROM. Lillian is the dam of Ch. Kaleko's Essence of Krishel, and Sophisticated Lady is the dam of Ch. Kaleko's Rocky Road, Ch. Bahntahai Prahrah, Ch. Kaleko's Noel and Kaleko's Miss Priss.

Miss Priss, when bred to Ch. Kai La Sha Sailor of Llenroc, produced Ch. Kaleko's Robo Cop.

Kaleko qualified to received the ALAC ROM breeders' award in 1989.

KIAN

Ann Lanterman, Kian Lhasa Apsos, purchased her first show and foundation bitch, Ch. San Jo's Tamara of Robtell ROM in a co-ownership from Marianne Nixon in 1972. Tamara, bred by Martell Roberts, was by Ch. Kyi Chu Manshifa of San Jo ROM out of Ch. Luty Party Doll of Robtell, CD.

When bred to Ch. Pu Gye Bo of Abbotsford, Tamara produced Ch. San Jo's Kian Tabbo and Ch. Bo's Little Peep of Kian ROM, and when bred to Ch. Zoroshah Morific of San Jo, she produced Ch. San Jo Kian Kandi Kan ROM★★.

Little Peep was bred to Ch. San Jo's Raaga Looki Mei ROM★ and produced Ch. Kian's The Peep Line and Ch. Kian's Hide 'N Go Peep★. When Go Peep was bred to Am. & Can. Ch. San Jo's Wellington Kandy Man ROM★, she produced Chs. Rah Hide, One 'N Only and Mindy of Tramdo. When bred to mulitple, BIS-winning Ch. San Jo's Shindig (Shenanigan x Group-winning Ch. San Jo's Tabatha), she produced Ch. Kian's Life of the Parti.

Parti was bred to Ch. San Jo's Blew 'Em Away to produce Ch. Kian Victory Parti.

Kian qualified to receive the ALAC ROM breeders' award in 1987.

KINDERLAND TA SEN

Kinderland Ta Sen is a breeding program resulting from the co-ownership of Ch. Kinderland's Chok's Seneca and all of her descendants and the formation of a partnership between Ellen Lonigro and Susan Giles.

Seneca, when bred to Ch. Ruffway T'Ang Chu ROM★★, produced Ch. Kinderland Ta Sen Avatar, and when bred to Ch. Kinderland's Ta Sen Dakini ROM★, sired by Intrepid out of Kinderland's Ta Sen Kangra, produced the record-producing bitch Kinderland's Ta Sen Isis ROM★★★★★.

The eighteen Kinderland Ta Sen champions from Isis were by four sires,

Intrepid, Gusto of Innsbrook, Play It Again Sam and Ch. Westgate's Give 'Em Hell Harry ROM★.

Another important producer for the Kinderland Ta Sen partnership is Isis' half brother, Group-winning Ch. Orlane's Scirocco ROM★, sire of more than sixteen champions, including the three Kinderland Ta Sen champions out of the Sam x Isis daughter Ch. Kinderland Ta Sen Mime O'Sam ROM. Scirroco is also the sire of the breed record holder multiple BIS Ch. Rufkins Chip Off the Ol Rock, whose dam is Ch. Ruffway Patra Tashi Tu ROM★★.

Kinderland was one of the charter recipients of the ALAC ROM breeders' award in 1973 and Ta Sen was awarded the ROM award in 1984.

KYMBA

Helen Ingel has bred and exhibited Lhasa Apsos since 1974. Her foundation bitch, first champion and namesake for Kymba Lhasa Apsos was Ch. Rimar's Kinda Kym-Ba, a litter sister to BIS Ch. Rimar Rumpelstiltskin ROM★ and Ch. Rimar Penny Candy. Kinda Kym-Ba had only one litter, which was by Ch. Yeti's Kula Kangri, and her son Ch. Kymba's Buster Brown was Mrs. Ingel's first homebred champion.

Mrs. Ingel also acquired Kinda Kym-Ba's sire, Ch. Yeti's Paper Tiger ROM, and Ch. Yeti's Cajun Devil, sister to Kula Kangri, when Patricia Pritchett retired.

When Cajun Devil was bred to Ch. Tabu's King of Hearts ROM★★★, she produced Ch. Kymba Yeti's Lady Alisa and Kymba's Nutmeg.

When Nutmeg was bred to Buster Brown, she produced Ch. Kymba's Just Mandy ROM★, who when bred to Ch. San Jo's Rusty Nail ROM★★ produced Ch. Kymba-Kailas Just Katie, Ch. Kymba-Kailas Just Abby and Kymba-Kailas Just Candy. When Candy was bred to Buster Brown, she produced Ch. Kymba-Kailas Cory Brown.

Mandy is also the dam of Ch. Kymba-Kailas Royal Flush by Ch. San Jo's Kian Black Jack ROM, and the Group winner Ch. Kymba-Kailas Majority of One by Ch. Anbara Rimar Raisin A Ruckus ROM.

Mrs. Ingel was awarded the ALAC ROM breeders' award in 1988.

MADOROS

Madoros started in 1970 when Marie and Don Ross obtained their first Lhasa Apso, Bandit, but became official when they bought a puppy bitch from Shirley Ruth and Liz Moseley in 1974. This puppy, a younger full sister of BIS Ch. Windsong's Gusto of Innsbrook ROM★, became Am. & Can. Ch. Windsong Madoros Mai Li Chin ROM★★. She produced Ch. Madoros DK's Sheih Lah, Group winner Am. & Can. Ch. Madoros Dah-Vieh of Flo J and Ch. Windsong's Mean Jean by Ch. Al Mar's Ala Kazam ROM★; Ch. Madoros He's Sofein and

Multiple Group winner American, Peruvian, South American World '88 Bi Peruvian, Mexican and International BISS Ch. Kinderland Ta Sen Bizzi Buzzi, bred by Ellen Lonigro and Susan Giles, Kinderland Ta Sen, and owned by Jerry and Vivian Henderson, Jeviehan. *Kernan*

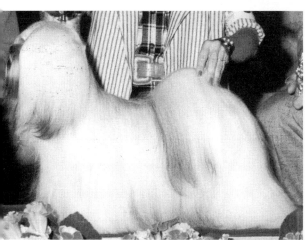

Ch. Kinderland Ta Sen Little Rock sired by Ch. Orlane's Scirocco out of Ch. Kinderland Ta Sen Mime O'Sam ROM, bred and owned by Ellen Lonigro and Susan Giles. Kinderland Ta Sen. *PJ*

Group winner Ch. Kymba Kailas Majority of One, bred and owned by Helen Ingel, Kymba, and Pauline Williams, Kailas. *Kernan*

Ch. Kymba's Buster Brown, bred by Helen Ingel, Kymba, and owned by Mrs. Ingel and R. M. Hoyt.

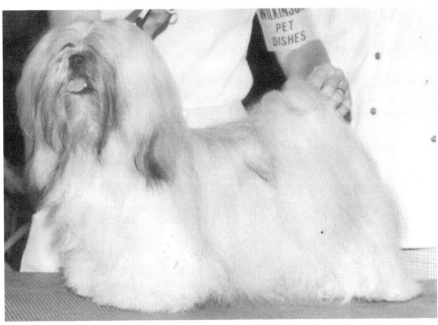

Am. Can. Ch. Windsong Madoros Mai Li Chin ROM**, the foundation bitch for the Madoros Lhasa Apsos of Don and Marie Ross. *Sosa*

Ch. Madoros Texas Taf Fieh by The Avenger and Ch. Madoros The Magician and Ch. Madoros The Sultan of Flo J by Ch. Madoros Solo of Orlane.

Madoros Misty Pebbles was bred to Ch. Orlane's Inimitable ROM★★★ to produce Ch. Madoros Encore of Fahlen and Ch. Madoros Misty Magic.

Mr. and Mrs. Ross acquired Orlane's White Knight II (Ch. Tabu's Music Man x Orlane's Solar Flair), and when bred to Orlane's Party Doll Of Madoros he sired Ch. Madoros Fireball of Orlane, and when to Madoros Saradepity, he sired Ch. Madoros Cover Up, the sire of Ch. Madoros Spotless Reputation out of Madoros Delta Dawn of Flo J.

The Madoros breeding program qualified to receive the ALAC ROM breeders' award in 1984.

MARDEL

Mary Ann and Darrell Strysick obtained their first Lhasa Apso in about 1975, fulfilled a showing and breeding contract, spayed their bitch and placed her in a good pet home. Their next was a better breed representative obtained from Nancy Coglianese.

Finishing easily, he became Ch. Tiffany's Won Kai Lee Senjen ROM (Bhran Dieh x Ch. Tiffany's Wendi La★) and Mardel's foundation sire. Bred to the foundation matron Woodlyn's Kishu ROM★, he produced Ch. Mardel's Cookie Monster, Ch. Mardel's Telula Tail Wiggle ROM, Ch. Mardel's My Girl Lolli Pup, Ch. Mardel's Hot Ta Trot and Ch. Mardel's Bratenella.

Mardel next acquired the male Ch. Kinderland's Ta Sen By Choice (Ch. Maran's Joshua O'Jen x Ch. Kinderland's Ta Sen Avatar). When bred to Lolli Pup, he produced the Group winner Ch. Mardel's Wee Willie Wonka ROM. Willie was bred to Hot Ta Trot and produced Ch. Mardel Northwind Hot Stuff and Ch. Mardel Northwind Instigator; to Mardel's House Mouse he sired Ch. Northwind Mardel Chia Mouse.

Telula was bred to By Choice to produce Ch. Mardel's Jabberwocky, and to BIS Ch. Woodlyn's Ruff and Ready ROM★ to produce Ch. Mardel's Miss Mischief and Ch. Woodlyn's Sassi of Mardel.

Mardel qualified to receive the ALAC ROM breeders' award in 1987.

MEILI

Meili Lhasa Apsos began in 1972 by Sue and Lynn Jamison, a mother-daughter team, with the purchase of a gold-and-white bitch from a pet shop. This puppy was to become the Jamisons' foundation bitch, Meili Jin Shaunyu ROM (Skipper Key x Chai Maida-La).

While attempting to get the AKC registration application for Jin Shaunyu, the Jamisons attended their first dog show, and as a result Jin Shaunyu was bred

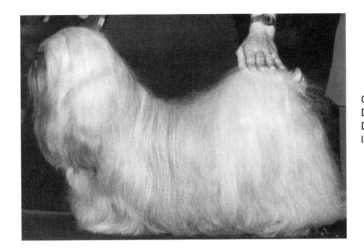

Group winner Ch. Madoros Dah-Vieh of Flo J, owned by Don Ross, Madoros, and the late Floy J. Thompson, Flo J.
Cott/Francis

Ch. Mardel's My Girl Lolli Pup, bred and owned by Mary Ann and Darrell Strysick, Mardel. *Olson*

Ch. Tiffany's Won Kai Lee Senjen, bred by Nancy Kretschmer, Tiffany, and Carolyn McKenna, the foundation dog for Mardel, he was owned by Mary Ann and Darrell Strysick.
Booth

Group winner Ch. Meili Gwongsin Jin Gwang, was bred and owned by Sue and Lynn Jamison, Meili. *Petrulis*

Ch. Meili Pippin Blakamoor, bred and owned by Sue and Lynn Jamison, Meili. *Olson*

Ch. Ming's Moondancer, bred and co-owned by Cheryl Zink, Ming, and owned by Victor Cohen, Victory. *Booth*

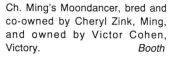

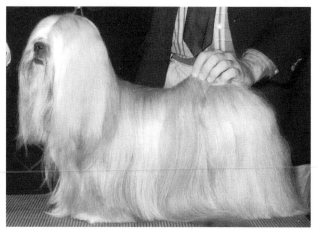

to Ch. Bel Air's El Toro Romeo★ (Ch. Zijuh El Toro x Beck's Parti Doll). The first puppy in this litter was Ch. Meili Jin Myanjyu Tufei, Meili's first champion.

Mrs. Jamison was so impressed by the black Lhasa Apso after seeing El Toro Romeo that Meili obtained a black son of his, Ch. Meili Romeo Yan Shen ROM, out of Ch. Kye Ho of Everglo.

Romeo Yan Shen produced five Meili champions, of which probably the best known was the Group-winning bitch Ch. Meili Gwongsin Jin Gwang, whose dam was Meili Tu Ti Miao.

Additional Meili champions sired by Romeo Yan Shen are Ch. Meili Myriah De Yan Shen and Ch. Meili Shaunyu De Yan Shen, both out of Jin Shaunyu, and Ch. Meili Gold Dust and Ch. Meili Pippin Bladamoor, both out of Meili Jimguiseng Mimi.

When Shaunyu De Yan Shen was bred to Gold Dust, she produced Ch. Meili Boss Hogg, and when bred to Meili Jubilation Kai-La-Sha, she produced Ch. Meili Kopper Beau.

Meili qualified for the ALAC Register of Merit breeders' award in 1987.

MING

Ming Lhasa Apsos of Cheryl and David Zink should not be confused with the foundation kennel of the same name that was owned by Judge Frank T. Lloyd and was retired in 1962.

In 1970, after attending a dog show, Mrs. Zink became interested in the sport, so the Zinks purchased their first foundation bitch, Amber Angel, sired by Arborhill's Ho Beau out of Lil Betsy Tu Shu. When bred to Shyr Lyz Little Caesar, she produced the Zinks' first homebred champion, Am. & Can. Ch. Ming's Lord Cognac ROM★, and Ming's foundation sire, having produced seven champions for the Zinks.

At the time Amber was mated to Caesar, the Zinks purchased their second foundation bitch, Am. & Can. Ch. Shyr Lyz Kim Chi (Shyr Lyz Bim-Boh Bov x Shyr Lyz Parti Girl) and Ming's first champion. When bred to Ch. Lingkhor Bhu of Norbulingka ROM★, she produced Ch. Ming's Chaka Khan of Danba. Kim Chi was also bred to Ch. Neika's Pleazing Pal to produce Ming's Gisella Leih, that when bred to Ch. Jampo's I'm Stepping Out of Syung ROM★ produced Ch. Ming's Anastasia ROM. When Anastasia was bred to Cognac, she produced the three Ming champions Angelique, Ambrosia and Twilight Mist.

The Zinks also purchased Shisedo's Spirit of Ming (Steppen Out x Everglo Autumn Amber), and when bred to Cognac, she produced Ch. Ming's Moonraker. When bred to Ming's Misty Morning, a daughter of Ch. Shisedo's Tochi Kele Tamaka and Somerset's Ciara of Ming, Moonraker produced Ch. Ming's Moondancer. Misty Morning was also bred to Cognac to produce Ch. Ming's Midnight Fantasy.

Another purchase that influenced the Ming program was the straight Hamilton-bred male Kai La Sha Ming The Real Thing, who when bred to Angelique

Group winner Am. Can. Ch. Ming's Lord Cognac ROM* bred and owned by Cheryl Zink, Ming. *Waugh, Inc.*

Ch. Mor Knoll's Alex-A-Hente ROM was bred and owned by Liz Morgan, Mor Knoll. *Klein*

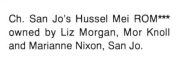

Ch. San Jo's Hussel Mei ROM*** owned by Liz Morgan, Mor Knoll and Marianne Nixon, San Jo.

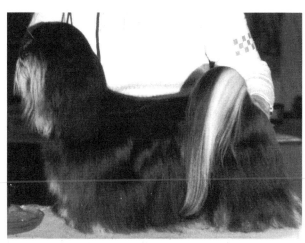

113

produced Ch. Ming's Rhiannon and Ming's Sugarfrost. Sugarfrost bred to Cognac produced Ch. Ming's Moonlight Madness.

Ming Lhasa Apsos qualified for the ALAC ROM award in 1986.

MOR KNOLL

Liz Morgan got her first Lhasa Apso in 1970 as a ten-week-old puppy. This puppy grew up to be Ch. Mor Knoll's Victoria, by Ch. Pan Chen Tonka Sonan ROM★ out of Hillside Acres Daffodil. From Victoria's first litter, by BIS Ch. Tibet of Cornwallis ROM★★★, came Mor Knoll's first homebred champion, Ch. Mor Knoll's Alex-A-Hente ROM, that when bred to Kinderland's Ginger Rgyal II ROM★ produced the bitch Ch. Mor Knoll Darlin of Rgyal ROM★.

Another foundation bitch for Mor Knoll was Chok's Joppa Bu Mo ROM★★★, obtained by Mrs. Morgan after having had two litters that produced four champions by Ch. Tabu's King of Hearts ROM★★★. Mrs. Morgan bred her again to King, and she produced Chs. Mor Knoll Encore Puffduster, Mor Knoll Rimar's Scarlet, Mor Knoll's Mahogany and Mor Knoll Ari Tova of Chiz. Joppa Bu Mo was also bred to BIS Ch. Orlane's Intrepid ROM★★ and produced Chs. Mor Knoll Chok's Grand Slam ROM★, Mor Knoll Chok's Farrah and Mor Knoll Chok's Line Drive ROM★.

In 1984, Mrs. Morgan became a co-owner of Ch. San Jo's Hussel Mei ROM★★★. When bred to four different San Jo studs, she produced eight champions carrying both the Mor Knoll and San Jo prefixes.

Mor Knoll qualified for an ALAC ROM breeders' award in 1977.

NORTHWIND

Cindy Butsic was introduced to the breed in 1974 when her husband, Larry, gave her Tasha Apso, a pet with typical Lhasa Apso charm. Participation in obedience eventually led to the conformation ring and an introduction to Sybil Joslyn Brennan, whose lines were a Pandan-Hylan-Cherryshore combination.

This friendship led to breeding Joslyn's Kizzy Wuz ROM to Group winner Ch. Ruffway Patra Dutch Treat and the acquisition of Ch. Ruffway Trademark (BIS Ch. Ruffway Patra Pololing x Ruffway Kusung). Trademark became Mrs. Butsic's first champion as well as the foundation for Northwind, and when bred to Kizzy Wuz produced Mrs. Butsic's first homebred champion, Ch. Northwind Nicoma ROM, as well as Ch. Northwind I Kina I Kan.

Mrs. Butsic obtained the bitch Mardel's House Mouse (Ch. Kinderland Ta Sen By Choice x Ch. Mardel's Telula Tail Wiggle ROM) from Mary Ann Strysick and an association was formed that produced many co-bred champions, including Ch. Northwind Mardel Chia Mouse, whose sire, a favorite of Mrs. Butsic, is the Group-winning dog Ch. Mardel Wee Willy Wonka ROM. Mrs. Butsic also bred Joslyn's Star Sapphire to Willy and produced Ch. Northwind Rampage.

The first homebred champion for Cindy Butsic, Northwind, was Ch. Northwind Nicomah ROM*.

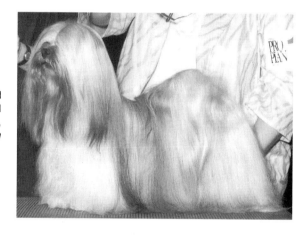

Ch. Northwind Sillieh Sallieh, bred by Cindy Butsic, Northwind, and owned by Barbara Walworth, Panchan, and Mrs. Butsic. *Booth*

Ch. Anbara Rimar's Toe Tappin Twiggy, bred and owned by Barbara Wood, Anbara, and Stephen Campbell, Rimar. *Klein*

Another bitch used in the Northwind breeding program was Delami Jolee's L'eggs ROM. (Ch. Delami Gangbusters x Shyr Lyz Devil Woman). L'eggs is the dam of five champions, including Ch. Northwind No Nonsense of Jolee by Trademark.

Mrs. Butsic's Northwind breeding program has produced many champions and qualified for the ALAC ROM breeders' award in 1987.

RIMAR

Stephen Campbell has been breeding Lhasa Apsos under the name of Rimar since 1970.

Mr. Campbell's foundation bitch was Rondelay Lhamo Zen-Ma (Ch. Karnes' Khambo x Ch. Rondelay Lhamo Kutra). When bred to Ch. Lingkhor Bhu of Norbulingka ROM★, she produced Ch. Rimar's Tipit ROM, Mr. Campbell's first homebred champion.

Rimar's foundation sire and first champion was multiple Group-winning Ch. Tabu's King of Hearts ROM★★★. He produced BIS Ch. J.G. King Richard, Ch. Rimar's Bee Twixt N Bee Tween and Ch. Rimar's U Bet Cha Buttons out of Tipit.

The second foundation bitch obtained by Mr. Campbell was the future Ch. Arborhill's Lho Lha of Rimar ROM (Bah Bieh Boi x Ch. Arborhill's Lhana ROM★). From Ch. Yeti's Paper Tiger ROM, she produced BIS Ch. Rimar's Rumpelstiltskin ROM★, Ch. Rimar's Kinda Kym Ba and Ch. Rimar's Penny Candy.

King Richard was bred to Penny Candy and produced Ch. Rimar's The Frivolus Fox ROM and Ch. Rimar's Gott Cha Num Bher.

Frivolus Fox was bred to the King son BIS Ch. Anbara Hobgoblin, whose dam was Ch. Anbara's Abra-Ka-Dabra ROM★, to produce Ch. Anbara Rimar's Footloose Fox ROM★★★, the dam of, among others, BIS Ch. Anbara Rimar Mary Puppins, Ch. Anbara Rimar Raisin A Ruckus ROM and Ch. Anbara Rimar Toe Tappin' Twiggy.

The Frivolus Fox was also bred to Ch. Anbara Justa Teddy Bear to produce BIS Ch. Anbara Rimar's Grin 'N Bear It ROM★ and Ch. Anbara Rimar's Magic Marker.

Mr. Campbell qualified to receive the ALAC ROM breeders' award in 1978.

SAMARA

Sami Brush bought her first Lhasa Apso, Neika Sassy Sadie Sings (Dunklehaven Mr. Spats x Neika Sing) as a pet in 1971, and six months later she bought Dunklehaven Honey Bear ROM★ (Ch. Berano's Moki-Tsu★ x Dunklehaven Tah-Ming★) just three weeks before she was due to whelp a litter by Ch. Orlane's Dieh Bieh★. Mrs. Brush kept from this litter the puppies who were to become multiple BIS Ch. Brush's Alvin of Samara ROM★ and his sister Ch. Brush's Abbi of Samara ROM.

BIS Am. Can. Ch. Rimar's J. G. King Richard (Ch. Tabu's King of Hearts x Ch. Rimar's Tipit), was a noted BIS winner bred by Stephen Campbell, Rimar.

BIS Ch. Brush's Alvin of Samara ROM*, owned by Sami Brush and bred by Elsie and Jim Dunkle, Dunklehaven. *Booth*

Ch. Sharbil Revelation, bred and owned by Sharon Russett, Sharbil. *Alverson*

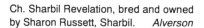

117

Sadie produced one Samara champion, Ch. Brush's Baretti of Samara when bred to Alvin, but it was through Honey Bear that the Samara breeding program advanced.

When Alvin was bred to Shalreign's Natasha (Orlane's Chip Of Spark x Shalreign You've Got A Lot), two champions were produced, one of which was Ch. Brush's Simon of Samara, who when bred to his granddam, Honey Bear, produced Samara's Sweet Shalom ROM. Shalom was bred to Ch. Innsbrook's Patrician O Sulan ROM★ and produced the sisters BIS Ch. Samara's Timekeeper Patti and Ch. Samara's Suger Is Sweet.

When Abbi was bred to Ch. Ruffway Mashaka ROM, the multiple Group-winning Ch. Samara's Koko Nor Of Knolwood resulted. Abbi was also bred to Ch. Samara's Quackers of Somerset and produced Ch. Samara's Gram Quacker and the multiple Group-winning Am. & Bda. Ch. Samara's Quacker Jack.

Samara qualified for the ALAC ROM breeders' award in 1984.

SHANGRELU

Wendy Penn established Shangrelu Lhasa Apsos when she purchased the two-month-old male puppy Sugarill Shangrelu (Ch. Orlane's Nyan Pa x Potala Keke's Sugarill Mini) that sired Mrs. Penn's foundation bitch, Shangrelu Tibbe Tu ROM when he was bred to Rise N' Shine Moppsy (Ch. Darroc's Charlie Boi x Darroc's Ama Su Lame).

Tibbe Tu, bred twice to Ch. Potala Keke's Tomba Tu ROM★, produced three champions, one of which was Mrs. Penn's first homebred champion, Ch. Shangrelu Sneak Preview ROM★. When Sneak Preview was bred to BIS Ch. Joi San's Golden Mocca Of Ky, the Group-winning bitch Ch. Shangrelu DB Sunshine★ resulted.

Mrs. Penn acquired BIS Ch. Potala Keke's Zintora and bred him to Tomba Tu daughters, which produced several Shangrelu champions. BIS Ch. Ja Ma's Rah Bieh of Karlan bred to Sneak Preview produced Am. & Can. Ch. Shangrelu Sneak Thief.

Shangrelu Mc Bizzieh Body ROM (Zintora x Sneak Preview) bred to Intrepid produced two champions, one of which was Ch. Shangrelu Show Biz, the sire of at least four champions, among them Ch. Orlane's Shot In The Dark ROM, whose dam is Orlane's Simplicity Of Geodan.

In 1981, Shangrelu Lhasa Apsos qualified for the ALAC ROM breeders' award.

SHARBIL

Bill and Sharon Russett started Sharbil with their purchase of a bitch, Dolsa Yamkos Tshi ROM (Ch. Dolsa Tsohks Sin-Don x Ch. May Ko Lew Ge-Mo) in 1974 on a co-ownership with Jean Kausch-Fergus.

Ch. Sharbil Shades of Autumn, bred by Samuel and Billie Shaver, Billies Follie, Toni Richmond and Sharon Russett, Sharbil, and owned by Mrs. Russett. *Alverson*

Am. Can. Ch. Sharil Joymarc Patent Pending, bred by Winifred Graye, Joymarc, and Cherlynn Jozwick, Sharil, and owned by Mrs. Jozwick and Becki Kraus, ArKay. *Booth*

BIS Ch. Sho Tru Hylan Namaste Top Gun, bred by Midge Hylton and Pat Keen and owned by Gillian Marks, Namaste, and Pat Keen. *Callea*

Multiple Group and BISS Ch. Sho Tru Hylan Stetson was bred by Pat Keen and owned by Pat Keen, Midge Hylton and Shirley Ray. *Callea*

119

This bitch was bred twice to Am. & Can. Ch. Dolsa Ringmaster ROM★ to produce Ch. Sharbil My Boi O'Dolsa; Am. & Can. Ch. Sharbil Precious Sabrina, the dam of Am. & Can. Ch. Sharbil Dolsa Fleetfoot Mac out of Am. & Can. Ch. Pawprints Pied Piper ROM, and Ch. Sharbil Angelique O'Dolsa, Sharbil's first homebred champion.

The Russetts then added a straight Hamilton male, Ch. Kai La Sha Sharbil Tsambo (Everglo Rempa ROM★ x Ch. Kai La Sha Dolma★) which was the first Sharbil-owned Lhasa Apso to finish owner-handled. When bred to Ocon Kara Moka of Sharbil (Sharbo Kashum Ba x Ch. Sharbo Zijuh Cha-II), he produced Am. & Can. Ch. Sharbil Tsam'son and Sharbil Sheshai Jachhen.

When Mac was bred to Jachhen, he produced Ch. Sharbil Revelation, and when bred to Chiz Ari Billie's Follie Bella ROM★, he produced three champions, including the multiple BIS bitch, Ch. Billie's Follie Preakness.

Bella was also bred to My Boi to produce Ch. Billies Follie Heidi, that when bred to Revelation produced Billies Follie Tasha. Tasha, when bred to Ch. BarCon's The Critics' Choice ROM★ (Ch. Kian's Rah Hide x BarCon's Rave Review), produced Ch. Sharbil Respect Yourself and Ch. Sharbil Shades of Autumn. Shades of Autumn was bred to Ch. Orlane's O J (Ch. Orlane's Incorrigible x Ch. Orlane's Early Bird★) to produce Ch. Sharbil's One Man Show.

Sharbil was awarded the ALAC ROM breeders' award in 1988.

SHARIL

Sharil Lhasa Apsos are owned by Cherlynn Jozwick.

In 1975, Mrs. Jozwick obtained her first Lhasa Apso, which became Can. Ch. Kizmit's Cricket Ici-Bon and later was placed as a pet because she was not of the quality to breed according to Mrs. Jozwick's standards.

Mrs. Jozwick next acquired the bitch Joymarc's Bonnie Belle (On Ba Lho Bho O'Joymarc★ x Joymarc's Topsi Tu), that when bred to Kai-La-Sha Rudi O'Tru Tyme (Licos Dicha La x Everglo Autumn Amber) produced Sharil's Sabrina and Sharil's first foundation sire, Ch. Sharil's Sebastian.

Next came the bitch that was to become Ch. Joymarc's Foxy Lady (Can. Ch. Ocon Joymarc Daredevil x Ch. Joymarc's Blama Claudia) and the dam of three champions out of her only litter, one of which was Ch. Sharil's Painted Lady, sired by Ch. Joymarc's Pretty Boy Floyd.

Mrs. Jozwick then became a co-owner of Everglo Joymarc Mary Mary (Everglo Rempa ROM★ x Everglo Red Ginger), that when bred to Daredevil produced Sharil's second foundation sire, Am. & Can. Ch. Sharil Joymarc Patent Pending, co-owned with and shown by Becki Kraus. When Patent Pending was bred to Joymarc's Dan Ba Cinnibar, he produced Ch. Dan Ba Sharil Natural High, and when bred to Painted Lady, he produced Ch. Sharil's Believe It Or Not and Ch. Sharil's Bubblicious.

Mary was also bred to Ch. Joymarc's Zorro of Willaday to produce Ch. Sharil's Second To None. Also bred to Zorro was Sabrina to produce Sharil's

Boom Boom, the dam of Chs. Sharil's Lady Luck of Barbo and Sharil's Quiet Riot out of Ch. Rin Po Che III. Sabrina was also bred to Ch. Zarrah San Jo's Hari Kari to produce Sharil Dan Ba Bu Mo Pa and Sharil Skal-Nor Kuba, that when bred together produced Ch. Sharil Dan Ba Ser Po Ke Rtse.

Sharil Lhasa Apsos qualified for the ALAC ROM breeders' award in 1988.

SHISEDO

Sandy Nyberg bought her first Lhasa Apso in 1973 as a pet, and it was this pet that was to become Krackerjack's Brandywine ROM★ (Orlane's Torchlight x Di-El's Shady Lady), the foundation bitch for Shisedo Lhasa Apsos. Krackerjack was bred twice to Ch. Jampo's I'm Steppen Out Of Syung ROM★ and produced Ch. Shisedo's Tochi Kele Tu, Ch. Shisedo's Kishma Ashe, Ch. Shisedo's Macho and Ch. Shisedo's Shi Ko Ko.

Kele Tu was bred to Ch. Tabu's Fame And Fortune to produce Ch. Shisedo's Tochi Kele Tamaka, and Ashe was bred to BIS Ch. Yojimbo Orion to produce Ch. Shisedo's Mecca.

Mrs. Nyberg obtained another foundation bitch as a puppy, which became Ch. Shisedo's Soo-Lai-Mon ROM★ (Ch. Donicia's Chim-Zu El Torro ROM★ x Ch. Donicia's Tai Suki Lu ROM★). When bred to Macho, she produced Ch. Shisedo's Ka Ba, Ch. Shisedo's Chewbacca of Jedi and Shisedo's Sa-Rii-Bu; the latter bred to Shen's Sushoka Rebo produced Ch. Shisedo's Prophecy.

Soo-Lai-Mon was also bred to Ch. Syung's Eureka (Ch. Schuman's Little John x Carnival Cameo of Orlane) to produce the BIS bitch Ch. Shisedo's Mo-Li.

Prophecy was bred to Mo-Li to produce Ch. Billies Follie Shisedo Simon, and to Soo-Lai-Mon to produce Ch. Shisedo's Noni.

Macho was also bred to Orlane's Griselda (Wynsippi's Pop-Over-R O Orlane x Tibb's Dream Rusty) to produce Ch. Shisedo's Omen, the sire of five champions, including Ch. Shisedo's Chynna Lee out of Shisedo's Ashley Amber Haze, by Ch. Kai La Sha Rahu-La O' Ja Ma out of Ch. Shisedo's Autumn Haze.

Mrs. Nyberg's Shisedo Lhasa Apsos qualified to receive the ALAC ROM breeders' award in 1981.

SHO TRU

Pat Keen, Sho Tru, obtained her foundation bitch in 1972 while living in California. This was Sunji Laitse of Krisna ROM, a Krisna Nor daughter out of Ch. Pandan Po Nya, that accompanied Miss Keen when she relocated in the Midwest. It was there that Laitse was bred to Ch. Orlane's Inimitable ROM★★★ to produce Ch. Sho Tru's Stardust Cowboy, and to BIS Ch. Orlane's Vindicator ROM★ to produce Miss Keen's first homebred BIS winner, Ch. Sho Tru The Main Event.

Stardust Cowboy was bred to Ch. Sakya Tabriz, and Miss Keen acquired Sho Tru Tabriz Of Orlane, that when bred to Intrepid produced Sho Tru's Kiss My Grits ROM★★, and when bred to Orlane's Intrigue produced Sho Tru Summer Breeze.

Sho Tru was awarded the ALAC ROM breeders' award in 1985.

HYLAN SHO TRU

Mrs. Midge Hylton and Miss Pat Keen formed the Sho Tru Hylan partnership when Miss Keen assumed the manager's position in the kennel run by Mr. Hylton before his death.

Although Sho Tru started with a predominately Hamilton foundation, at the time the partnership with Hylan started, the Sho Tru line was mostly Orlane, so joining with Hylan was a new cross of Hamilton and Orlane.

Miss Keen brought to the partnership Kiss My Grits, that was bred to Ch. Orlane's Impudent of Windwick★ to produce the Group-winning Ch. Sho Tru Hylan Stetson and Ch. Sho Tru Hylan Crystal Sue. Additionally, she was bred to Group-winning Ch. Orlane's Scirocco ROM★ and produced champions Sho Tru Hylan Tak'm By Storm, Image of Ta Sen, Roc'm-Sock'm and the top-winning brace Rocks Anne and Rock A Bye Baby.

Also contributed by Sho Tru was Summer Breeze, that when bred to Impudent produced Chs. Hylan Sho Tru Impetuous and Sho Tru Hylan Joanie.

The straight Hamilton-bred Hylan bitch Ch. Hylan Hoshira Kiss Me Kate ROM★ (Ch. Hylan Tallisyn x Hylan Chanda), co-owned by Shirley Ray, Mrs. Hylton and Miss Keen, contributed Chs. Hoshira Hylan Anthing Goes and Hylan Hoshira All That Jazz when bred to Ch. Shangrelu Show Biz; and Chs. Hoshira Hylan Music Man, Hylan Hoshira Sweet Charity, Hoshira Hylan Hello Dolly and Hylan Hoshira Starlitexpress when she was bred to Ch. Light Up's Red Alert ROM★.

Stetson bred to Sho Tru Hylan Peppermintstik (Ch. Orlane's Double Treat x Sho Tru Heavenly Star) produced Ch. Sho Tru Hylan Namaste Topgun and Sho Tru Hylan Ace of Spades.

TALIMER

Terre Mohr, Talimer, purchased her first Lhasa Apso in 1977. Known as Miniver Cheevey, she was never bred but was a wonderful companion and was the reason that Ms. Mohr became involved in the breed.

In 1980, the bitch Syung's Rendition In Black ROM★★ was acquired along with two BIS Ch. Arborhill's Rapso Dieh ROM★★ sons, Ch. Ja Ma's Wenles The Wiz out of Ch. Joval's Midnight Lace ROM★ and Am. & Can. Ch. Ja Ma's Rhe Bhel Yen of Jabu ROM out of Ch. Lifelong's Stolen Hours ROM★.

Rendition produced two champions by The Wiz, Ch. Talimer Sorceress and

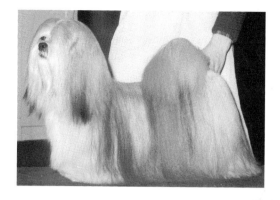

Ch. Talimer Kin No Hina of Son-Del, bred by Terre Mohr and owned by Carmen Watson Temple and Terre Mohr, Talimer.
A Ritter Photo by Kathy

Ch. Talimer Show Off, bred by Terre Mohr and owned by Toni Richmond, Terre Mohr and Harry Bennett. *Ashbey*

Group winner Ch. Tall Oaks Somethin Special, Best of Breed at the National Capital Lhasa Apso Club Specialty, 1985 under judge Carolyn Herbel, Tabu. *Kernan*

Belgian BIS Am. Belgian Ch. Kyilee Cunba Kam ROM**, the foundation bitch for Tall Oaks Lhasa Apsos was bred by Bobbie Lee, Kyilee, and owned by Paul and Kay Shaner, Tall Oaks. *Gilbert*

Ch. Talimer Kin No Hina of Son-Del, five champions by Rhe Bhel Yen, Ch. Talimer Sleuth, Ch. Talimer Mataba Mingpo, Ch. Syung's Knolwood Ahmerdeen Joy, Ch. Talimer Serendipity and Ch. Talimer Scoundrel, and one champion by Can., Am. & Bda. Ch. Ja Ma's Rennegade★, Ch. Talimer Irlees Surprise.

Both Sorceress and Serendipity were bred to Ch. Orlane Ja Ma All The Rage, with Sorceress producing Ch. Talimer and Carovale's T Magnum, and Serendipity producing Ch. Talimer Show Off.

Talimer qualified and received the ALAC ROM breeders' award in 1989.

TALL OAKS

Kay and Paul Shaner became interested in the Lhasa Apso with the purchase of a pet bitch in 1977. This interest led them to a dog show and the purchase of a male puppy from Bobbie Lee, Kyilee Double Dip (Ch. Tabu's Rags To Riches x Ch. Tabu's Indian Summer), which was bred to their original bitch, Shaner's Precious Mia (Bruno x Ming Ling Chen).

The continued acquaintance with Mrs. Lee gave the Shaners the opportunity to purchase their foundation bitch, Belgian BIS American & Belgian Ch. Kyilee Cunba Kam ROM★★ (BIS Ch. Tulku's Yeti of Milarepa x Kyilee Tiglecan of Maru).

Mrs. Shaner showed Cunba Kam to her American championship and then bred her to Gar-San's Dutch Apple, which produced Ch. Tall Oaks Quiet Breeze and Tall Oaks Shady Lady. Cunba Kam was next bred to Ch. Everglo Eager Beaver to produce Ch. Tall Oaks Suns-Horizon and Ch. Tall Oaks Gypsy In My Soul.

Quiet Breeze was bred to Suns-Horizon to produce Ch. Tall Oaks Just A Whisper, and Shady Lady was bred to Llenroc's Amigo to produce Ch. Tall Oaks Merrily Moppin.

Cunba Kam was bred the third time to Ch. Karma Rgyal Po Chan (Karma Cordova Tsan-Dan x Karma A-Le-Kam-Bu) to produce Ch. Tall Oaks Ramblin Man and Ch. Tall Oaks Smoken Bandit.

Cunba Kam was also bred to Ch. Shen Pa Ni-Khyim ROM★ to produce Group-winning Ch. Tall Oaks Somethin Special, Ch. Tall Oaks Magnificent Obsession and Ch. Tall Oaks Midnight Lace.

Ch. Tall Oaks Jus-Fur Fun was bred to Tall Oaks Little Day Dreamer to produce Ch. Tall Oaks Eighties Lady.

Tall Oaks received the ALAC ROM breeders' award in 1988.

TARA HUFF

Although charmed by the breed since 1968, it was not until 1970 when Peggy Huffman and her husband, an air force officer, relocated in Hawaii that they obtained their first Lhasa Apso, a beautiful red that turned out to be a pet.

Ch. Stonewall's Gung Ho ROM*, owned by Peggy Huffman, Tara Huff, photographed in Hawaii.

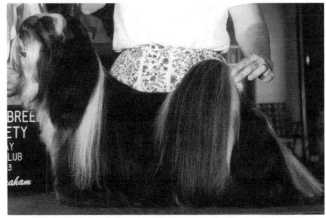

Ch. Tara Huff Black Magic bred by Peggy Huffman, Tara Huff.

Graham

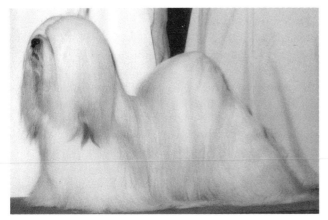

Multiple BIS Ch. S. J. W. Waffle Stomper ROM** was co-bred by Paul and Lois Voigt and Leslie Ann Engen (the S. J. W. stands for San Jo Wellington) and was owned by Mrs. Engen and her mother, Marianne Nixon, San Jo. Whelped in 1980, Waffle Stomper, sired sixteen champions before his premature death in 1983. *Petrulis*

125

Because Australian imports do not have to go through quarantine in Hawaii, the bitch Udelwar Tara was imported from that country. Additionally, Mrs. Huffman imported Ch. Stonewall's Gung Ho ROM★ (Orlane's Ming Kyi x Orlane's Su Lin) from the mainland.

The next import was also from the mainland and a joint effort between Valiene Weathers-Heckart and Mrs. Huffman when they imported Ch. Kuchi's Tara of Wynsippi★★ in whelp to Ch. Ruffway T'Ang Chu ROM★★ to become a foundation dam for both kennels.

Ch. Tara Huff Maapo, Ch. Tara Huff Derf and Ch. Hale Alii Kupono were the three champions produced by Tara and T'Ang Chu.

In 1975, Tara Huff moved back to the mainland, and this move expanded access to dog shows and accelerated activities that led to Mrs. Huffman becoming a professional handler and producing additional Tara Huff champions.

Gung Ho's daughter, Tara Huff Taa, out of Golden Honey Miegie, was bred to Ch. Potala Keke's Bhutan to produce Ch. Tara Huff Keepo, that when bred to Maapo produced Ch. Clay's War Lord of Tara Huff.

Gung Ho was bred to Carolyn's Rika Shah to produce Ch. Tara Huff Windieh O Tamara, that when bred to Ch. Shyr Lyz That Magic Moment produced Ch. Tara Huff Black Magic.

Mrs. Huffman acquired and bred Tycan Kuro Roku Hua (Ch. On Ba Khabul Khan of Sharbo ROM x Loch Ness Ming Baityan Banye) to Intrepid to produce Tara Huff Sophy De Tikah, that when bred to Ch. Hale Alii Dragonslayer ROM★ produced Ch. Tara Huff Georgette De Tikal and Ch. Tara Huff Suyeta O Hale Alii.

When Georgette was bred to Ch. Kikyru Quentan-Tzu, she produced Ch. Tara Huff Trishna Tikal and Ch. Tikal Tara Huff's Tyrin.

Tara Huff's breeding program was awarded the ALAC ROM breeders' award in 1985.

WELLINGTON

Wellington Lhasa Apsos is owned by Paul and Lois Voigt, who purchased their first Lhasa Apso in 1972.

In 1976, the Voigts obtained a bitch from Madeline Chizever Durholz that became their first champion as well as the foundation of their breeding program. This bitch was Ch. Chiz Ari Sehilot ROM★★★★★ (Tonka Sonan x Kinderland's Winne of Chiz ROM★) and purchased in a co-ownership breeders' terms arrangement. She was bred first to BIS Ch. Little Fir's Shel Ari of Chiz ROM★★, which produced six champions carrying the Chiz Ari Wellington names.

In 1977, the Voigts purchased a puppy bitch in co-ownership with Leslie Ann Engen that was the second foundation bitch for Wellington, and she became Group-winning Ch. San Jo's Kian Kandi Kan ROM★★. Bred only to San Jo sires, Kandi produced seven champions, including littermates BIS Ch. SJW Waffle Stomper ROM★ and Group-winning Ch. SJW Whipper Snapper.

In addition to the six champions out of Shel Ari, Sehilot produced eight champions by Ch. San Jo Shenanigan ROM★★, among them Ch. Wellington's Veri Blackberi (dam of Ch. Wellington San Jo Tokyo Rose by Ch. San Jo's Shindig ROM★), Ch. Wellington's Wish On A Star and Ch. Wellington's Shady Deal CD. When Sehilot was bred to Ch. San Jo's Soshome Up ROM★, she produced Ch. Wellington's Comeuppance, Ch. Wellington's Up 'N Attum and Ch. Wellington's Live It Up.

The Wellington Lhasa Apsos qualified for the ALAC Register of Merit breeders' award in 1981.

WYNDWOOD

Wyndwood Lhasa Apsos are owned by Kay and Bobby Hales. Although the first involvement in Lhasa Apsos for Wyndwood was in 1976, it was not until 1978 when the foundation bitch Orlane's Sweet Finale ROM★ (BIS Ch. Orlane's Vindicator ROM★ x Orlane's Lolly Pop O Luty) was purchased that a successful breeding program began. Also purchased from Orlane was the male Innsbrook's Orville Gufen Bacher (Gusto of Innsbrook x Sakya Fan Fare of Orlane), that when bred to Finale sired Wyndwood's first homebred champion, Ch. Wyndwood's Goofus Too.

Finale was also bred to Ch. Madoros Solo Of Orlane to produce BIS Ch. Wyndwood's Here Come D'Tank, and to Inimitable to produce Ch. Wyndwood's Poquita Mas ROM★.

Goofus Too was bred to Ginseng's Morningstar to produce Wyndwood's Crystal Pistol, the dam of Chs. Wynwood's Krystle Bear and Shilos Sir Goofus Bear, both out of Ch. Light Up's Red Alert ROM★.

Additionally, Ch. Orlane's 'Nana Pudd'n O'Wyndwood was purchased from Orlane and bred to Ch. Gingseng's Nocona to produce Ch. Wyndwood's Honeysuckle Rose ROM★★ and Wyndwood Kandi Kisses O'Gypsy.

It was at this time in the breeding program that Mr. and Mrs. Hales purchased from San Jo the young sire that became Ch. San Jo's Wingtips ROM★ (Waffle Stomper x San Jo's Shome Nangel). When bred to Poquita Mas, he produced Ch. Wyndwood's Summer Wine, Ch. Moonwalker's Fuzz R O'Wyndwood and Ch. Wyndwood's Best Foot Forward. Wingtips was also bred to Honeysuckle Rose to produce Ch. Wyndwood's Ain't Misbehavin, and to Kandi Kisses to produce Chs. Wyndwood's Stormy Weather and Gypsy's Nilla Wafer.

Honeysuckle Rose was bred to Ch. San Jo's Out O' The Blue ROM★★ to produce Ch. Wyndwood's Sundance Of Mai Li, Ch. Wyndwood Gypsy Blue Denim, Wyndwood's Double Trouble and BIS Ch. Wyndwood's Fuzzbuster. Honeysuckle Rose was also bred to Red Alert to produce Ch. Wyndwood Piwacket Honey Bear and Ch. Wyndwood's Call To Glory, and to Ch. Wellington's Wyndwood E L Fudge to produce Ch. Wyndwood's Born To Boogie and Ch. Chiran N Wyndwoods Tbet Ur Lif.

BIS Ch. Wyndwood's Here Come D' Tank, bred by Kay Floyd (Hales), Wyndwood, and Dorothy Kendall, Orlane, and owned by Sandra Hamann and Mrs. Hales.

BIS Ch. Wyndwoods Fuzzbuster, bred and owned by Kay and Bobby Hales, Wyndwood, changed ownership several times during his show career. The primary handler throughout Fuzzbuster's show career was C. L. Eudy. *Olan Mills*

Ch. Zarrah's Snap-To-It O'Anbara, bred by Roberta Richardson and Nathalie Heskett and owned by Mrs. Richardson and Barbara Wood, Anbara. *Callea*

Sundance and Kandi Kisses were bred together to produce Ch. Wyndwood's Jiminy Cricket.

Poquita Mas was bred to Ch. Wellington's Up 'N Attum to produce Ch. Wyndwood's Ginger Bits.

Double Trouble was bred to Wyndwood's Sushi Parti, sired by Wingtips out of Wyndwood's Sabrina, to produce Ch. Wyndwood's Sudien Catch Th' Wind.

Wyndwood Lhasa Apsos received the ALAC ROM breeders' award in 1986.

ZARRAH

Zarrah Lhasa Apsos was founded in 1973 when Roberta Richardson was given a puppy by Evelyn Finney. He was by Ch. On Ba Jo Bo ROM★ out of Farana of Zoroshah, and became Ch. Antar of Zoroshah when he was handled to his championship title at fifteen months of age by Mrs. Richardson.

Am. & Can. Ch. Zarrah Lynsgo Tarbaby and Ch. Zarrah San Jo's Hari Kari were produced when the bitch Sharbo Kalika was bred to Everglo Rempa ROM★.

The next acquisition was Naomi of Zoroshah (Ch. Everglo Sir Tom x Everglo Fanfare), that when bred to Group-winning Ch. Everglo Zijuh Tomba ROM★★ produced Zarrah's foundation bitch, Zarrah's Ya Mar Ta ROM. Mar Ta produced Ch. Zarrah's Ted Terrific and Ch. Zarrah's Ya Na-Ra of Tena out of Lyngso Sharbo Me-O-Tan of Tena. Ted Terrific produced Ch. San Jo Zhantor Blackgammon when bred to Mykara San Jo's Tar N' Feathered, and Ya Na-Ra produced Ch. Tacin Zarrah Tuff Stuff when bred to Ch. Sharbo Zijuh Kamaru★.

Mar Ta also produced Ch. Zarrah's Omar when bred to Ch. On Ba Me Go. Omar is a foundation sire for Mrs. Richardson and the sire of Ch. Zarrah Krisna Mischief Maker, whose dam is Zarrah's Dar-Ba. Mischief Maker is the dam of Ch. Krisna Zarrah Minda by Ch. Anbara Rimar Raisin' A Ruckus, and Ch. Zarrah's Tailor Made O'Kara by Ch. Zarrah Tena Snap-To-It O'Anbara.

Zarrah Lhasa Apsos qualified for the ALAC Register of Merit breeders' award in 1987.

ZHANTOR

Don and Naomi Hanson, Zhantor, purchased their first foundation bitch from Raul and Cassandra de la Rosa in 1975. She was Ch. Suntory Sonata ROM (Ch. Kyma of Abbotsford ROM★★ x Ch. Chen Krisna Tsoma Nor ROM★). When bred to Ch. San Jo's Soshome ROM★, she produced Ch. Zhantor Maestro and Ch. Zhantor Songbird ROM★★.

Songbird became Zhantor's second foundation bitch, and when bred to Ch. San Jo's Raaga Looki Mei ROM★ produced Ch. Zhantor Grand Ol' Parti, and

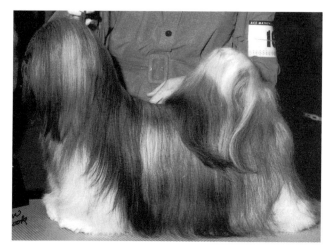

Ch. Zarrah's Taylor Maid O'Kara, bred by Roberta Richardson and owned by Mrs. Richardson and Phyllis Hebrard. *Cook*

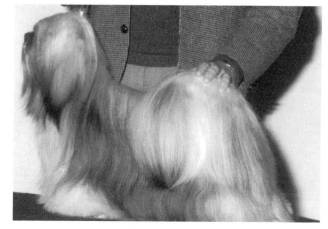

Ch. Zhantor Epiphany, bred and owned by Don and Naomi Hanson, Zhantor. *Roberts*

BIS Ch. Zhantor Joint Venture, bred by Don and Naomi Hanson, Zhantor, was owned with them by Leslie Engen, San Jo, and Kay and Bobby Hales, Wyndwood.

130

when bred to BIS Ch. SJW Waffle Stomper ROM★ produced Ch. Zhantor Epiphany.

Epiphany was bred to Ch. San Jo's Rusty Nail ROM★★ to produce BIS Ch. San Jo Zhantor Joint Venture and Ch. Zhantor Daydream Believer.

Songbird was also bred to Ch. San Jo Soshome Up ROM★ to produce Ch. Zhantor Hark Herald and Ch. San Jo Zhantor Sugarplum ROM★. Songbird's final litter was out of Ch. San Jo's Out O' The Blue ROM★★ and produced Ch. Zhantor Red Lollipop, Ch. Zhantor Cranberry Truffle and Ch. San Jo Zhantor Cinnamon Chews.

Zhantor qualified for the ALAC ROM breeders' award in 1986.

BIS Ch. Tibet of Cornwallis ROM**** is the top producing sire in the history of the breed with forty-eight champion offspring to his credit. Among these are at least seven Group winners, and three BIS winners. He was born in March, 1966, and died eleven days before his sixteenth birthday. He was bred by Paul Williams, Cornwallis, and owned by Norman and Carolyn Herbel, Tabu.

Multiple BIS winner Am. Bda. Ch. Kinderland's Tonka ROM*, bred by Ellen Lonigro, Kinderland, owned by Mr. and Mrs. Norman L. Herbel, Tabu, and handled by Robert Sharp, Sharpette.

Gilbert

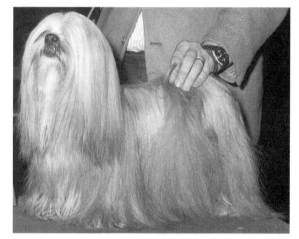

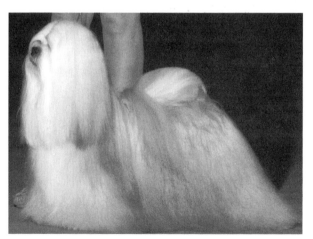

Multiple BIS Ch. Sulan's Master Blend was bred by Suzette Michele and Marlene Kimbrel and owned by Manya Greif and Miss Michele. Handled throughout his memorable career by Emily Gunning, Master Blend won nineteen all-breed Bests.

Ashbey

7

The Lhasa Apso
Record Holders

RECORDS ARE MADE and records are broken. This chapter is a review of the record producers and the record show winners.

THE LHASA APSO RECORD PRODUCERS

The STAR (★) PRODUCER rating system was developed by the authors in an effort to evaluate to some extent the producing ability of sires and dams. The Register of Merit (ROM) system sponsored by the American Lhasa Apso Club is limited because it only includes members' dogs and was not established until 1973 with no retroactive inclusion. The Star Producer system is all-inclusive from the first champion to current time.

Stars (★) are added in the proper number at the end of the Lhasa Apso's name and titles based upon the following table.

The Star Producer rating system for sires and dams is:

Sires

One-Star Producer	★	6–16 champion offspring
Two-Star Producer	★★	17–27 champion offspring

Three-Star Producer ★★★	28–38 champion offspring
Four-Star Producer ★★★★	39–49 champion offspring
Five-Star Producer ★★★★★	50–60 champion offspring

Dams

One-Star Producer ★	4–6 champion offspring
Two-Star Producer ★★	7–9 champion offspring
Three-Star Producer ★★★	10–12 champion offspring
Four-Star Producer ★★★★	13–15 champion offspring
Five-Star Producer ★★★★★	16–18 champion offspring

Top Ten Star Producing Sires

No. of
Chs. *Name of Sire*

48	Ch. Tibet of Cornwallis ROM★★★★
44	Ch. Everglo's Spark of Gold ROM★★★★
40	Ch. Orlane's Inimitable ROM★★★★
36	Ch. Tabu's King of Hearts ROM★★★
29	Ch. Orlane's Intrepid ROM★★★
29	Ch. Ruffway Mashala Chu ROM★★★
28	Ch. Cherryshores Bah Bieh Boi ROM★★★
27	Ch. Windsong's Gusto of Innsbrook ROM★★
24	Ch. Chen Korum Ti ROM★★
24	Ch. Orlane's Dulmo ROM★★

Top Ten Star Producing Dams

18	Kinderland's Ta Sen Isis ROM★★★★★
17	Ch. Chiz Ari Sehilot ROM★★★★★
13	Cordova Sin Sa ROM★★★★
12	Ch. Gindy of Norbulingka ROM★★★
12	Ch. Ruffway Tashi★★★
11	Chok's Joppa Bu Mo ROM★★★
10	Ch. Anbara Rimar's Footloose Fox ROM★★★
10	Ch. San Jo's Hussel Mei ROM★★★
9	Ch. Char Ru's Double or Nothing ROM★★
9	Ch. Kinderland's Sang Po ROM★★
9	Ch. Kyi Chu Kira, CD, ROM★★
9	Ch. San Jo's Hussel Bussel ROM★★
9	Ch. Shyr Lyz Misa Cun-Tia Kai-Lei ROM★★

GROUP WINNER CH. ARBORHILL'S BHRAN DIEH ROM★★ 20 (aka Bhran Dieh), sire: Sparky, dam: Lee Sah.

BIS AM. & CAN. CH. ARBORHILL'S RAH KIEH ROM★ 15 (aka Rah Kieh), sire: Rapso Dieh, dam: Ch. Arborhill's Lhana ROM★ (Kham x Ch. Arborhill's Karoling Karolyn ROM★).

BIS AM. & CAN. CH. ARBORHILL'S RAPSO DIEH ROM★★ 19 (aka Rapso Dieh), sire: Sparky, dam: Lee Sah.

BIS CH. BARCON'S THE AVENGER ROM★★ 20 (aka The Avenger) sire: Sparky, dam: BarCon's Madam Eglantine (Ch. Keke's Petruchio x Can. Ch. Keke's Little Ginger).

BIS AM., CAN. & BDA. CH. BIHAR'S REVENGER OF SAMMI RAJA★ 14 (aka Revenger), sire: The Avenger, dam: Am. & Can. Ch. Khabachen Kasha's Thetis★ (BIS Ch. Chen Korum Ti ROM★★ x Ch. Kasha's Tsonya Of Tal Hi ROM★).

BIS CH. CHEN KORUM TI ROM★★ 24 (aka Korum Ti), sire: Nyun Ti, dam: Ch. Chen Karakorum (Ch. Panda Bear of Kyi Chu x Kara Nor).

GROUP WINNER AM. & CAN. CH. CHEN KRISNA NOR ROM★★ 22 (aka Krisna Nor), sire: Nyun Ti, dam: Chen Pho-Nimo (Seng Tru x Chen Himalayan Hanah Nor ROM★).

CH. CHEN NYUN TI ROM★★ 21 (aka Nyun Ti), sire: Ch. Chen Makalu Nor Dzungar (Ch. Licos Omorfo La ROM★ x Kara Nor), dam: Licos Gia La (Ch. Licos Chulung La ROM★ x Chen Himalayan Hanah Nor ROM★).

MULTIPLE GROUP WINNER CH. CHERRYSHORES BAH BIEH BOI ROM★★★ 28 (aka Bah Bieh Boi), sire: Ch. Kyi Chu Kaliph Nor★ (Americal's Sandar of Pamu★ x Ch. Karma Ami Chiri), dam: Ch. Cherryshores Mah Dahm★ (Ch. Chu-La's Mieh T'u x Green Diamond Decidedly).

CH. COLARLIE'S SHAN BANGALOR ROM★★ 17 (aka Shan Bangalor), sire: Rincan Of Kelea (Ch. Las-Sa-Gre's Manchado Dorado x Karma Rinpoche), dam: Ai Wu Ting (Hsiao-Ti Sambo of Teri Tot x Ch. Fu La Simpatica).

CH. DONICIA'S CHIM ZU EL TORO ROM★ 11 (aka Chim), sire: Ch. Bel Air's El Toro Romeo★ (Ch. Zijuh El Toro x Beck's Parti Doll), dam: Golden Rule's Mel-O-Ne O' Everglo (Chulung La x Everglo Buttercup ROM★).

CH. DORJON'S CHAMPAGNE EDITION ROM★★ 19 (aka Champagne Edition), sire: Shel Ari, dam: Ch. Mor Knoll Rgyal Tiffany ROM★ (Ch. Potala Keke's Golden Gatsby ROM★ x Ch. Mor Knoll Darlin of Rgyal ROM★).

CH. EVERGLO'S CHARLIE BROWN ROM★ 12 (aka Charlie Brown), sire: Frosty Knight, dam: Kambu of Everglo ROM (Cubbi Kyeri Of Everglo x Ch. Kyima Of Everglo ROM★).

EVERGLO'S REMPA ROM★ 11 (aka Rempa), sire: Karma Sha-do of Everglo ROM (Ch. Karma Lobsang x Karma Zim Po), dam: Everglo Buttercup ROM★ (Ch. Licos Omorfo La ROM★ x Ch. Kyima of Everglo ROM★).

BIS CH. EVERGLO'S SPARK OF GOLD ROM★★★ 44 (aka Sparky), sire: Ch. Kai Sang's Clown of Everglo (Glen Pines Chagpo-Ri x Kai Sang's Tzi-Ren of Miradel), dam: Tibetan Cookie of Everglo (Ch. Kai Sang's Clown of Everglo x Ruffway Hun-Nee-Bun).

GROUP WINNER CH. EVERGLO ZIJUH TOMBA ROM★★ 22 (aka Tomba), sire: Frosty Knight, dam: Kambu Of Everglo ROM (Cubbi Kyeri Of Everglo x Ch. Kyima Of Everglo ROM★).

CH. HALE ALII DRAGONSLAYER ROM★ 10 (aka Dragonslayer), sire: Gusto of Innsbrook, dam: Ch. Hali Alii Kupono (T'Ang Chu x Ch. Kuchi's Tara of Wynsippi★★).

CH. HAMILTON JIMPA★ 12 (aka Jimpa), sire: Ch. Hamilton Kalon (Tatsienlu x Hamilton Tughar), dam: Ch. Hamilton Samada★ (Tatsienlu x Hamilton Lachen).

CH. HAMILTON TATSIENLU★ 10 (aka Tatsienlu), sire: Hamilton Yangchen (Hamilton Kusog x Hamilton Kyi Chu), dam: Hamilton Novo (Hamilton Dakmar x Hamilton Maru).

CH. INNSBROOK'S PATRICIAN O'SULAN ROM★★ 21 (aka Patrician), sire: Inimitable, dam: Ch. Innsbrook's Scarlett Lady (Gusto of Innsbrook x Ch. Innsbrook's Shades Of Crissy).

CH. JAMPO'S I'M STEPPEN OUT OF SYUNG ROM★ 11 (aka Steppen Out), sire: Jampo's Krisna Kin Cor Of Dolsa ROM (Krisna Nor x Sin-Sa), dam: Shalu's Po-Go Toshi ROM (Krisna Nor x Ch. Shalu's She La).

CH. KARMA DMAR PO★ 15 (aka Dmar Po), sire: Americal's Sandar Of Pamu★ (Ch. Hamilton Chang Tang x Lady Pamu), dam: Am. & Mex. Ch. Karma Sangpo (Ch. Hamilton Kung★ x Ch. Hamilton Karma★).

BIS CH. KARMA FROSTY KNIGHT O EVERGLO ROM★ 16 (aka Frosty Knight), sire: Ch. Karma Kushog★ (Hamilton Shi-Pon x Ch. Hamilton Karma★), dam: Ch. Hamilton Sha Tru (Ch. Hamilton San-dupa★ x Hamilton Ghar Pon).

CH. KARMA RUS-TI★ 12 (aka Rus-Ti), sire: Dmar Po, dam: Hamilton Gyo-Tru (Ch. Hamilton Sandupa x Hamilton Mala).

CH. KASHGAR OF GAR TEN★ 16 (aka Kashgar), sire: Hamilton Shi Pon (Ch. Hamilton Sandupa★ x Ch. Hamilton Den Sa), dam: Tengin of Gar Ten (Ch. Karma Getson x Lou-Lan Gar Ten).

BIS CH. KHAM OF NORBULINGKA ROM★★ 20 (aka Kham), sire: Licos Khung La (Ch. Hamilton Achok★ x Ch. Licos Nyapso La ROM★★), dam: Karma Kosala (Ch. Hamilton Sandupa★ x Am. & Mex. Ch. Karma Sangpo).

BIS AM., CAN., BDA. & MEX. CH. KYI CHU FRIAR TUCK ROM★ 14 (aka Friar Tuck), sire: Ch. Quetzal Feyla Of Kyi Chu★ (Jimpa x Miss Shandha), dam: Miss Shandha.

BIS Ch. Karma Frosty Knight O Everglo ROM was bred by Dorothy Cohen and used in the kennels of Everglo and Ruffway before he was finally purchased by Tsung Kennel. It was Tsung that campaigned Frosty to his history-making record.

BIS Am., Bda., Can., Mex. Ch. Kyi Chu Friar Tuck ROM won thirteen Bests in Show and two ALAC Specialties. Tuck was a past record holder for the breed and the top-winning parti color of all time. He was shown by Robert Sharp for owner Marvin Frank.

GROUP WINNER AM. & CAN. CH. KYMA OF ABBOTSFORD
ROM★★ 18 (aka Kyma), sire: Sinbad, dam: Ch. Chuli Of Abbotsford
(Am. & Can. Ch. Teako of Abbotsford x Yu La Of Abbotsford).

CH. LARRMAR DE TSEN ROM★ 10 (aka De Tsen), sire: BIS Ch. Licos
Kulu La (Ch. Americal's Leng Kong ROM★ x Ch. Americal's Rika
ROM★), dam: Ch. Shangri La Tibetan Butterfly (Ch. Tenzing of Lost
Horizon x Lynchaven Tangla★).

CH. LICOS CHULUNG LA ROM★ 11 (aka Chulung La), sire: Ch. Hamil-
ton Achok★ (Tatsienlu x Hamilton Dobra★), dam: Ch. Licos Nyapso
La ROM★★ (Ch. Americal's Leng Kong ROM★ x Ch. Americal's Rika
ROM★).

CH. LIGHT UP'S RED ALERT ROM★ 13 (aka Reddy), sire: Intrepid,
dam: Light Up's Soda's My Pop (Rapso Dieh x Tashi Truly Scrump-
tious).

BIS CH. LITTLE FIR'S SHEL ARI OF CHIZ ROM★★ 17 (aka Shel Ari),
sire: Marpa, dam: Ch. Orlane Meling Of Ruffway (Sparky x Ruffway
Khambu ROM★).

CH. MING TALI II, CD★ 10 (aka Ming Tali), sire: Ch. Wu Tai (Hamilton
Dakmar x Ch. Ming Lu), dam: Ch. Ming Kyi (Pedro x Ch. Ming Lu).

BIS CH. MISTI'S PLAY IT AGAIN SAM ROM★★ 21 (aka Play It Again
Sam), sire: Misty Acres Sailor (Ch. Kinderland's Ta Sen Dakini ROM★
x Ch. Misti's I've Got Da Spirit), dam: Ch. Misti's Shesa Ladi (Ch.
Sakya Kamaru x Schu Schu).

ON BA LHO BHO O'JOYMARC★ 10 (aka Lho Bho), sire: Tomba, dam:
Zim Zim.

BIS AM. & CAN. CH. ORLANE'S BE SPARKY OF AL MAR ROM★
14 (aka Be Sparky), sire: Ch. Orlane's Dieh Bieh★ (Sparky x Ch. Orlane
Chitra Of Ruffway ROM★★), dam: Orlane's Holly Berry (Sparky x Ch.
Kai Sang's Flame Of Everglo ROM★).

CH. ORLANE'S DULMO ROM★★ 24 (aka Dulmo), sire: Sparky, dam:
Ch. Orlane's Chitra Of Ruffway ROM★★ (Frosty Knight x Ruffway
Khambu ROM★).

CH ORLANE'S IMPUDENT OF WINDWICK ROM★ 14 (aka Impudent),
sire: Inimitable, dam: Orlane's Dah-Li★★ (Ch. Madoro's Dah-Vieh Of
Flo J x Orlane's Marmalade).

CH. ORLANE'S INIMITABLE ROM★★★★ 40 (aka Inimitable), sire:
Gusto of Innsbrook, dam: Yorktown's Sassy Satin (Sparky x Orlane's
Of Golden Chrisma).

AM. & ENG. BIS AM. & ENG. CH. ORLANE'S INTREPID ROM★★★
29 (aka Intrepid), sire: Gusto of Innsbrook, dam: Orlane's Brandywyne★
(The Avenger x Orlane's Mi Ti Jenny).

BIS CH. ORLANE'S SPAN-KIEH, CD, ROM★ 10 (aka Span-Kieh), sire:
Gusto of Innsbrook, dam: Ch. Green Pond Sparkle Plenty (Ch. Golden
Rule's Kyi Chu Sankor x Ch. Tiffany's O-Bin-An of Green Pond, CD).

AM. & CAN. CH. ORLANE'S SCIROCCO ROM★★ 19 (aka Scirocco),

sire: Ch. Kinderland Ta Sen Dakini ROM★ (Intrepid x Kinderland's Ta Sen Kangra), dam: Orlane's Brandy-Mine★ (Gusto of Innsbrook x Ch. Orlane's Brandywyne★).

CH. PAN CHEN TONKA SONAN ROM★ 16 (aka Tonka Sonan), sire: Nyun Ti, dam: Ch. Pandan Choshe Tsen (Seng Tru x Choshe Tsona).

GROUP WINNER CH. POTALA KEKE'S TOMBA TU ROM★ 12 (aka Tomba Tu), sire: Tomba, dam: BIS Ch. Potala Keke's Yum Yum ROM★ (Seng Tru x Ch. Keke's Bambo ROM★★).

CH. RUFFWAY MARPA ROM★ 14 (aka Marpa), sire: Sparky, dam: Ch. Ruffway Kara Shing ROM (Ch. Ruffway Chogal x Ch. Ruffway Lholung).

GROUP WINNER CH. RUFFWAY MASHALA CHU ROM★★★ 29 (aka Mashala Chu), sire: BIS Ruffway Mashaka ROM (Sparky x Ch. Ruffway Kara Shing ROM), dam: Ruffway Doshala (T'Ang Chu x Ruffway Blaise of Darno).

GROUP WINNER CH. RUFFWAY T'ANG CHU ROM★★ 19 (aka T'Ang Chu), sire: Ch. Reiniet's Roial Chanticleer★ (Ch. Americal's Sing Song x Reiniet's Silver Nymph), dam: Ch. Ruffway Kham Chung (Frosty x Kambu Of Everglo ROM).

CH. SAN JO'S OUT O' THE BLUE ROM★★ 19 (aka Out O' The Blue), sire: BIS Ch. Anbara Rimar's Grin 'N Bear It ROM★ (Am., Ger. & Int. Ch. Anbara Justa Teddy Bear x Ch. Rimar's The Frivolous Fox ROM), dam: Hussel Bussel.

CAN. BIS AM. & CAN. CH. SAN JO'S RAAGA LOOKI MEI ROM★ 13 (aka Looki Mei), sire: Ch. San Jo's Tonsen Me Of Sheridan (San Jo's Senge Me x Tonka Me Of Sheridan), dam: Ch. San Jo's Lena ROM (Ch. Kyi Chu Manshifa of San Jo ROM x Am. & Can. Ch. Kyi Chu Kissami ROM★).

CH. SAN JO'S RUSTY NAIL ROM★★ 22 (aka Rusty Nail), sire: BIS Ch. Anbara Rimar's Grin 'N Bear It ROM★ (Am., Ger. & Int. Ch. Anbara Justa Teddy Bear x Ch. Rimar's The Frivolous Fox ROM), dam: Hussel Bussel.

GROUP WINNER CH. SAN JO SHENANIGAN, CD, ROM★★ 23 (aka Shenanigan), sire: Ch. Zoroshah Morific Of San Jo (Ch. Everglo Sir Tom ROM x Everglo Tangerine), dam: San Jo's Pandora (Ch. San Jo's Tonsen Me Of Sheridan x San Jo's Mi Luv).

CH. SAN JO SOSHOME UP ROM★ 16 (aka Soshome Up), sire: Can. BIS Am. & Can. Ch. San Jo's Soshome ROM★ (Ch. Sa Mar Of Abbotsford★ x San Jo's Sassafras), dam: Hussel Bussel.

CH. SAN JO'S WINGTIPS ROM★ 12 (aka Wingtips), sire: Waffle Stomper, dam: San Jo's Shome Nangel (Ch. San Jo's Soshome x Ch. San Jo's Almost Angel).

BIS CH. SHARBO ZIJUH ZER KHAN ROM★ 14 (aka Zer Khan), sire: Tomba, dam: Ch. Zijuh Jinda★ (Ch. Zijuh Tsam★ x Donna Cardella's Tsng★).

SINBAD OF ABBOTSFORD ROM★ 16 (aka Sinbad), sire: Am. & Can. Ch. Teako Of Abbotsford (English Import Brackenbury Kandron x Kalula Of Abbotsford), dam: English Import Brackenbury Dochen (Ramblershot O'Tuan x Brackenbury Min-Nee).

BIS CH. SJW WAFFLE STOMPER ROM★ 16 (aka Waffle Stomper), sire: Looki Mei, dam: Ch. San Jo's Kian Kandi Kan ROM★★ (Ch. Zoroshah Morific of San Jo x Ch. San Jo's Tamara Of Rob-Tell ROM).

MULTIPLE GROUP WINNER CH. TABU'S KING OF HEARTS ROM★★★ 36 (aka King), sire: Seng Tru, dam: BIS Am. & Bda. Ch. Kinderland's Tonka ROM★ (Tibet x Sang Po).

CH. TATLI SU'S FLYING TIGER ROM★ 10 (aka Flying Tiger), sire: Ch. Tatli Su's Star Ship Enterprise (Ch. Syung's Chico The Cocaine Kid★ x Ch. Tatli Su's Star Trek 'n Trib'l), dam: Knolwood's Shanay Adams (Ch. Brush's Tiko Of Samara x Ch. Samara's Knolwood Kharisma).

BIS CH. TIBET OF CORNWALLIS ROM★★★★ 48 (aka Tibet), sire: Karma Tharpa (Karma Yon-Ten x Karma Kam-Bu), dam: Ch. Licos Cheti La (Ch. Licos Chaplia La ROM x Ch. Licos Nyapso La ROM★★).

BIS CH. TIFFANY'S QUA-LA-TI ROM★ 15 (aka Qually), sire: The Avenger, dam: Ch. Tiffany's Wendi-La★ (Royal Crescent Majah Rajah x Beranos Peggy Chu).

MULTIPLE GROUP WINNER CH. TN HI ZEUS THE DETHRONER ROM★ 12 (aka Zeus), sire: Ch. Cameo's Khor-Ke San O' Honeydew (Ch. Donicia's Chim-Zu El Torro x Honeydew Krissie Ku), dam: Tn Hi Me'N My Shadow (Ch. Ocon Karba Sang x Ch. Tn Hi Pah Ti Shyshy).

BIS CH. TOM LEE MANCHU OF KNOLWOOD ROM★★ 20 (aka Tom Lee Manchu), sire: Inimitable, dam: Ch. Ruleo's Peppermint Patti (Ch. Donicia's Chim-Zu El Torro ROM★ x Anstead's Golden Heather).

CH. TRA MAR TANGLELOFT COZMIK RAZ★ 13 (aka Cozmik Raz), sire: Ch. Ja Ma's Bohemian Rapso Dieh ROM (Rapso Dieh x Ch. Donicia's Tai Suki Lu ROM★), dam: Lazsefare Ho-Lee Ter-Rah (Ch. Berano's Smo Kie Tsu★ x Berano's Bar Bieh Lin of Pami).

BIS CH. WINDSONG'S GUSTO OF INNSBROOK ROM★★ 27 (aka Gusto of Innsbrook), sire: Ch. Annie's Golden Fluff ROM★ (Orlane's Inky of Sagemont x Golden Flair ROM), dam: Cajohn's Buffieh of Windsong ROM★ (Ch. Sakya Top Drawer ROM★ x Gillot Gold Shansi).

CH. ZIJUH SENG TRU ROM★★ 21 (aka Seng Tru), sire: Hamilton Toradga (Ch. Hamilton Kalon x Ch. Hamilton Den Sa), dam: Ch. Hamilton Shim Tru★ (Ch. Hamilton Sandupa★ x Hamilton Saung).

Top Star Producing Dams

CH. ANBARA RIMAR'S FOOTLOOSE FOX ROM★★★ 10 (aka Footloose Fox), sire: BIS Ch. Anbara Hobgoblin (King x Ch. Anbara's Abra

Ka Dabra ROM★), dam: Ch. Rimar's The Frivolous Fox ROM (BIS Ch. Rimar's J G King Richard x Ch. Rimar's Penny Candy).

CH. ARBORHILL'S LEE SAH ROM★★ 8 (aka Lee Sah), sire: Bah Bieh Boi, dam: Ch. Arborhill's Karoling Karolyn ROM★ (Ch. Jimpa's Kana Rinpoche x Gser Jo-Mo of La-Sari).

CH. ART EST SHE MA★★ 8 (aka She Ma), sire: BIS Ch. Qua-La-Ti's Makara ROM★ (T'Ang Chu x Ch. Tiffany's Yolanda La-Tsu ROM★), dam: Gene's Flaming Mame (Paso De Rojo El Tojo x Shandy of Brunning).

CH. CHAR RU'S DOUBLE OR NOTHING ROM★★ 9 (aka Double or Nothing), sire: Ch. Char Ru's Happiness Is (Ch. Bara's Bigwig x Hayden's Princess Mang Mami ROM), dam: Ch. Char Ru's Roulette (Ch. Bara's Wags to Witches ROM★ x Char Ru's Its A Bingo).

CH. CHIZ ARI SEHILOT ROM★★★★★ 17 (aka Sehilot), sire: Tonka Sonan, dam: Kinderland's Winne of Chiz (Ch. On Ba Jes Su Khan x Crest O Lake Ming Lee).

CHOK'S JOPPA BU MO ROM★★★ 11 (aka Joppa Bu Mo), sire: Ch. Kinderland Tim Pa (Marpa x Ch. Kinderland's Sang Po ROM), dam: Ch. Ming Toy's Ku Su Bar Ba (Ch. Chen Kimmi's Srin-Po x Ch. Kinderland's Tara Lu).

CH. COLARLIE'S MISS SHANDA ROM★★ 8 (aka Miss Shanda), sire: Shan Bangalor, dam: Miradel's Ming Fu Chia, CD (Ming Tali II x Ch. Fu La Simpatica.)

CORDOVA SIN SA ROM★★★★ 13 (aka Sin Sa), sire: Karma Kacho (Dmar Po x Hamilton Druk Tru), dam: Karma Sakyi★ (Ch. Karma Kushog★ x Ch. Karma Sanga II).

CH. GINDY OF NORBULINGKA ROM★★★ 12 (aka Gindy), sire: Kham x Ch. Karma Muffin of Norbulingka (Dmar Po x Hamilton Chang Tru★★).

HAMILTON CHANG TRU★★ 8 (aka Chang Tru), sire: Tatsienlu, dam: Hamilton Nirvana (Ch. Hamilton Sandupa★ x Hamilton Amdo).

CH. KARMA RUS TIMALA ROM★★ 8 (aka Rus Timala), sire: Rus-Ti, dam: Karma Mingma (Ch. Karma Kushog★ x Lady Pamu).

CH. KINDERLAND'S SANG PO ROM★★ 9 (aka Sang Po), sire: Kham, dam: Ch'ha-Ya-Chi (Dzin Pa Rinpoche x Ron Si Rinpoche).

KINDERLAND'S TA SEN ISIS ROM★★★★★ 18 (aka Isis), sire: Ch. Kinderland's Ta Sen Dakini ROM★ (Intrepid x Kinderland's Ta Sen Kangra), dam: Ch. Kinderland's Choks Seneca (Seng Tru x Ch. Kinderland's Mi Terra ROM★).

CH. KYI CHU KARA NOR ROM★★ 8 (aka Kara Nor), sire: America's Sandar of Pamu★ (Ch. Hamilton Chang-Tang x Lady Pamu), dam: Ch. Karma Ami Chiri (Hamilton Shi-Pon x Ch. Hamilton Karma★).

CH. KYI CHU KIRA, CD, ROM★★ 9 (aka Kira), sire: Ch. Hamilton Jimpa★ (Ch. Hamilton Kalon x Ch. Hamilton Samada), dam: Ch. Colarlie's Miss Shandha (Shan Bangalor x Miradel's Ming Fu Chia, CD).

BELGIUM BIS AM. & BELG. CH. KYILEE CUNBA KAM ROM★★ 8 (aka Cumba Kam), sire: BIS Ch. Tulku's Yeti of Milarepa (Tibet x Carter's Tara Of Everglo ROM★★), dam: Kyilee Tiglecan Of Maru (Ch. Dixie's Beau Of Everglo ROM★ x Ch. Everglo Ma-La Bu★).

MIRADEL'S MING FU CHIA, CD★★ 8 (aka Chia), sire: Ming Tali II x Ch. Fu La Simpatica (Chiang Foo x Ch. Fardale Fu Ssi★).

CH. RUFFWAY TASHI★★★ 12 (aka Tashi), sire: Ruffway Kadar (T'Ang Chu x Ruffway Khanda), dam: Ch. Ruffway Byang-Kha (Sparky x Ruffway Drimo).

BIS CH. SAN JO HUSSEL BUSSEL ROM★★ 9 (aka Hussel Bussel), sire: Ch. San Jo's Sorta Sooty (Ch. On Ba Jo Bo ROM★ x Ch. Dexella's Tara Dee), dam: Ch. King's Brandi Kyi of San Jo (Ch. Kyi Chu Manshifa Of San Jo x San Jo's Bandi of Gartok).

CH. SAN JO'S HUSSEL MEI ROM★★★ 10 (aka Hussel Mei), sire: Waffle Stomper, dam: Hussel Bussel.

CH. SHYR LYZ MISA CUN-TIA KAI-LEI ROM★★ 9 (aka Misa Cun-Tia), sire: Ch. Kai-Cee A Lighter Shade of Pale (Bah Bieh Boi x Cherryshores Dahr Kyz), dam: Kol-Ba Sem-Cun Tia (Ch. Licos Singi La x Drax Ka-Ba Kol-Ba).

SYUNG'S RENDITION IN BLACK ROM★★ 8 (aka Rendition), sire: Ch. Jampo's I'm Steppen Out Of Syung ROM★ (Jampo's Krisna Kin-Cor Of Dolsa x Shalu's Po-Go Toshi), dam: Ch. Innsbrook Champagne Of Syung ROM (Gusto of Innsbrook x Ch. Innsbrook's Shades of Crissy).

CH. WYNDWOOD'S HONEYSUCKLE ROSE ROM★★ 8 (aka Honeysuckle Rose), sire: Ch. Ginseng's Nocona (Ch. Ginseng's Winterhawk x Ch. Ginseng's Lotta Class), dam: Ch. Orlane's 'Nana Pudd'n O'Wyndwood (Patrician x Ch. Orlane's Whimsy of Innsbrook★).

CH. ZHANTOR SONGBIRD ROM★★ 8 (aka Songbird), sire: Ch. San Jo's Soshome ROM★ (Ch. Sa Mar of Abbotsford★ x San Jo's Sassafras), dam: Ch. Suntory Sonata ROM (Kyma x Ch. Chen Krisna Tsoma Nor ROM★).

ZIJUH ON BA ZIM ZIM ROM★★ 8 (aka Zim Zim), sire: Chen Changri Nor (Seng Tru x Chen Himalayan Hanah Nor ROM★), dam: Tai Foon (Ch. Chen Makalu Nor Of Dzungar x Zijuh Ngor).

RECORD SHOW WINNERS

In the spring of 1935, the American Kennel Club sanctioned Lhasa Apso participation in all-breed shows. Twenty-two years later, on October 26, 1957, at the Two Cities Kennel Club, Yuba City, California, **Ch. Hamilton Torma** became the first Lhasa Apso to win Best in Show at an all-breed show. Mitch Wooten handled her this day as he had throughout her successful career.

Torma was whelped on February 6, 1952, at Hamilton Farm Kennel. She was bred by Mr. and Mrs. C. S. Cutting and was owned by Mrs. Marie Stillman

BIS Ch. Hamilton Torma made history for the breed by being the first Lhasa Apso to win an all-breed BIS. The show was the Twin Cities KC, Yuba City, California, October 26, 1957. Torma was bred by Mr. and Mrs. C. S. Cutting and proudly owned by Marie Stillman. Torma was handled by Mitch Wooten to the history-making win under judge Maurice Baker.

BIS Ch. Kham of Norbulingka ROM, owned and bred by Phyllis Marcy, the winner of five all-breed Bests in Show and the Best of Breed winner at the first ALAC Specialty. He is shown here winning a BIS under Heywood Hartley, handled by Jane Kay.

of Americal Kennel. Her sire was Ch. Hamilton Tatsienlu★ and her dam was Hamilton Lachen. Torma was the dam of three champions.

Torma's record stood until 1961 when her grandson **BIS Ch. Licos Kulu La**, sired by Ch. Americal's Leng Kong ROM★ out of Torma's daughter, Ch. Americal's Rika ROM★, under the capable handling of Maxine Beam, won four Bests in Show.

Born May 26, 1956, Kulu La died May 21, 1963. He was the sire of three champions.

BIS Ch. Kham of Norbulingka ROM★★ set a new record with five Bests in Show in 1966, only five years after Kulu La had set his record. Kham, bred by Mrs. Phyllis Marcy of Norbulingka kennel and sired by Licos Khung La out of Karma Kosala, was whelped in June 1961 and died in August 1974. Kham was the sire of twenty champions.

BIS Ch. Karma Frosty Knight O Everglo ROM★ followed Kham as the winner of most Bests in Show. He was bred by Mrs. Dorothy Cohen of Karma Lhasa Apsos. His sire was Ch. Karma Kushog★ and his dam was Ch. Hamilton Sha Tru. Mrs. Cohen sold him to Mrs. Gloria Fowler of Everglo Kennel. Mrs. Georgia Palmer of Ruffway Lhasa Apsos guided Frosty Knight to his championship for Mrs. Fowler. He was later purchased by the Misses Aspuru and Rossie of Tsung Kennel, who campaigned him to his first six Bests in Show setting a new record. Frosty Knight was retired with eleven BIS awards in 1970. He is the sire of sixteen champions.

BIS Am., Bda., Can. & Mex. Ch. Kyi Chu Friar Tuck ROM★ was the next to set the record for the most Best in Show wins. He was bred by Jay Amann and Mrs. Ruth Smith. Friar Tuck, born January 30, 1965, was a son of Ch. Quetzal Feyla of Kyi Chu★ and Ch. Colarlie's Miss Shanda ROM★★.

Robert Sharp, who handled Friar Tuck so effectively during his career, bought him in 1967 and in 1970 handled him to his thirteenth and final top award to set the new record for Best in Show wins. Friar Tuck is the sire of fourteen champions.

BIS Ch. BarCon's The Avenger ROM★★ became the next Best in Show record holder in 1974 by amassing fourteen victories. Mr. and Mrs. Barry Tompkins bred and owned him, and Mrs. Dorothy Kendall, owner of his sire, BIS Ch. Everglo's Spark of Gold ROM★★★, co-owned and handled him. His dam is BarCon's Madam Eglantine. He is the sire of twenty champions.

BIS Ch. Yojimbo Orion, owned and bred by Elaine Spaeth, was campaigned during 1977 and 1978 by John Thyssen to win fourteen Best in Show awards, which tied the record. His sire is Ch. Dolsa Yojimbo ROM★, and his dam is Blackbay Sass A Fhrass. He is the sire of five champions.

BIS Ch. Sulan's Master Blend, bred by Suzette Michele and Marlene Rykiel and owned by Suzette Michele and Manya Greif, was handled by Emily Gunning. He was campaigned in 1987 and 1988, and retired after setting a new record of nineteen Best in Show wins. Additionally, his 106 Group firsts in just two years make him the top Group winner in the history of the breed.

144

BIS Ch. BarCon's The Avenger, winner of the 1973 and 1974 Eastern ALAC Specialties was the son of BIS Ch. Everglo's Spark of Gold ROM and BarCon's Madam Eglantyne and was owned and bred by Barry and Connie Tompkins. He is shown winning one of his fourteen Bests in Show this one under Dr. Malcolm Phelps, handled by his co-owner Dorothy Kendall.

BIS Ch. Yojimbo Orion shown winning Best in Show at the San Gabriel Valley KC under Derek Rayne and handled by John Thyssen for breeder-owner Elaine Spaeth. "Ryan" was the son of Ch. . Dolsa Yojimbo and Blackbay Sass A Fhrass. He won Best of Breed at the 1977 Western ALAC Specialty, and was the first Lhasa Apso to win the Group at Westminster.

145

BIS Am. Can. Ch. Potala Keke's Yum Yum ROM was the winner of both the 1976 Eastern and Western ALAC Specialties. She is shown here with judge Robert Berndt, her handler Carolyn Herbel and her breeder-owner Keke (Blumberg) Kahn.

BIS Am., Can. Ch. Kyi Shara ROM shown winning a Group under Heywood Hartley, handled by Jane Kay. Shara was bred by Terry Smith and owned by Keke Blumberg. She was Best of Breed at the 1967 ALAC Specialty, was a daughter of Ch. Karma Kanjur and Ch. Kyi Chu Kira, CD and was the dam of six champions.

Sired by Ch. Wellington Comeuppance out of Ch. Sulan's Tapestry Weaver, Master Blend is himself the sire of five champions to date.

BIS Am. & Can. Ch. Rufkins Chip Off The Ol Rock won his record-breaking 20th Best in Show award late in 1990, handled by Clay Coady. Owned and bred by Roberta Lombardi, he was co-bred by Georgia Palmer and is co-owned by Canadian Arlene Oley.

His sire is Ch. Orlane's Scirocco ROM★★ out of Ch. Ruffway Patra Tashi Tu ROM★★.

THE BEST IN SHOW BITCHES

The story of the record holders for Bests in Show by bitches has been different from that of the males.

BIS Ch. Hamilton Torma won the first Best in show in 1957, and even when her grandson BIS Ch. Licos Kulu La broke her record for any Lhasa Apso in 1961, her record for most Bests in Show for bitches remained. It was not even matched until 1966. Then in three successive years it was matched but not surpassed by three bitches.

BIS Am. & Can. Ch. Kyi Chu Shara ROM★, owned by Mrs. Keke Blumberg, won Best in Show in December 1966. Shara was whelped July 4, 1964, and her sire was Ch. Karma Kanjur of Hamilton background, and her dam was Ch. Kyi Chu Kira, CD, ROM★★. Shara is the dam of six champions.

BIS Am., Can. & Mex. Ch. San Saba Chi Chi Jimi won Best in Show on September 3, 1967, Jimi, owned and handled by Mrs. Edna Voyles, was bred by Mrs. Bettye K. Scott. Her sire was Ch. Lui Gi Shigatzoo★, and her dam was Hamilton Chodon★.

BIS Am. & Can. Ch. Orlane's Good As Gold was the fourth to become a joint holder of the then record for bitches of one Best in Show. Whelped May 8, 1965, she was bred, owned and handled by Mrs. Dorothy Kendall. Goody's sire was Ch. Quetzal Feyla of Kyi Chu★, and her dam was Ch. Kai Sang's Flame of Everglo ROM★.

Torma's record, matched by Shara, Jimi and Goody, remained until June 1972 when **BIS Ch. Kili's Katara of Ke Tu** won Best in Show awards on successive weekends.

In the fall of 1972, **BIS Am. & Bda. Ch. Kinderland's Tonka ROM★** won three Bests in Show to become the new record holder for bitches.

Katara won a third Best in Show in the spring of 1973 to tie Tonka. Later in the fall of 1973, Tonka won a fourth Best to become the undisputed record holder for bitches.

Katara was bred and owned by Lisbeth C. and E. Kiefer Labenberg and handled to her record by the late Marvin Cates. Her sire was Ch. Choshe Ke Tu of Pandan, and her dam was Kili's Fol Dol★. Katara was the dam of three champions.

Tonka was bred by Ellen Lonigro, owned by the authors and handled to her record by Robert Sharp. She was sired by BIS Ch. Tibet of Cornwallis ROM★★★★ out of Ch. Kinderland's Sang Po ROM★★. Tonka was the dam of four champions.

Tonka's record stood until **BIS Ch. San Jo's Hussel Bussel ROM★★** won her fifth Best in Show award in May 1984. Hussel Bussel was bred, owned and handled by Marianne Nixon and Leslie Ann Engen. Her sire was Ch. San Jo's Sorta Sooty, and her dam was Ch. King's Brandi Kyi of San Jo. She was the dam of nine champions.

BIS Ch. Kili's Katara of Ke-Tu was Best in Show at the Oakland Kennel Club show. She was handled by Marvin Cates for her breeders-owners Lisbeth C. and E. Kiefer Labenberg.

BIS Am., Can., Mex. Ch. San Saba Chi Chi Jimi was a daughter of Ch. Lui Gi's Shigatzoo and Hamilton Chodon. Jimi was bred by Bettye Kirksey Scott and was handled and owned by Mrs. Edna Voyles.

8

Official Standard of the Lhasa Apso

A BREED STANDARD is a definition of the ideal specimen of the breed described. It is a word pattern by which dogs of that breed are judged at shows. The American Kennel Club view is that a Standard of a given breed is not aimed at a person who has never seen a specimen of that breed. It is meant as a guide to help the person who has some familiarity with dogs in general and with the breed in particular.

Conversely, it is not an anatomical study that would enable one who has never seen a specimen of the breed to know exactly what that breed looks like.

When you read a Standard, remember that it is only an elementary description of a breed. It points out the qualities that make the breed unique. It also indicates areas where judges should be alert for problems. Some detail may be necessary, but too much detail can be confusing and difficult to remember. Overemphasis may even cause unexpected problems.

BACKGROUND OF THE STANDARD

The American breed Standard for Lhasa Apsos, approved April 9, 1935, by the American Kennel Club and revised July 11, 1978, by the American Lhasa Apso Club and approved by the American Kennel Club, defines the ideal specimen of the breed. The Lhasa Apso Standard on which many countries based

149

their standards was the English version approved by the Kennel Club in 1934 when the Tibetan Breeds Association defined the various Tibetan breeds.

We are dwelling on where the wording for the 1934 English Standard originated because of its influence on most standards throughout the world, and more specifically because the American Standard was adopted almost word for word.

In the English *Kennel Gazette*, December 1901, on pages 373 and 374, there is an article by Lionel Jacobs entitled "Bhuteer Terrier," in which he discusses the various names connected with the small Tibetan dog that was known at that time in England as the Bhuteer Terrier. He states that it is his "opinion that the term Llassa Terrier, is preferable to any other."

Having viewed many of the "small dogs of Llassa" or "the terriers of Thibet," he believed that they should be recognized by The Kennel Club (England) and proposed the following description (Standard), which contains some familiar words and phrases.

> "*Head*—Distinctly Terrier-like. *Skull narrow, falling away behind the eyes in a marked degree, not quite flat, but not domed or apple-shaped. Fore face of fair length*, strong in front of the eyes, the nose, large, prominent and pointed, not depressed; *a square muzzle is objectionable*. The stop, size for size, about that of a Skye Terrier. *Mouth* quite *level*, but of the two a slightly overshot mouth is preferable to an undershot one. The teeth are somewhat smaller than would be expected in a Terrier of the same size. In this respect, the breed seems to suffer to an extraordinary degree from cankered teeth. I have never yet seen an imported specimen with a sound mouth.
>
> *Ears*—Set on low, and carried close to the cheeks, similar to the ears of a drop-eared Skye.
>
> *Eyes*—*Neither very large and full nor very small and sunk, dark brown* in colour.
>
> *Legs* and *Feet*—The *fore legs* should be *straight*. In all short-legged breeds there is a tendency to crookedness, but the straighter the legs the better. There should be good bone. Owing to the heavy coat the legs look, and should look, very heavy in bone, but in reality, the bone is not heavy. It should be round and of good strength right down to the toes, the less ankle the better. The hocks should be particularly well let down. *Feet should be round and cat-like, with good pads*.
>
> *Body*—There is a tendency in England to look for a level top and a short back. All the best specimens have a slight arch at the loin and the back should not be too short; it should be considerably *longer than* the *height at the withers*, note the measurements given of the bitch Marni. The dog should be *well ribbed-up*, with a *strong loin* and *well developed quarters and thighs*.
>
> Stern—*Should be carried well over the back* after the manner of the tail of the Chow. All Thibetan dogs carry their tail in this way, and a *low carriage of stern* is a sign of impure blood.
>
> *Coat*—Should be *heavy, of good length and very dense*. There should be a strong growth on the skull, falling on both sides. The legs should be well clothed right down to the toes. On the body, the hair should not reach to the ground, as in a show Yorkshire; there should be a certain amount of daylight. In general appearance the hair should convey the idea of being much harder to the eyes than it is to the touch. It should look *hard, straight* and strong, when to the touch it is soft, but

not silky. The hair should be *straight* with no tendency to curl. Colour—Black, dark grizzle, slate, sandy, or an admixture of these colours with white.
Size—About 10 inches or 11 inches height *at shoulder for dogs*, and 9 inches or 10 inches for bitches.

The emphasis is the authors'.

Marni was a bitch owned by Colonel Walsh and considered by many authorities, at the time she lived, as the best representative of her breed. Mr. Jacobs saw her and made note of her measurements as follows:

Length of head—6 ¼ inches
Length of back—19 inches
Length of ear—2¼ inches
Height at shoulders—10 inches

Mr. Jacobs' description of the breed can also be found in W. D. Drury's *British Dogs*, Volume 1, Third Edition, published circa 1903; Ellie Bauman's *Onba Opus*, published circa July 1978; Sally Helf's *Lhasa Lore*, published by Alpine Publications, 1983; Ann Lindsay Wynyard's article "Some Lhasa Echoes of the Past, Part II," published by the magazine, *Lhasas Unlimited,* Sept./Oct. 1985.

In the English *Kennel Gazette*, March 1934, is an article by G. Hayes entitled "A Review of the Apsos, Tibetan Terriers and Spaniels at Cruft's Show." This article is the judge's critique of these breeds, which were exhibited at the 1934 Cruft's show. The following are Mr. Hayes' comments on Apsos and appear to be another source for the Standard wording.

"APSOS.——I decided to go for type. In body, rather like a Border Terrier, slightly longer if anything. In head, shape very like one, *skull* slightly *narrower* and side ear-carriage though. The distinctive coat and undercoat. The *head furnishing* in the shape of dark ear tips, the *beard* of the predominant colour (Preferably heavily mixed with black like the ear tips). The long *whiskers* on either side of the muzzle, and the *heavy head* hair hanging over the face. The *tail* is a very distinctive feature being carried *screw*ed tight *over the back*. Those country bred have a peculiar *kink* at the tip, which is very noticeable. I ignored this latter, as I do not yet know the origin or perhaps cause.

The eye should not be too prominent, and the typical expression of the face really requires to be seen, as it is difficult to describe.

I did not stress the golden colour as this is not fixed for the breed, also I know that parti-coloured sometimes throw golden puppies and vice versa.

I use the word Lhasa dog as indicative of distinctiveness of type. There are small dogs all over Tibet, of course. I did not find a dog with the complete combination of the characteristics I was looking for. Type I found, and then lack of coat and of *furnishings*. Nice coats in two or three cases, and then slight lack of type in eye, face and tails. The *character* of the dog is rather *gay and assertive*, though *chary of strangers*. Some dogs would not stand up properly for their owners. It is hard to judge a dog or bitch which is doubled up like a boiled shrimp. This is not characteristic of the breed. Leg hair was not thick enough all through. When the standard is fixed and type is known, a dog out of coat and without *head furnishings*, and lacking leg hair, will have little or no chance, of course. Two or three dogs and bitches low down in the placings were in much better coat than some of the higher ones.

One white dog which took my fancy in the ring very much at first glance, I could not place on examination. The round eye, *domed* head and flat face, also the tail, made it of different type altogether, the outlook being nearer to that of the Japanese Spaniel or Pekingese. Though I did not know this at the time I ascertained afterwards this dog had been bred from a dog and bitch imported from China.

I give below my rough notes made just after judging; taken with the above remarks they should speak for themselves without elaboration.

Dogs——Winner, Zizi; just sufficient type, with good condition of coat and *good head furnishings*. Second, Taktru; good type and size, better golden colour than first; not in good coat and a little out of condition. Third, Lhasa; an old dog, parti-coloured, put up on account of Lhasa type over better conditioned and *furnished* dogs (I would like to see in condition). Reserve, Langtru; nice little dog, good coat and correct *head furnishings*; would not hold tail up.

Bitches——Winner, Drenjong Droma; nice type, not in best coat; good golden colour, typical head though this lacked *furnishings*; placed on type. Second, Lamo; like first, younger, should *furnish* up later. Third, Lugu; better *head furnishings* than those above, *coat* in better condition; eye not so good, and shy. Reserve, Sona; another shy one; *good coat*, head nice, typical *furnishings*, a nice little bitch.

In Special Breeders the bitch Lamo was placed over Taiping; this on type. The latter, a taking little dog; too *domed* in *skull*, too round in eye, too flat in *foreface* for Tibetan type.''

The emphasis is the authors'.

It is the opinion of the authors that the drafters of the Standard not only attempted to describe the Lhasa Apso, but there was also emphasis on those traits that differentiate the Lhasa Apso from the Shih Tzu.

THE AMERICAN STANDARD

Character: Gay and assertive, but chary of strangers.

Size: Variable, but about ten inches or eleven inches at shoulder for dogs; bitches slightly smaller.

Colors: All colors equally acceptable with or without dark tips to ears and beard.

Body Shape: The length from the point of shoulders to point of buttocks longer than height at withers, well ribbed up, strong loin, well-developed quarters and thighs.

Coat: Heavy, straight, hard, not woolly or silky, of good length and very dense.

Mouth and Muzzle: The preferred bite is either level or slightly undershot. Muzzle of medium length; a square muzzle is objectionable.

Head: Heavy head furnishings with good fall over eyes, good whiskers and beard; skull narrow, falling away behind the eyes in a marked degree, not quite flat, but not domed or apple-shaped; straight foreface of fair length. Nose black, the length from tip of nose to eye to be roughly about one-third of the total length from nose to back of skull.

Eyes: Dark brown, neither very large and full, nor very small and sunk.

Ears: Pendant, heavily feathered.

Legs: Forelegs straight; both forelegs and hind legs heavily furnished with hair.

Feet: Well-feathered; should be round and catlike with good pads.

Tail and Carriage: Well-feathered; should be carried well over back in a screw; there may be a kink at the end. A low carriage of stern is a serious fault.

THE SIGNIFICANCE OF TYPE

The general definition of the word *type* is "a kind, class or group that is distinguished by some particular characteristic; the general form, structure, style or characteristic common to or distinctive of a particular kind, class or group; a person or thing embodying the characteristic qualities of a kind, class or group; a representative specimen."

The biological definition of the word *type* is "a form of being having the morphological (the form and structure of an organism considered as a whole) and physiological (the functions of the organs and parts of a living being) characteristics by which a number of individuals may be classified together."

Possibly a simpler sounding definition of the word *type* is "a genus or species that most nearly exemplifies the essential characteristics of a higher group; the one or more specimens on which the description and naming of a species is based."

We have labored to define the word because, in the language of the dog world, one of the most misused words is *type*, perhaps because many fanciers and breeders *interpret* the word rather than *define* it. This is a polite way of saying that many who use the word really do not know what it means. More frequently than not the word is improperly used. All too often we hear the expression "that dog is not *my* type" or "is *my* type," as though the speaker were the authority specifying the essential characteristics of the breed. Sometimes correct movement is said to be "good type" or "typey." At other times elegance is equated to soundness or proper type. Those phrases conceal the fact that *at most* the speaker is stating *his preference*, which may or may not coincide with the official description of the essential characteristics of the breed. Obviously a statement of preference is of value only to the extent of the speaker's knowledge, information and experience, and all the other words on that subject hidden in the cliché "expertise."

Before written Standards, owners tested their dogs in a contest to determine their ability to perform the function for which they were bred. The dog which most consistently had the qualities to perform his allotted function had *type*. When more people became interested in the different breeds, it was no longer possible to rely on oral statements. Hence written statements or Standards came into use.

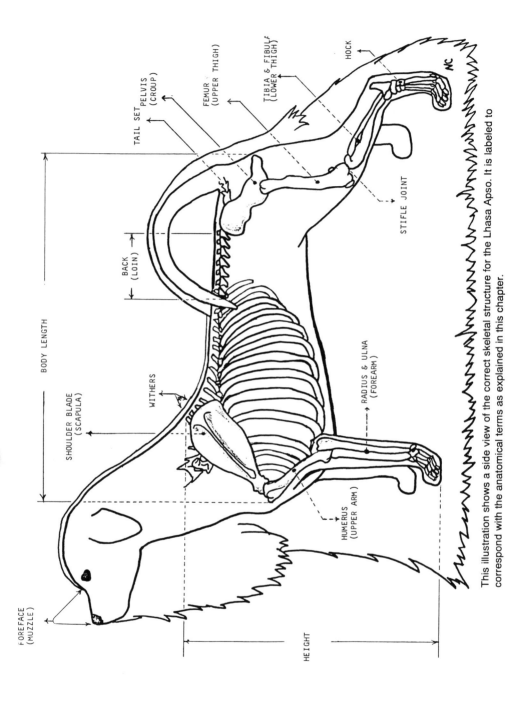

This illustration shows a side view of the correct skeletal structure for the Lhasa Apso. It is labeled to correspond with the anatomical terms as explained in this chapter.

FOREFACE (MUZZLE)

HEIGHT

HUMERUS (UPPER ARM)

RADIUS & ULNA (FOREARM)

SHOULDER BLADE (SCAPULA)

WITHERS

BODY LENGTH

BACK (LOIN)

TAIL SET

PELVIS (CROUP)

FEMUR (UPPER THIGH)

TIBIA & FIBULA (LOWER THIGH)

HOCK

NC

STIFLE JOINT

154

9

Blueprint of the Lhasa Apso Standard

T HE LHASA APSO attracts attention by its appearance, and its character retains it. The breed appeals to both men and women because it was bred to be a companion. Upon first observation, persons unfamiliar with the breed are struck by the unique qualities of a typical Lhasa Apso, but not until they get to know one personally are they able to appreciate the total charm of the breed.

CHARACTER

The first paragraph of the Standard describes the character (temperament) of the Lhasa Apso as *"gay and assertive, but chary of strangers."* These words in the Standard are of utmost significance in understanding the breed.

The three key words are *gay, assertive* and *chary. Gay* is used in the traditional sense of merry or bright. *Assertive* means positive but neither aggressive nor vicious. Just as the Tibetans are physically strong, emotionally courageous and independent, so is the Lhasa Apso. That is what the word *assertive* connotes. Tibetans are also merry and fun-loving with their friends. So is the *gay* Lhasa Apso.

Chary is the word which has caused the most confusion. It means cautious, circumspect, wary, but not shy or timid. Borrowed from the original English Standard, the word *chary* has caused confusion among Americans unaccustomed to the English precise use of language. The word has a multiplicity of connotations, such as (1) careful, (2) wary, (3) shy of, but not shy, (4) fastidious and (5) sparing. Any assumption that it means shy or cowardly is erroneous and overlooks some fine shades of meaning complimentary to the dog.

The word *chary* describes a confident dog that should not be immediately friendly to strangers rather than a timid animal. Lhasa Apsos are unself-conscious with and courteous to strangers but should not immediately make up to them. Because the Lhasa Apso was originally a companion and indoor sentinel dog for monks and wealthy nobles, it is easily understood why the breed is not effusively friendly to strangers. The Lhasa Apso is, however, a basically friendly dog once it has decided that the stranger is not a threat to it or its master. It has a good, even temperament characteristic of many larger dogs.

The Lhasa Apso's *chary* trait is not the cause of reticence or timidity in the show ring. That stems from the owner's failure to school the dog and accustom it to sounds and practices of the show ring and the day-to-day bustle outside the home. Once Lhasa Apsos have become accustomed to life outside their home and are properly trained for the show ring, many will take no notice of a dog show's turmoil until required to perform.

The unknown can upset a Lhasa Apso. If it never rides in automobiles, goes to stores, meets strangers outside of, or in, the home or sees children of all ages, it cannot be expected to be an extrovert. Lhasa Apsos possess the calmness and gracious aplomb that goes with a keen sense of dignity. In the show ring that dignity is manifest, although often leavened with a touch of the "ham."

UNTYPICAL CHARACTER (TEMPERAMENT)

Lhasa Apsos should not be yappy, high strung or vicious. The Lhasa Apso is not cowardly, shy or retiring even when it is most recalcitrant in accepting a new situation. If a particular animal is morose or seemingly a "loner," it is not typical of the breed and possibly the unfortunate result of some bad experience or improper training and handling.

Lhasa Apsos are not generally snappish. If molested, they try to avoid the molester; but, if hurt, they bite as any dog would under similar circumstances. Only if a Lhasa Apso has been improperly treated or poorly trained will it exhibit undesirable behavior traits.

SIZE

Size, defined only as height, in the Standard is *"variable, but about ten inches or eleven inches at shoulder for dogs; bitches slightly smaller."* The word *variable* indicates that a dog should be considered the correct height if it measures *between* ten and eleven inches at the withers.

The word *about* indicates that there is permissible tolerance above and below the ten or eleven inches specified in the Standard. This means that precise size is secondary as long as the dog displays the other important breed attributes. The Lhasa Apso should never, however, vary more than one half inch over or under to be the ideal height stated in the Standard.

"Bitches slightly smaller" means that the females should not only be smaller but also have the femininity that distinguishes them easily from males—thereby displaying secondary sex characteristics. Males should be masculine without being coarse and females should be feminine without being overly refined.

Weight is not mentioned in the Standard but should be commensurate with a well-muscled, strong, sturdy, small dog. A Lhasa Apso in the proper condition should be in good, hard flesh, neither too fat nor too thin, although a tendency toward leanness in the slow-maturing youngster is not uncommon or incorrect. Proper weight should be sixteen to eighteen pounds for dogs and twelve to fourteen pounds for bitches.

During the last decade there has been a trend toward larger Lhasa Apsos. A trend that has continued primarily because many breeders show their dogs at outdoor shows where the grass is often too high. The taller Lhasa Apso usually wins because it makes a better picture in the tall grass both proportionately and moving. Continued breeding to and for these larger Lhasa Apsos has developed a majority of larger competitors.

This makes the ten-inch-tall, sixteen-pound Lhasa Apso appear too small to many judges who may find size difficult to evaluate, because without disqualifications the Lhasa Apso cannot be measured or weighed in the show ring. This lack of disqualification does not mean size is any less important, just harder to evaluate.

COLOR

The Standard states that all colors are equally acceptable with or without dark tips to ears and beard. The original Standard contained a color preference. The removal of this preference means that breed type and sound structure should always take precedence over color.

BODY SHAPE

Body shape is not only a study of the anatomy of a Lhasa Apso but also a study of locomotion. This is because structure reflects movement.

The Standard calls for *"The length from the point of shoulders to point of buttocks longer than height at withers, well ribbed up, strong loin, well-developed quarters and thighs."*

We derived this description of body shape by allowing form to be determined by performance; therefore, we believe the correct movement for a Lhasa Apso should be an effortless, ground-covering trot without laboring, bouncing or rolling.

According to the Standard, the length of the Lhasa Apso measured from the *"point of shoulders to point of buttocks"* is *"longer than height at withers."* The *withers* form the highest point of the shoulders immediately behind the neck. The *point of shoulders* is the articulation of the upper arm (humerus) and the shoulder (scapula). *Buttocks* is defined as the articulation of the pelvis and femur which comprises the hips.

The paragraph on size has established the ideal height at the withers as ten or eleven inches, with further provision for variation with bitches slightly smaller. We prefer the rectangular body shape to be a ratio of 7.5 to 10. This means that our preference for height of ten and a half inches at the withers requires the length to be fourteen inches. Another way to express this ratio is 33⅓ percent longer than tall or 25 percent shorter in height than in length.

This ratio of height to length allows the Lhasa Apso to have the reach and drive necessary for the desired effortless, ground covering gait. A shorter body may cause interference between the front and rear feet as they meet under the body or may cause restricted reach and drive.

A longer body will cause loss of power transference from rear to front and will usually interfere with the smoothness of the gait, thus causing bouncing, rolling or roaching of the backline. The backline (the part of the topline that begins directly behind the withers and ends at the tailset) should always be firm and level in movement.

The Standard requires the Lhasa Apso to be *"well ribbed up."* That phrase comes from the horse world and means that the Lhasa Apso should have long ribs angling backward at approximately 45 degrees as they reach from the spinal column to the brisket. Viewed from the side, a well-ribbed-up Lhasa Apso will have a rather long rib cage compared with the length of the loin. Viewed from the front, the rib cage should be oval-shaped with the width at the top. The Lhasa Apso should not have barrel-shaped ribs.

A *"strong loin"* refers to that region of the body on either side of the vertebral column behind the last ribs and in front of the hindquarters; that is between the thoracic section and the pelvis or croup. The loin has seven vertebrae with their processes slanting forward to support the muscles that transfer the rear thrust forward, which propels the entire body. This transfer of power requires strong muscles for a firm, level backline. Strong muscles prevents an undesirable roach or soft back both standing and moving.

Finally, the Standard calls for *"well developed quarters and thighs."* The word *thigh*, according to the AKC Glossary, means hindquarters from hip to stifle. To understand the thigh, it is necessary to consider the combined assemblies of the back legs and croup.

From the top down the rear assembly is: (1) pelvis or croup (sacrum vertebrae); (2) upper thigh (femur); (3) stifle joint or knee (patella); (4) lower thigh (tibia and fibula); (5) hock assembly and (6) foot. (See illustrations A and

B page 172). The function of the rear assembly is not just weight support when standing, but power generation in movement.

The foundation of the back leg drive is the pelvis or croup. The pelvis consists of three bones fused together on each side of and fastened to the spinal column, where it forms the *croup*. The proper slope of the croup to develop the greatest power is 30 degrees to the horizontal. A lesser slope or flat croup will cause too much kick up behind, which wastes energy. A steeper slope will cause the rear action to be too far under the dog, and the follow-through of the rear legs will be limited.

The femur is attached to the pelvis in a ball-and-socket joint. The femur extends downward and forward to the stifle joint. The stifle joint is the dog's knee. It is the joint between the upper thigh and lower thigh. A well-bent stifle is one in which the inside angle between the upper thigh and lower thigh is about 120 degrees, regardless of the croup angle.

The lower thigh consists of the tibia and fibula, and extends from the stifle to the hock joint.

The hock is the area between the lower thigh and the foot; the dog's true heel. It should be perpendicular to the ground when standing. Hocks that are ''well let down,'' a term synonymous with hocks close to the ground, means there is a relatively short distance between the hock joint and the ground. This contributes to ease of movement and reduces the leverage on the Achilles tendon, thus lessening fatigue.

The foregoing summarizes the meaning of ''*well-developed quarters and thighs*'' and their relationship to the rest of the rear assembly.

The Standard gives guidance to the correct front assembly mostly by silence. This means the front should be the normal or basic canine front, which has a ''well laid back'' shoulder—a term meaning that the shoulder blade inclines backward from the point of shoulder to the top of the blade at an efficient angle, 45 degrees being the most efficient angle. If the angle of the shoulder blade is less than 45 degrees, it will result in less reach by the front legs. If the angle of the rear assembly is equal to this straighter front, the result, all other things equal, may be a smooth gait, but more steps will be taken than the longer stride of the 45 degree layback. It is rare to find a Lhasa Apso with this preferred angulation, which has led to a theory that the 45 degree layback is not correct or desirable. We believe that to stop reaching for this as a goal would be to compromise canine anatomy and would further contribute to the deterioration of correct structure.

The upper arm and the shoulder blade should be equal in length and the elbow should reach to the bottom of the rib cage. An upper arm that is shorter than the shoulder blade may result in a paddling or high-stepping movement in front and is to be avoided.

The Standard states that the forelegs should be straight, which means that the front legs from the elbow to the ankle are straight, although the front feet may turn out slightly. The Lhasa Apso is not achondroplastic and any dwarflike traits should be considered faults.

A standing Lhasa Apso is supported by all four legs with the pads planted at the corners of a quadrangle. The support by all four legs does not appear at any time when the Lhasa Apso is moving. As the speed increases, the legs gradually angle inward until the pads are finally falling on a line directly under the longitudinal center of the body. The hind legs form a V with the hips as the upper points and the pad marks as the apex of the V on the ground. The legs slant from the hips to the ground as the Lhasa Apso moves faster, but the hocks should turn neither in nor out.

The Standard's silence on describing movement means that the Lhasa Apso should have normal or basic canine movement as judged by the trot. The normal or basic canine movement is not restricted by exceptions, which do not exist in the Lhasa Apso Standard.

COAT

The Standard describes the Lhasa Apso's coat as "*heavy, straight, hard, not woolly or silky, of good length and very dense*".

Although Lhasa Apsos can be very beautiful when well groomed, it must be remembered that the Standard's description of the coat requests characteristics that protected this little dog from the extreme temperatures and harsh environment in its country of origin. Beauty, acquired by grooming, should therefore be a plus only if the coat is correct according to the Standard.

The coat, when *heavy, straight* and *hard*, is easy to care for because it is resistant to tangles and does not easily mat. Additionally, it repels rain and snow and does not collect dirt.

Heavy means the coat has weight to it and when lifted away from the body will fall quickly back into place. This weight is what creates the drape of hair on each side of the body as it falls to the floor from a part that extends down the middle of the back from the nose to the tail. The Standard's request for a heavy coat means that a soft, fine, light, flyaway texture is unacceptable.

Hard means the coat should be strong, resilient, durable and will not break off easily when rubbed against grass, carpet, bushes, stones or other abrasive objects that are encountered in normal life. Obviously, silky, fine, thin or fragile hair is not a correct characteristic for the Lhasa Apso.

Straight means the shafts of hair are straight and thus coupled with the request for *heavy* and *hard* helps to keep natural debris from sticking to the coat. Additionally, dirt and tangles tend to slide off the ends of the hair. Obviously a woolly, kinky, curly or wavy coat is uncharacteristic for both performance as well as appearance.

In summation, the correct texture for the Lhasa Apso's coat should be similar to straight human hair. When the Lhasa Apso is correctly coated, there will be some soft undercoat close to the body even when most of the undercoat has been stripped out. This soft undercoat should be easily distinguished from the heavy, hard, outer coat. Usually when a coat is too soft or silky, there will be little or no definition between outer coat and undercoat.

Coat *of good length* means that the coat should be long enough to protect the body and legs, acting like an overcoat. The normal length of coat for a mature Lhasa Apso is floor length, although because the Lhasa Apso is slow to mature it may take two or three years before the coat is long enough to reach the floor. A Lhasa Apso of any age should not be faulted for lack of coat length so long as the texture and density is correct. Additionally, the Lhasa Apso is to be shown naturally without any trimming, shaping or scissoring; however, if the body coat grows long enough to interfere with the dog's movement, the ends should be trimmed to floor length.

The term *very dense* means that there should be a lot of the *heavy, straight, hard* coat making it thick enough to form a protective cover for the small body when temperatures are extreme. The correctly textured coat provides protective insulation for both cold and hot temperatures.

We have put considerable effort into explaining what the correct Lhasa Apso coat is because there is a current trend toward profuse, soft, exaggerated coat that can be made to look very glamorous with innovative new grooming products and methods. It should be noted that although a well-groomed Lhasa Apso can and should be very beautiful, this beauty is not all the Standard requires.

MOUTH AND MUZZLE

The current Standard states under the heading of Mouth and Muzzle as follows: *"The preferred bite is either level or slightly undershot. Muzzle of medium length; a square muzzle is objectionable."*

Controversy about the Lhasa Apso bite has abounded for many years and often is elevated to a position that deletes appreciation for all other traits. For this reason the authors are attempting to provide a background from which to make an educated decision about the correct bite.

Mr. Jacobs's original description of the breed, from which much of the Standard's language was copied, states, "Mouth quite level, but of the two a slightly overshot mouth is preferable to an undershot one."

On April 11, 1970, the first Tibetan Apso show ever organized with Tibetan judges officiating was held at the Tibet House in New Delhi. These five Tibetan judges, along with members of the Apso show committee, presented a paper which contained definitions and comments on the various breeds of Tibetan dogs and the standard by which Tibetans judge these breeds. This paper stated: "Mouth: Short muzzle with roundish mouth—not pointed. Lower jaw should not protrude neither should nose be long."

The breed's first Standard stated under the heading of *Mouth* and Muzzle as follows: *"Mouth* level, otherwise slightly undershot preferable. Muzzle of medium length; a square muzzle is objectionable." (Empasis is authors'.)

Simply stated, *mouth level* means upper and lower jaws are of equal length.

Apparently the drafters of the 1978 revision did not understand that the words *mouth* and *bite* are not always synonymous, as they left the heading the same (*Mouth* and Muzzle) but in the first sentence changed the word *mouth* to *bite*.

We believe it is incorrect to assume that the words *mouth* and *bite* are always synonymous, because there is strong evidence that both *scissors* and *level* are considered the correct bite in a *level mouth*, and if these bites are not present, then a *slightly* undershot bite is preferable to an *extremely* undershot bite or an overshot bite. This means that changing the word *mouth* to *bite* elevated what originally was the third-choice bite to one of the two preferred bites.

Substituting the word *bite* for *mouth* also eliminates any description of the mouth and jaw. We believe that the use of *mouth level* in the original standard described the jaws as well as the bite and depicted the normal canine jaw with six upper incisors and six lower incisors, forming either a scissors or level bite placed in strong well-aligned jaws of equal length.

According to the current Standard, all bites are acceptable with only a preference for level or slightly undershot noted.

In our search for a reason that the undershot bite was elevated to a position of preference, we deduced that one possible reason was the inclusion of the phrase "otherwise slightly undershot preferable" in the first Standard. This phrase was frequently misunderstood or misread and believed to mean that the undershot bite was preferable to the other bites. We believe it was included because there was a shortage of foundation stock at the time the Standard was drafted and the early fanciers of the breed felt all traits were equally important in the perpetuation of the breed, and although mouth, teeth, and bite were noted, there was no desire to eliminate an otherwise good specimen because of an undershot bite.

Another reason for undershot preference appears to be the desire for an Oriental expression, which of course is incorrect because all research on the earliest imports from Tibet leads us to believe that the Oriental (tendency to brachycephalic skull) was linked to the Shih Tzu, not the Lhasa Apso. Early writings depict the correct expression for the Lhasa Apso to be more Terrier-like, which would not need an undershot bite for correct expression.

It appears that modern breeders without historical knowledge have tended to perpetuate the bite to their liking, not the way it was originally intended to be, i.e., level mouth, not undershot bite.

According to the AKC Glossary, the definition of *muzzle* is: "The head in front of the eyes—nasal bone, nostrils, and jaws. Foreface." "*Muzzle of medium length*" as called for in the Standard indicates that the muzzle should not be short nor should it be long.

According to the dictionary, *square* means: "A four-sided plane figure having all its sides equal and all its angles right angles."

We conclude from this definition that no matter which view one takes (top, frontal or side), the muzzle should not be square. This means the underlying bone structure and should not be confused with the illusion given by good whiskers and beard. In other words, the muzzle should taper slightly toward the nose.

HEAD

The Standard describes the head as follows: *"Heavy head furnishings with good fall over eyes, good whiskers and beard; skull narrow, falling away behind the eyes in a marked degree, not quite flat, but not domed or apple-shaped; straight foreface of fair length. Nose black, the length from tip of nose to eye to be roughly about one-third of the total length from nose to back of skull."*

The first three phrases in the Head section are simply an extension of the Coat section, describing the coat on the head.

In his land of origin, the small Lhasa Apso needed the protection provided by the *heavy head furnishings, the good fall over the eyes* and the *good whiskers and beard.* Primarily a house companion in this country, the Lhasa Apso rarely needs his coat for survival, but because his protective head covering is so effective, he likes to romp in the snow or let the cold wind blow in his face.

The head furnishings, fall, whiskers and beard are characteristics that when coupled with the correct head structure provide the distinctly unique Lhasa Apso expression.

The additional phrases in the Head section (except *nose black*) describe the type of skull the Lhasa Apso should have. In order to define these phrases it is necessary to understand the skull types.

The canine skull is categorized into three types as follows:

1. Dolichocephalic—long and narrow. The muzzle is long, sometimes more than half the total length of the skull.
2. Mesaticephalic—intermediate in form.
3. Brachycephalic—very broad and short; known as "short-faced." The muzzle is usually quite a bit less than half the total length of skull.

The dolichocephalic skull type can be ruled out, because although the Lhasa Apso Standard calls for a narrow skull, it does not call for a muzzle as long as it is synonymous with the dolichocephalic skull type.

There is conjecture by some that the Lhasa Apso has a brachycephalic skull type. The Standard's phrase *narrow skull* is in direct disagreement with this concept. The phrase *falling away behind the eyes in a marked degree* also suggests that the Lhasa Apso skull is not brachycephalic in type. Although this phrase is considered difficult to understand, when careful study is given to visualizing the canine skull, the meaning of this phrase becomes quite clear and definitely helps to understand the Lhasa Apso's head structure.

In order to understand this phrase, *falling away behind the eyes in a marked degree*, gently press the hair down on either side of the skull, locating the zygomatic arches, which will appear to be curved bones on either side of the head between the eyes and the ears. Actually they are the continuation of the malar bones that are located under the eyes. Midway along the arches the malar bones fuse with the temporal bones that protrude from the sides of the skull just below the ear set.

In the broad skull type (brachycephalic) the malar bones arc out almost perpendicularly to the muzzle, forming an arch that is about as wide at the front as at the back of the skull.

In the narrow skull type there is a definite narrowness in the arch immediately behind the eyes or a *falling away behind the eyes in a marked degree*. The arch then tends to widen as it becomes the temporal bone that arcs back to the skull in front and below the ears.

Study of the different skull types makes it apparent that this narrowing or falling away behind the eyes will require a less frontally placed eye than will the broad skull type with the *widening* of the skull immediately *behind* the eyes.

According to the AKC Glossary:

Foreface: The front part of the head, before the eyes. Muzzle.''

Muzzle: The head in front of the eyes—nasal bone, nostrils, and jaws. Foreface.''

Reference to the muzzle is made again in the Lhasa Apso Standard under the Head section: "*straight foreface of fair length*." Described as "of fair length" and "of medium length," never does it indicate that the muzzle should be short, as described in the definition of a brachycephalic skull type as "short-faced." As a matter of fact the Mouth and Muzzle section states "*a square muzzle is objectionable*," a trait that along with short and broad is most often requested by the standards of the brachycephalic breeds.

The muzzle or foreface is mentioned in the Standard for the third time after "*nose black*," and gives yet another guideline for the length of the muzzle by comparing the length of the muzzle to the total length of the skull, i.e., "*the length from tip of nose to eye to be roughly about one-third of the total length from nose to back of skull*."

In discussing the muzzle length it should be noted that the original Standard stated that the ideal length for the muzzle or foreface was about one and a half inches from the tip of the nose to the eye. We believe that the 1978 revision removing the phrase "about one and a half inches long" was a mistake because it stated a measurement that worked like a safety valve to help control size.

Nature tends to produce balance and symmetry; therefore, if the length of muzzle changes, the remainder of the animal tends to follow that change. It was especially important in the case of the Lhasa Apso, because in its country of origin there was evidence of a variation in size and type in what was termed the Apso breed. The Western world attempted to make the Lhasa Apso a specific breed and the one-and-a-half-inch muzzle requirement was an integral part of the Lhasa Apso Standard and should have remained as a part of the current Standard.

In addition to being of fair length, the foreface is to be *straight*, which means that it is not to have a dish face nor a Roman nose.

The Head section also states that the nose should be black and thus excludes a brown or liver nose, a Butterfly nose or a Dudley nose.

Also described in this section is the basic shape of the top of the skull or head as follows: "*[skull] not quite flat, but not domed or apple-shaped.*" These terms are self-explanatory and describe nothing that classifies the skull type.

Not mentioned in the description of head is the stop, which is located between the eyes and is where the muzzle joins the head. The definition of the stop depends largely on the skull type, with the narrow, long muzzle types tending to have less definition of stop than the short-faced types, which have the most marked stops. It is our opinion that the Lhasa Apso should have a shallow but apparent stop.

EYES

The Standard describes the eyes as follows: "*Dark brown, neither very large and full, nor very small and sunk.*"

Dark brown describes the desired color for the Lhasa Apso's eyes and is self-explanatory. The phrases *neither very large and full, nor small and sunk* indicate what is incorrect and leave the impression that the proper eye is almond-shaped and medium in size.

As described in the Head section, the correct skull construction requires the eyes to be placed less frontally and more obliquely than the heavy head fall makes them appear at first impression.

EARS

The Standard says that the ears are "*pendant*" and "*heavily feathered.*" This simply means that the Lhasa Apso should have drop ears that hang down the side of the Lhasa Apso's head, laying close to the cheek, and the ears should be profusely covered with long hair.

The ears are set somewhat back on the head and about level with the eyes; however, the ear set is important only to the extent that it should not interfere with the symmetry of the head structure and expression.

LEGS

The Standard states as follows: "*Forelegs straight, both forelegs and hind legs heavily furnished with hair.*"

Forelegs straight means that the forearms or front legs when viewed from the front should be straight, although the forefeet or front feet may turn out slightly.

Both forelegs and hind legs heavily furnished with hair is an additional

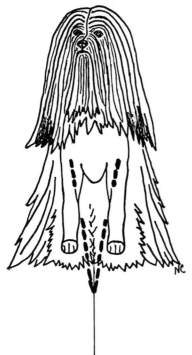

The front view illustrates the correct position of the legs standing and the broken lines illustrate the position of the legs during movement. Note converging pattern.

The rear view illustrates the correct position of the legs and hocks standing, and the broken lines illustrate the position of the legs during movement.

description of the coat, and obviously the legs needed the same protection from the extreme climate of Tibet as did the rest of the Lhasa Apso's body.

FEET

The Standard states that the feet should be *"Well-feathered, should be round and catlike with good pads."*

Well-feathered is a description that continues to describe that the Lhasa Apso should be totally covered from head to toe with a protective coat.

According to the AKC Glossary, a cat foot is, "The short, round compact foot like that of a cat. The foot with short third digits." Cat feet, the most common shape for the canine foot, coupled with the Standard's request for *good pads*, provide the Lhasa Apso with efficient feet that carry it over the roughest of terrains or the living room carpet.

TAIL AND CARRIAGE

The Standard describes the tail and carriage as follows: *"Well-feathered, should be carried well over back in a screw; there may be a kink at the end. A low carriage of stern is a serious fault."*

Well-feathered is further describing the coat and has been well explained in previous sections.

Should be carried well over back in a screw means that the tail should set on high enough that it *can* be carried well over the back in a screw or a tight or spiral curl, the end of which falls to the loin area and may have a kink at the end.

We believe that the reference made to a *low carriage of stern is a serious fault* means that the tail should be carried well over the back during movement, indicating that the tail *can* be carried high. It should not be considered a serious fault if the tail is dropped when the dog is standing, bored or startled. The tail should, however, flip up well over the back as soon as the Lhasa Apso begins to gait.

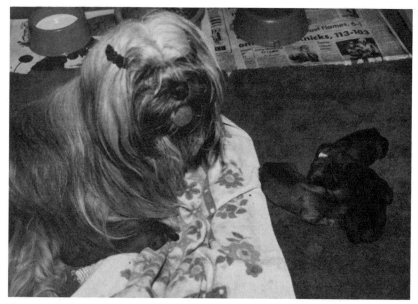

Ch. Tabu's Bronze Bonanza owned by Martin and Elaine Fisher is the proud mother of this week-old litter.

Lhasa Apso puppies at two weeks of age.

10

Choosing a Lhasa Apso Puppy

SELECTING A PUPPY for your family requires careful research. The puppy you select will hopefully be a member of your family for at least ten years or more. The more carefully you plan before making your selection, the more likely it is that you will avoid the disappointment of having to live with a dog that does not suit your household.

Before you look at any puppies, look at your environment and try to visualize it containing an adult dog of the breed you are considering.

FIRST CONSIDERATIONS

If you choose the Lhasa Apso, consider its characteristics so that your final selection will not be a mistake. The responsibility of maintaining the long coat may be a liability to an extremely busy, active family. The Lhasa Apso is a hardy breed but should not be considered either a stuffed toy or a wrestling partner for young children. Although a small dog, the Lhasa Apso will require the same discipline and training as a large dog. If, after considering these characteristics, you and your family have decided upon the Lhasa Apso, it is time to select your individual puppy.

FINDING THE RIGHT PUPPY

It is advantageous and enjoyable to be able to see one or both of a puppy's parents, and at some kennels you may even see grandparents, aunts, uncles and cousins. Observation of its relatives can give you an insight as to the temperament and stableness you may expect from your puppy.

The Lhasa Apso is a breed noted for longevity; therefore, it is usually slower to mature than many other breeds. Because of slow maturity Lhasa Apso puppies should not go to new homes until they are at least twelve weeks old.

MALE OR FEMALE

Your selection of sex is not important as both sexes make excellent pets and companions. Assuming that you are buying your Lhasa Apso as a family pet, it may be advisable to have him castrated or her spayed. The altering of your female pet will eliminate the twice-yearly job of keeping her confined for three weeks while she is in season. A male will not be inclined to roam in search of a female if he has been altered.

The matter of reproducing the Lhasa Apso should be the responsibility of the experienced, knowledgeable and properly equipped breeder.

WHAT TO LOOK FOR

It is difficult to tell much about a very young puppy except that it appears to be healthy. A healthy puppy should be alert, lively and plump, but not potbellied. A potbelly may be a sign of poor nutrition or worms. The healthy puppy will have clear eyes with no discharge. His ears should be clean and free of irritation. The skin and coat should be clean with no signs of parasites. Beware of the puppy that has a runny nose and eyes.

Temperament is very important and should be considered strongly when making your selection. The proper attitude for young Lhasa puppies is happy, friendly and outgoing. As the puppies get older they will begin to show the aloof reserve with strangers that is typical of the adult Lhasa Apso temperament.

Sometime between twelve and sixteen weeks you can catch a glimpse of what the puppy promises to be structurally; but you must have considerable knowledge of and experience with dogs generally and the breed specifically to be able to make a lasting evaluation as to show quality.

For the next few months the puppy goes through a series of constantly changing, somewhat awkward stages. Then between eight and twelve months an expert can give you a reasonably valid opinion about the dog's structural potential as a show dog.

If you are looking for a show puppy, you will obviously want to wait until the puppy is at least twelve to sixteen weeks old, and will not make a choice then without help. Preferably you will wait until the puppies you are considering are between eight and twelve months old.

While it is true that the older the puppy, the higher the price may be, the increase in price is what you are paying for more probability of success when you begin to show.

If you are buying a Lhasa Apso with the intent of showing in Conformation, we suggest that you check the animal against the breed Standard and try to make an informed judgment as to how he or she measures up to the Standard requirements.

For your convenience we have listed some of the ratios, measurements and angles we use in evaluating the structure of our Lhasa Apsos.

The following is meant as a guide to be used in conjunction with the Standard and to evaluate adults or nearly full-grown puppies while standing still (illustration A).

1. Height of ten and a half inches at top of shoulder (withers) for a dog, a bitch slightly smaller.

2. Ratio of the height at withers to length from point of shoulder to point of buttocks is 7.5:10.

3. Muzzle about one and a half inches long.

4. Ratio of length of muzzle (from tip of nose to eye) to length of skull is 1:2.

5. Ratio of length of head from muzzle to back of skull to length of body is 1:3.

6. Length of neck and head from point of attachment of neck to body is slightly less than height at the withers.

7. Length of neck from point of attachment of neck to body to base of skull slightly less than length of head.

8. Angle of neck approximately 90 degrees to shoulder blade.

9. Angle of layback of the shoulder blade 45 degrees to a horizontal.

10. Angle of upper arm 90 degrees to shoulder blade.

11. Length of upper arm nearly as long as length of shoulder blade.

12. Front legs perpendicular to a horizontal base.

13. Angle of tibia and fibula 120 degrees to femur (i.e., stifle joint).

14. Hock perpendicular to ground.

15. Tailset straight above articulation (joint) of pelvis and femur.

16. Withers is the highest point in the topline, which slopes gradually back to the croup.

The final test for proper structure is to observe the dog moving at a trot. If it appears to move like the dog in illustration B, it means that it has the proper ratios, angles and measurements enumerated above.

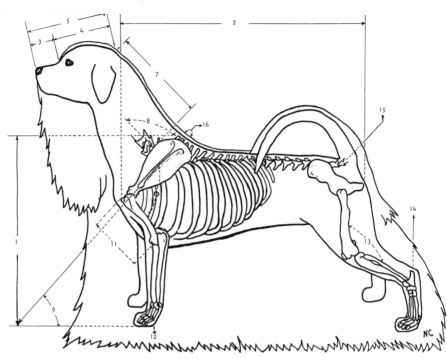

Illustration A: Ratios, angles and measurements used in evaluating structure.

Illustration B: Lhasa Apso with proper structure should give this appearance.

ESSENTIAL DOCUMENTS

Purchasers of a show puppy generally are looking into the future to the time their Lhasa Apso will be bred. For this reason it is important to request the explanation of the puppy's pedigree. You should be supplied with this document, along with the official American Kennel Club registration form, when you buy your puppy.

The pedigree is not an official document of registration but is a record of your puppy's ancestors. When the time comes for mating your Lhasa Apso the pedigree will be an invaluable aid in the selection of a proper mate. You should, however, learn as much as possible about the dogs appearing in the pedigree— their strong and weak breeding points—long before breeding.

Do not forget to ask for health records so that you can supply your veterinarian with this information and keep his records complete for your dog.

Whether you are selecting your Lhasa Apso puppy for a pet, a show dog or both, remember that a healthy structurally and mentally sound puppy will be more easily trained to fit into your environment as the companion dog the Lhasa Apso was developed to be.

When you buy a dog that is represented as being eligible for registration with The American Kennel Club, you are entitled to receive an AKC application form properly filled out by the seller, which—when completed by you and submitted to the AKC with the proper fee—will enable you to effect the registration of the dog. When the application has been processed, you will receive an AKC registration certificate.

Under AKC rules, any person who sells dogs that are represented as being AKC registrable must maintain records that will make it possible to give full identifying information with every dog delivered, even though AKC papers may not yet be available. *Do not accept a promise of later identification.*

The Rules and Regulations of The American Kennel Club stipulate that whenever someone sells or delivers a dog that is said to be registrable with the AKC, the dog must be identified either by putting into the hands of the buyer a properly completed AKC registration application, or by giving the buyer a bill of sale or a written statement *signed by the seller*, giving the dog's full breeding information as follows:

Breed, sex, and color of the dog
Date of birth of the dog
Registered names of the dog's sire and dam
Name of the breeder

If you encounter any problems in acquiring the necessary registration application forms, it is suggested that you write The American Kennel Club, 51 Madison Avenue, New York, NY 10010, *giving full particulars*, and the difficulty will be reviewed. All individuals acquiring a dog represented as being AKC registrable should realize it is their responsibility to obtain complete identification of the dog as described above sufficient to identify in AKC records, or *they should not buy the dog*.

Lhasa Apsos are good with children which is obvious when it is bedtime at the authors' during a visit from granddaughters. Lacey and Kelli. These puppies are twelve weeks old.

11

How to Groom the Lhasa Apso

T HE LHASA APSO'S profuse coat is one of its hallmarks. You are apparently attracted to "hairy dogs" to have chosen it. If you decided on the Lhasa Apso because you saw a beautiful specimen with a floor-length coat in a photo or at a dog show, you should realize the dog did not just happen to look like that. Many hours of grooming and care were spent to make the coat so beautiful.

Proper grooming is quite easy if done correctly, and can be fun for both you and your dog. Learning from a book is possible if you read the descriptions carefully and think about what the words suggest, not just what they say. With the proper tools, patience and common sense, much can be accomplished in a few hours of grooming each week.

TOOLS

Here is a list of the necessary equipment for grooming your Lhasa Apso:

The Mason Pearson brush
Slicker brush
Fine-and medium-tooth steel comb
Hemostat
Nail clipper

Photo 2. Grasp the front and back legs on his opposite side.

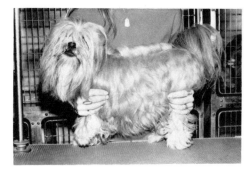

Photo 1. Grooming Tools—1. Knitting needle; 2. Fine and medium tooth comb; 3. The Mason Pearson Brush; 4. Slicker brush; 5. Nail clipper; 6. Scissors; 7. Hemostat.

Photo 3. Lift him slightly and push him over and away from your body.

Photo 4. Lean over him while speaking softly until he relaxes in the desired position.

Photo 5. Slip your hands and body away so he lies still without being held.

176

Good quality barber's scissors
Knitting needle
Hair dryer
Spray applicator
Small latex bands and barrettes
Styptic powder

The Mason Pearson brush is manufactured in England and is expensive and hard to obtain. It has a combination of natural bristles and nylon pin bristles. It is highly prized for show grooming because it effectively removes tangles without damaging the coat. It may be substituted by a cushioned metal pin brush, and there are many serviceable imitations of the Mason Pearson brush on the market.

The right grooming equipment for a Lhasa Apso can usually be obtained from a well-stocked dog supply shop or at dog shows from a concession stand.

PREPARATION FOR GENERAL GROOMING

Grooming can be fun if your Lhasa Apso is trained to allow it without a struggle. This training should start as early as possible. One of the first things a puppy should learn is to lie quietly on its side on a grooming table or flat surface. This surface should be comfortable for you while standing, or sitting if you prefer.

You should be comfortable while grooming or you tend to rush the job. Do not try to groom your Lhasa Apso from a disadvantageous position on the floor or on your bed. Neither you nor the dog will be comfortable and the grooming results will be disappointing.

Allow your dog to relieve itself before you start grooming to avoid restlessness. Give the dog a break frequently if its coat condition requires a long session.

To lay a Lhasa Apso on its side, stand it sideways in front of you on the grooming surface. Now grasp the front and back legs on its opposite side (photo 2), lift slightly and push the dog over and away from your body (photo 3). At the same time, lean over and hold it while speaking softly, until the dog relaxes (photo 4). Then gently and slowly slip your hands and body away so it lies still without being held (photo 5). If your dog struggles and stands up, repeat the process until you have convinced it that it will not be hurt while lying on its side. You may have to use a little force to hold the dog down the first few times it struggles. Otherwise, it will assume it can get up any time it desires. Practice lying your dog on its side until it will stay there without being held. This frees your hands for grooming. When you have finished a practice session, praise and play with the dog to make it feel rewarded for having pleased you. The early grooming sessions are more for the benefit of training than grooming.

In the beginning you will spend more time teaching your dog to be quiet than grooming it. A puppy's coat mats very little the first few months. By the time it starts the matting-tangling change of coat, at six to nine months, the dog has been trained to lie still while you brush.

Some Lhasa Apsos during grooming will try to bite or growl. This is a no-no and must be stopped immediately by any method necessary. Try a sharp, loud No!, a slap on the table with No! or if necessary a sharp slap on the muzzle or the rump with a No!

GENERAL GROOMING

When your Lhasa Apso has learned to lie down without struggling or getting up, the real grooming process begins.

Start by pushing all the hair away from you, exposing the skin of the stomach. Having a starting point helps to avoid getting the hair caught in your brush or comb, and allows you to see the area to be groomed. The exposed skin of the stomach forms a horizontal part in the hair (photo 6). The part need not be perfectly straight, but if you do not make a part, you may not get to the skin or you may miss some areas entirely.

Before brushing, spray with a fine mist of water or a commercial coat conditioner. This will help to lubricate the dry coat, protect the ends and help to control the static electricity, thus making the coat more manageable.

After spraying the coat, use the Mason Pearson brush to brush it down. Keep the brush flat on the hair, avoiding any twisting, turning or flipping action, which tends to break the ends of the hair (photo 7). Brush a small portion of hair down toward the stomach, continuing horizontally from the front to the back of the body. Take care to brush only a small amount of hair, thus moving the part a fraction of an inch up the side of the body.

After moving the part up about an inch with the brush, use a medium-tooth steel comb on the same area, making sure there are no tangles or mats that were missed with the brush. Do not flip, twist or turn the comb either but simply pull it gently straight through the hair. If the comb is stopped by a snarl, simply lift it straight up and out of the hair and start over very gently, working the tangle to within a few inches of the ends of the hair. Use the brush to gently work the snarl out the last few inches. Continue this inch-by-inch grooming process until you have groomed the entire body on one side of your Lhasa Apso, including its chest and rear.

If you discover a mat too large to work out with the comb or brush, use your fingers to spread the mat apart. After separating the mat with your fingers, use the brush to work out the mat. Plenty of patience is a definite asset when working out mats. The more you separate the mat into smaller mats or tangles, the less damage you will cause to the hair.

Another way to remove a large mat is to use the corner of a slicker brush in a "picking" action, gently pulling hair bit by bit loose from the mat.

Grooming the legs requires you to hold the foot and most of the leg hair at the same time (photo 8). Start at the base of the leg next to the body. Brush

Int. Ch. Troubadour de Gandamak (France) on a 17th Century prayer table.

Ch. Sharbo Topguy with handler Carol Smith.

Ch. Chen Krishna Nor with co-owner Wendy Har[

Ch. Everglo Sundance with handler Marvin Cates.

Ch. Ahisma A Tantras with handler Carolyn Herbel.

Ch. Karma Kushog with Darby McSorley.

Ch. Tabu's Appleseed Annie with owner Susan Gehr.

Ch. Tabu's Bric A Brac, owned by Charles and Barbara Steele and handled by Carmen Herbel, is shown winning under judge Leota Vandeventer.

Ch. Anbara's Abra-Ka-Dabra and Ch. Anbara's Ruffian, owned and handled by Barabara Wood, were Best Brace in Show six times during 1977. They are shown making one of these wins at the Farmington Valley KC under judge Lorna B. Demidoff.

Ch. Arborhill's Bhran-Dieh, owned by Shirley Ruth, shown in a win under judge George Payton, handler Thelma Sloan.

Ch. Tabu's Miss Chimney Sweep, owned and handled by Nancy Clarke, was BW at Westminster enroute to her championship. The judge was Edd Embry Bivin.

Ch. Potala Keke's Tomba Tu, owned and bred by Keke Blumberg, is shown winning BB at Queensboro under Katherine E. Gately, handler Carmen Herbel.

Ch. Balrene Chia Pao with his owner-breeder-handler, Dr. Ellen Brown.

Ch. Potala Keke's Golden Gatsby, owned by Barbara Chevalier, is shown winning the Non-Sporting Group at Quebec under judge A. Peter Knoop, handler Garrett Lambert.

Tabu's Jazz Man, bred, owned and handled by
Carolyn Herbel.

Ch. Potala Keke's Kelana, owned by
Jeanne and John Hope and shown with
handler Carolyn Herbel.

Ch. Tabu's Fame and Fortune, owned by Gerri and Ann Goldberg, shown winning under Dr. Harold Huggins, handler Carmen Herbel.

Ch. Everglo Zijuh Tomba (left) winning a stud dog class under judge Graham Head. Tomba was handled by Sharon Rouse. His progeny shown are Ch. Sharbo Topguy (center) with Darby McSorley and Ch. Sharbo Me-Shanda Ba with Lynn Morgan.

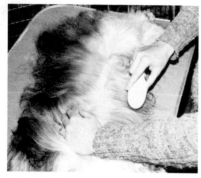

Photo 6. The horizontal part that moves up the side of the body as you brush small amounts of hair.

Photo 7. Keep the brush flat on the hair avoiding any twisting or flipping action which tends to break the ends of the hair.

Photo 8. Grooming and the leg requires you to hold the foot and most of their leg hair in one hand while brushing with the other.

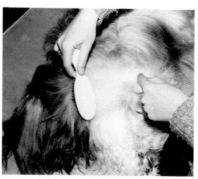

Photo 9. The proper way to hold the leg and brush when brushing the front of the leg.

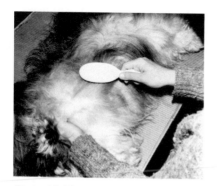

Photo 10. The proper way to brush the sensitive area under the leg next to the body.

the hair away from the foot and toward the body. By following the same technique as you did on the body, the part should appear completely around the leg (photo 9). The area under your Lhasa Apso's leg next to the body tends to mat quickly, so be sure to get all the mats from this area. As this area is one of the most sensitive areas to groom, be gentle to prevent any discomfort (photo 10). Brush the leg until you have reached the foot. Be careful not to use long brush strokes that damage the body coat. After all the leg hair has been completely brushed and detangled, lightly brush the coat downward toward the foot so it falls in its natural direction.

The whiskers and beard, another sensitive area, should be groomed with care. The facial area requires special attention because food particles may adhere to the hair around the mouth and matter accumulates under the eyes. Brush the ends of the beard carefully to avoid harming the eyes or scratching the lips or nose. After brushing the beard and whiskers thoroughly, use the fine-toothed steel comb close to the eye, pulling gently away from the eye (photo 11). Remove all eye matter with the comb. If the matter has dried, use a wet cotton swab to moisten it before combing. A toothbrush is also a good tool for cleaning this area. Two drops of eye wash solution in each eye will help to rinse away any matter in the eyes. Cleaning this facial area should be done frequently to eliminate a buildup of eye matter or food particles. Cleaning this area also helps to eliminate odor, infection and a generally untidy appearance.

The head, ears and tail should be groomed with special care because this portion of your Lhasa Apso's coat can suffer damage more readily than the rest of the coat, as it is usually of different texture. It also tends to be longer and the ends break more easily.

The head is groomed the same as the body, by using the part, brush and comb method. Be sure to groom under the chin and neck too.

The ears may be sticky from being dragged in food. It may be necessary to spray their ends until wet and then gently brush to remove residue. After brushing the ears, gently comb to be sure no tangles have been missed. Be careful not to scratch the ear leather or damage the hair ends with the teeth of the comb.

The tail should be groomed by taking all the tail hair from the base of the tail to its end and making a part down one side (photo 12). Fold all the hair over to one side and then spray and brush. After gentle brushing, comb near the tail but never comb the hair ends.

CLEANING EARS

Because the Lhasa Apso is a long-coated dog, it has hair in its ears. This hair can easily become embedded with dirt, causing infection or odor. It should be removed about once each month or as needed. Frequent ear hair removal helps eliminate irritation to the skin. A hemostat is ideal for pulling hair from the ears. With your Lhasa Apso on its side, the task will be much easier, as you can use both hands.

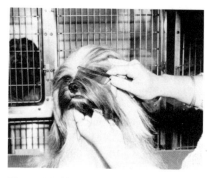

Photo 11. Use the fine-toothed comb close to the eye; pulling gently away from the eye to remove eye matter.

Photo 12. The tail should be groomed by taking all the hair from the base of the tail to its end.

Photo 13. While holding the ear leather with one hand, to expose the ear canal, use the hemostat to pull the hair from the ear.

Photo 14. Swab the ear with a piece of cotton, on the end of the hemostat, that has been dipped in alcohol.

181

By holding the ear leather with one hand, the ear canal can be exposed and made accessible. Use the hemostat to pull a few hairs with one stroke; do not jerk (photo 13). A steady pull is less painful as the ear canal does not have a great deal of sensitivity. Do not try to pull too much hair with one stroke. Instead, make several attempts to remove all the hair. Don't probe too deep into the ear canal; allow the hair to grow out long enough to grasp.

After the hair has been removed, place a piece of cotton on the end of the hemostat. Dip the cotton in alcohol and swab the ear (photo 14). This process should be repeated until the cotton is clean when removed from the ear. The cotton should not be stained after more than three times if the ear is healthy. The alcohol helps to remove any infectious particles from the ear and dissolves accumulated wax. Ears should be cleaned with alcohol every time your Lhasa Apso is groomed.

CLIPPING TOENAILS

Your Lhasa Apso's toenails should be clipped frequently enough to keep the nails short. The nails should never be allowed to grow long enough to absorb the pressure of walking. This pressure should be absorbed by the toes. If the nails are allowed to grow too long, they can cause splaying of the feet and discomfort to your dog. The frequency of clipping depends on the kind of surface your Lhasa Apso runs on. Concrete will tend to wear nails short, but a dog exercised on grass or a soft surface will have longer nails from lack of abrasive contact to wear them short.

Lay your Lhasa Apso on its side and grasp one of its feet in your hand. Use your index finger to push the hair away from the nails and place your thumb between the pads. With the nail clipper in your other hand, clip the tip off the nail a little at a time until the blunt end of the nail appears pink or, in the case of a black nail, moist (photo 15). If you clip too deep, the nail will bleed. The bleeding can be stopped by applying pressure on the end of the nail. Keep styptic powder available and apply it to stop the bleeding immediately.

SPECIAL CLEANING

If your Lhasa Apso messes his genitals or anus, you will want to clean them as part of regular grooming and on special occasions. Spray the area until it is fairly wet. Sprinkle a little baby powder on the area and brush until it is fairly dry. The powder helps to absorb moisture, removes stain and controls odor. If your Lhasa Apso is too messy in either area, bathe it. Dirt makes your dog uncomfortable and causes problems, infections and work for you. Check each time it eliminates for any fecal material that may adhere to its coat. Lhasa Apsos often report such problems to their owners; they really do not like to be untidy!

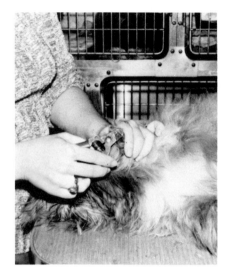

Photo 15. The proper way to hold the foot and clippers while clipping nails.

Photo 16. Clipping the hair from between the pads with an electric clipper.

Photo 17. This Lhasa Apso's face furnishing has grown long enough to drape down the side of the muzzle so that it does not irritate the eyes.

TRIMMING

The Lhasa Apso should have the hair between its pads trimmed approximately every two or three weeks. Lay the dog on its side and, using a pair of scissors or an electric clipper with a #15 blade, trim all excess hair that is between the pads (photo 16). Do not trim on top of the feet or between the toes. Trim only the bottom of the foot between the pads. Sometimes it is desirable to *even* the hair on the top of the feet if it grows so long as to flop under the feet and create a handicap to the dog when he is moving. This trimming should be done with care and never too close to the feet. A rounded, neat appearance is desired.

The hair growing within one quarter inch of the anus may be trimmed to eliminate the collection of fecal material.

Trimming the hair under the eyes or on the muzzle may result in irritation to the eyes, especially as it grows out. The hair under the eyes, if allowed to grow long enough, will drape down the side of the muzzle and will not irritate the eyes (photo 17). Sometimes puppies will have excessive tearing when their hair has not grown long enough to drape down the muzzle away from the eyes. During this stage the puppy's eyes should be cleaned often. Keeping the area under the eyes clean helps promote the growth of the hair.

FINISH GROOMING

Your Lhasa Apso has been thoroughly brushed. Its ears, eyes and genitals are clean. Its toenails and pads are trimmed. Now it is ready to have its hair parted neatly from the tip of its nose to the base of its tail and to have its topknot put up.

To get the part centered and straight, your Lhasa Apso should be standing four-square and facing you. Use a knitting needle to make the part down the back. Starting at the nose, center the part between the eyes and over the skull, aiming for the base of the tail. Attempt only about four inches with each stroke of the needle. Continue a straight line from the skull down the neck and back to the base of the tail, following the spinal column to center the part. Spray the part lightly and brush the hair straight down on both sides of the body (photo 18).

This part is rather difficult to keep straight in puppies. In the longer, adult coat the part tends to remain orderly for several days.

Before putting up the topknot, you must determine if your Lhasa Apso has enough headfall for one or two topknots. The longer, thicker headfall requires two topknots. With less headfall one will stay up better.

If you use one topknot, make a part from the outer corner of the eye to the back of the skull or occiput, just above the ear. Do not make the part below the eye or ear because it will stretch the skin and cause discomfort, and your Lhasa Apso will probably scratch the topknot. Use the same process on each side of the head. Brush the two portions of hair straight back from the face to the top

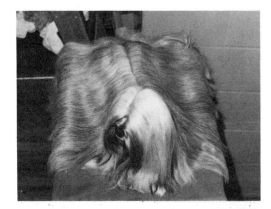

Photo 18. BIS Ch. Potala Keke's Yum Yum ROM models the proper part; straight from the tip of her nose to the base of her tail.

Photo 19. These Lhasa puppies are modeling the one topknot style. The puppy on the left is wearing a barrette and the other one an elastic band.

Photo 20. Ch. Thang-Ka Simhanada shows the proper two topknot style with barrettes.

of the head, making one strand or ponytail of hair. Secure this strand of hair with a latex band or barrette. Do not tie the hair too tight as it will pull the dog's skin causing discomfort and scratching again (photo 19).

When using two topknots, follow the same process as above, except that the portions on each side of the head are kept separate, leaving the part in the center of the skull. Each side is secured in a strand or ponytail just above the ear, allowing the hair to hang down over the ear. Be careful not to catch any hair on the ears in the latex band or barrette, as this may also cause discomfort and scratching (photo 20).

Either style of topknot should be taken down and redone several times a week. Do not allow the topknot to remain up for more than one week or skin irritation resulting in sores may occur.

In the show ring for Conformation and Obedience the Lhasa Apso is shown without tying the hair back from the face; however, most exhibitors prefer to keep the hair secured away from the eyes and face when their dogs are not in the show ring, to allow for better vision and for cleanliness. Securing the headfall in topknots prevents the Lhasa Apso from chewing on the long hair and reduces eye irritation.

When introducing your Lhasa Apso to a topknot, divert its attention from the strange new thing on its head. One fairly successful plan is to tie the hair up just before going for a walk or a ride.

BATHING

Your Lhasa Apso should be bathed as often as needed to keep it tidy. The frequency of bathing will depend on the environment it lives in. A dog running on a big concrete or gravel patio will not need bathing as often as one walked on oily city streets.

Prepare your dog for its bath by performing a routine general grooming as described before. When all its mats and tangles have been removed, place it in a sink or bathtub. Keep the bathtub drain open and, using a spray attachment or dipping container, completely saturate the coat. Be careful not to get water in the ears. Apply a recommended dog shampoo to the coat with a squeeze bottle, keeping soap out of the eyes. You may wish to use a tearless shampoo for the head and around the eyes. Do not rub the shampoo into the coat. Squeeze it in as you would in washing a fine sweater. Rinse the shampoo out of the coat and apply a second time if needed. Always rinse *all* shampoo out of the coat. Otherwise, skin irritation and problems may result. After rinsing, apply a cream rinse according to directions, if desired. Cream rinse helps when brushing tangles from the wet coat but will not alone demat a coat. Dematting should be done before the bath, as getting mats wet makes them tighter and harder to remove.

If there are any fleas or ticks on your Lhasa Apso, use a flea or tick rinse on it. Be sure to follow mixing directions to avoid irritation by applying too strong a mixture. Ask your veterinarian to recommend a flea and tick rinse. This rinse should not have an offensive odor and may be used if you anticipate having your Lhasa Apso in a location, such as a park, dog show or wooded area, where fleas or ticks are present. Do not use a flea and tick rinse routinely after every bath.

After the rinses have been applied and your dog is ready to be dried, wrap it in a large terry cloth towel to blot all excess moisture. You may want to use two towels, but never rub your Lhasa Apso when drying. To do so will create tangles and mats that are difficult to remove.

Now remove the towel and lay your dog on its side on the grooming surface. Turn the hair dryer on warm and direct it toward the stomach. Start to brush as you dry, following the method used in general grooming, forming the horizontal parting of the coat and brushing until dry down to the skin.

After your Lhasa Apso is dry, put the finishing touches on it by making a straight, neat part from its nose to its tail and securing its headfall into one or two topknots.

Patience is a virtue at all times during a grooming session. With practice your judgment and knowledge will increase and your Lhasa Apso will look better and better. If you groom your dog regularly and thoroughly, its beautiful coat will make you proud.

WRAPPING THE COAT

Wrapping to obtain a long, luxurious, floor-length coat is not necessary. There are some circumstances, however, where it might be desirable. Wrapping does not make the hair grow faster but keeps the ends from being damaged by normal activity. If your Lhasa Apso is exercised on a rough surface, the ends of the hair will be damaged. Some dogs step on their coats while playing and pull out hair or break it off. Observing your Lhasa Apso's daily routine will help you decide if wrapping will be beneficial.

Before wrapping your Lhasa Apso, groom it very thoroughly, making sure it is clean and free of mats and tangles.

The use of coat oil before wrapping is optional. If you use oil, it should be applied according to directions. Commercial coat oil helps promote a healthy coat and improves the coat texture. Apply the oil only to the coat. Do not saturate the skin, as excessive oiling of the skin causes it to flake and peel as though it had been sunburned.

Wrappers are made of many different materials. Some popular materials are paper towels, Handi-Wipes, silk squares, waxed paper, bakery tissues or plastic bags. You should experiment with different materials and choose the one you find easy to work with and that holds the coat best. The size of each wrap varies with the length of the coat. Ten inches square is the average.

With your Lhasa Apso standing squarely on the grooming surface before you, make the first section to be wrapped by parting the coat. Assuming you have the part straight down your Lhasa Apso's spine, make a perpendicular part

Photo 21. The first of coat section for wrapping.

Photo 22. The hair brushed together into one strand with the lengthwise folded wrapper around it.

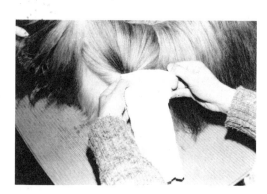

Photo 23. The second lengthwise fold of the wrapper.

Photo 24. A third and fourth lengthwise fold of the wrapper.

188

Photo 25. The lengthwise folded wrapper folded in half crosswise.

Photo 26, The first wrap finished and secured with a rubber band.

Photo 27. Section of coat for the middle wrap.

Photo 28. The third and final section for wrapping one side.

from just in front of the withers to the bottom of the shoulder blade. Holding this part, make another part from the bottom of the shoulder blade across to just above the elbow. Finish parting this section by making a part perpendicular to the spine (photo 21). You should have approximately one third of your dog's body coat above the elbow and below the spine in this square. Avoid getting any leg hair in this section, as this causes discomfort. Brush the hair together into one strand and fold the wrapper in half lengthwise around the strand of hair (photo 22). Making sure the hair stays together in the first fold, fold the now doubled wrap in half lengthwise (photo 23). You may wish to make a third and fourth fold to make the wrap smaller (photo 24). With the strand of hair securely wrapped in the lengthwise-folded wrapper, fold this wrapper in half crosswise (photo 25) and then in half again crosswise, forming a neat little package with the strand of hair tucked securely inside. Take a rubber band and wrap it horizontally around the package so that it holds firmly but not tightly (photo 26). Grasp the finished wrap and gently pull to loosen the tightness all over but not so hard as to pull or loosen the hair from the wrap. This is done to ease uncomfortable tension on the skin.

To form the next section make a horizontal part straight across from above the elbow to the loin or flank area and perpendicular up to the spine (photo 27). Wrap this section as described above.

The third and final section on this side of your dog is formed by making a horizontal part from the loin area across to meet a perpendicular part straight down from the anus (photo 28). When making the perpendicular part down from the anus do not get any hair from the opposite side. If you do, it will cause a pocket that will catch fecal material. Do not catch any hair attached to the genitals or beyond the base of the tail.

Repeat the wrapping process on the other side of your Lhasa Apso (photo 29).

If your Lhasa Apso has never been wrapped, introduce it to wearing wraps slowly. Keep your dog wrapped only when you can observe it closely. If the dog tries to chew them out or scratches at them, reprimand it and draw its attention away from them. Never allow a wrapped Lhasa Apso to run free where there are objects that can catch the hair above the wraps.

Braids may be substituted for wraps (photo 30). If you feel that you are not satisfied with the results of wrapping your dog's coat, you may want to try braiding. Some types of coat will respond better to braids. In making the decision between wraps or braids, experiment to see which is most satisfactory for you.

If braids are preferred, secure them with latex bands because rubber bands will damage the coat.

Use the same method for braiding as in wrapping by parting the hair into sections. After braiding each section secure the end with a latex band and fold it in half crosswise and then in half crosswise again. Secure this folded braid with a latex band.

The wraps or braids on your Lhasa Apso should be changed when the

Photos 29 and 30. The Lhasa Apso above is modeling wraps used to protect the ends of his coat. For contrast, the model on the right wears braids. Note that the braid on the right is not folded to show where it begins and how the end is secured.

Photos 31 and 32. Multiple Group winner Ch. Potala Keke's Tomba Tu ROM before trimming (left) and after trimming (below).

191

underside of the hair, just above the wrap or braid, begins to tangle. This could be as often as every other day for some dogs.

Wrapping or braiding entails a considerable amount of time and effort. It should be done only under controlled conditions and after a considerable amount of grooming experience is obtained.

Wrapping or braiding the coat prevents wear to the ends of the coat caused by dragging on the surface your Lhasa Apso walks on. It may be necessary to trim the body coat when it grows long enough to interfere with movement (photo 31). Trimming this coat should be done with care so that it does not look trimmed. When trimming, your dog should be standing as in the show ring. Trim so that the coat is not just touching the floor but is one inch longer (photo 32). Improper trimming can ruin a coat so have it done by an expert the first time to see the proper way.

PET (OR NECESSITY) CLIPPING

If you have difficulty keeping your Lhasa Apso properly groomed or live where your dog picks up brambles and burrs, you may wish to have the dog clipped. Lhasa Apsos are long-coated and much of their initial charm is in their coats. They do have wonderful personalities, and with the proper clip lose none of their charm. Any professional grooming shop can probably clip your Lhasa Apso or you may learn to clip it yourself.

There are several ways to clip your Lhasa Apso and your choice depends on your taste and the reason the dog is being clipped. If you clip your dog because you do not want to cope with the long coat, clip the hair on the back and sides short and leave the legs, tail, ears and whiskers longer. This clip is much the same as a pet Schnauzer clip and is very attractive and easy to maintain.

Another style is to clip all the hair on the back and legs the same length. This is good for Lhasa Apsos that walk with their owners in fields and woods where stickers, leaves and brambles catch in a long coat. It also serves as a necessity clip, if your dog gets extremely matted, instead of brushing. Trying to brush a very badly matted coat is very painful, and the end result can be disappointing and leave it with a thin, straggly, unkept look.

Whether you choose one of these clips or choose one styled especially for your dog, a clipped Lhasa Apso can be handsome and easy to care for.

12

How to Show
a Lhasa Apso

In THIS CHAPTER we will tell you of the special techniques customary in showing a Lhasa Apso in the Conformation ring. You will derive more benefit from our suggestions if you study them after you have read at least one good general text on showing dogs, [such as *The Winning Edge* by George C. Alston with Connie Vanacore, 1992, Howell Book House, New York, N.Y.] It will also help to have attended at least one dog show where you can watch the handling of Lhasa Apsos, the conduct of the judge and stewards and general ring routine.

After you and your dog have practiced at home, enter a few match shows so that you can practice your showing technique under simulated show conditions. With this preliminary practice you will feel more confident when you enter an AKC point show.

These are the special techniques customary in showing a Lhasa Apso in the Conformation ring.

POSING

To set a Lhasa Apso in a show pose, first place the front legs squarely under and supporting the front assembly. The front feet should not toe in or out.

Next stretch the rear legs back enough to express angulation with the hocks perpendicular to the ground and parallel to each other about four inches apart. If

Proper way to set up a Lhasa Apso in the show ring.

Improper way to set up a Lhasa Apso in the show ring.

Improper way to set up a Lhasa Apso in the show ring.

your Lhasa Apso has a proper structure and is posed correctly, the topline should be slightly higher at the withers sloping to the croup without a sag or a roach. The head should be held proudly with its position straight ahead or slightly away from you. The tail should be held over the back naturally; however, you may hold it. If you hold the tail, it should be done in a manner so as not to detract from the dog's natural appearance.

After you have your dog posed, use a brush or comb to give the coat a neat, just-groomed appearance.

You may find it difficult to see your Lhasa Apso set up as others do when you are the handler. This problem can be easily solved by practicing the above procedure in front of a mirror. When he looks good to you in the mirror, then look down on him and make a mental note of how he looks when viewing him from your angle.

GAITING

Before gaiting your Lhasa Apso, be sure to alert it in some way so it knows that it is time to move. Because Lhasa Apsos are shown with the headfall free, sometimes they are unable to see all of your movements, therefore a communication other than visual should be established.

Lhasa Apsos should not be "strung up" (held on an extremely tight lead) when gaited, as this will hamper natural movement. However, because of their obstructed vision many will move more confidently with the security of a firmly held lead to guide them.

DEVELOPING A SHOWMAN

A Lhasa Apso that is to be shown should be introduced to strange sights, sounds and surprise conditions and be introduced to strange people and dogs as early in its life as possible. We are not suggesting that you take an unimmunized baby puppy out among the public. Neither are we suggesting that you send an older dog out alone and ignore it. We are advising that you familiarize your dog with situations away from home so that it does not become shy and unhappy when away from the security of the environment and things it is most accustomed to.

Remember your Lhasa Apso should be, according to the Standard, gay and assertive but chary of strangers. Therefore it may need a little more socializing than some of the other breeds. If your dog is like most others, it will learn to enjoy these outings. Its tail is a good barometer of its feelings—down when your dog is unhappy or afraid and up well over his back when happy and confident.

Showing your own Lhasa Apso can be fun and enjoyable if you keep it groomed properly and practice showing techniques so that you feel comfortable in the ring.

13

Special Care and Training of a Lhasa Apso

THE SUBJECT of care and training of dogs is so broad that a chapter in this breed book can only sketch instructions relating specifically to the Lhasa Apso and rely upon you to refer to other books that cover the subject in greater depth.

You probably bought or are considering buying a Lhasa Apso because you liked the way it looked or its personality and underlying character appealed to you.

These characteristics create the need for special care and training for your Lhasa Apso.

LIVING WITH A BORN SENTINEL

As you have read a number of times in this book, the Lhasa Apso was developed as a companion and warning sentinel. Hence it is friendly with those it knows but wary of unknown sights and sounds, and of strangers. That is not to say it is aggressive or bites. Simply that everything strange alerts the dog and you are kept informed by its barking and scurrying around.

If your Lhasa Apso has a tendency to be overzealous in sounding alarms, discipline is necessary. Decide which warnings are not valid and give it the voice command *no*. In the early stages of training you may need to enforce the voice command with a physical reprimand such as a gentle shake or a stamp of your foot to get its attention. Generally as your Lhasa Apso puppy develops its mature personality it will have better judgment as to what you need to be warned about.

THE COAT

Because your Lhasa Apso is a long-coated breed, it requires special care not required for many other breeds. In chapter 11 we have completely explained how to groom your Lhasa Apso; however, we have listed below some hints that will help to make that grooming easier.

1. Do not allow your dog to run in lawns covered with leaves, weed patches or tall grass, as its coat will become embedded with burrs, grass seed and dried leaves. If it runs into such an area the debris should be brushed out immediately so as not to cause irritation.

2. Do not allow the dog to run in the rain or snow. If it does be sure to immediately dry with a hair dryer, brushing at the same time to eliminate matting and tangling. If muddy, rinse the mud from its coat before drying.

3. Your Lhasa Apso's excessive rear coat can become soiled with fecal material, so check after its exercising periods.

Because your Lhasa Apso is not only comparatively small but also has heavy, long hair, it is usually not a good fighter even though the spirit is there. The dog is independent and will not back down from any dog, so protect it from the risk of injury by preventing your pet from fighting.

Keep your Lhasa Apso from swimming pools, fish ponds or horse troughs. Even though it may like the water its long coat will weigh it down and cause its stamina to be drained quickly. Unless it can walk out of the pool or is rescued at the first sign of weakness, the dog may drown.

Do take your dog driving with you as often as you can, but observe the weather so as not to submit it to extremes of temperature while left in the car. Always lock the car with the windows open, only far enough so that it cannot jump out, to allow ventilation in warm weather. Although the car is not burglar-proof with the windows open, the locked doors will deter an accidental opening of the doors that may allow your Lhasa Apso to jump out.

ON SMALL CHILDREN

Children find it very tempting to pull the hair of a Lhasa Apso, particularly the attractive topknots. If you have a small child, teach him or her early to respect every pet's rights. Teach the child to be gentle and loving and your dog will reciprocate.

VETERINARY CONCERNS

If your Lhasa Apso must be tranquilized or anesthetized, we suggest that you inform your veterinarian that some Lhasa Apsos have a tendency to react erratically to such treatment. The tendency is to react to the drug slowly and then not to regain conciousness as soon as they should. Also, repeated anesthesia is crucial as there may be retention within the body from one time to the next.

Do not worm your Lhasa Apso as a matter of routine. Worm it only when the veterinarian has made a diagnosis and determined that parasites exist. Frequent worming can cause a buildup of the drugs within the body, causing improper functioning of vital organs.

One final word regarding care. Keep you Lhasa Apso trim and muscular, *not overweight*. This will make it a healthier, happier animal and will allow it to use its structure properly.

14

The Lhasa Apso in Canada

THE DOMINION of Canada and the United States have always enjoyed a very close relationship in connection with Lhasa Apsos.

The first Lhasa Apsos registered with the American Kennel Club were the Canadian imports Tarzan of Kokonor and Empress of Kokonor, who were descendants of what were probably some of the breed's first imports into Canada. These were the dog Taikoo of Kokonor, whelped in China in 1930, and Dinkie, a bitch whelped in China in 1928. Both arrived in Canada in 1933.

Their owner, Miss Margaret Torrible, Victoria, British Columbia, bred Taikoo and Dinkie together to produce Chang Daw and Ching Ming, who when bred together produced Empress. A repeat litter of Taikoo and Dinkie produced Tarzan.

We do not have the necessary information to determine how much Miss Torrible's breeding program influenced the modern Canadian Lhasa Apso.

Although Lhasa Apsos were imported into Canada a few years before they came to the United States, the vastness of Canada tended to polarize the Canadian breeders. The breeders from the western provinces did not readily exchange stock with breeders from the eastern or central provinces and vice versa, but instead often found American breeders nearer to them from which to obtain and sometimes exchange stock.

The famous ABBOTSFORD line of Georgia and James Roberts was founded in British Columbia in 1954 when a puppy bitch was purchased from

Mrs. Ritchie. The puppy was to become Can. Ch. Ping and was by Am. Ch. Karandale Dakmar out of Can. Ch. Karandale Tangee.

The first Abbotsford-bred Lhasa Apsos were from Ping, who when bred to Ch. Ming Tali II, CD, produced Ch. San Yu Ti of Abbotsford. Ping was also bred to Can. Ch. Miradel's Que Tee and produced Ch. Jomo Dkar-Po of Abbotsford.

In the next twenty-seven years the Abbotsford breeding program became very successful, with the epitome of their expectations, according to Mrs. Roberts, being the multiple Best in Show-winning Can. & Am. Ch. Teako of Abbotsford. Teako's sire was the English-bred Brackenbury Kandron, and his dam was Kalula of Abbotsford. Teako was the first Lhasa Apso to win a Best in Show in Canada and went on to win seven during his career, as well as winning Best of Breed at the American Lhasa Apso Club's first western Specialty in 1969.

A Canadian Register of Merit kennel, the Abbotsford name appears in the pedigrees of many of the top Lhasa Apso kennels both in Canada and in the United States.

When Mrs. Roberts died in 1981, Bonnie Hubert, SHANKARA, of British Columbia, got Can. & Am. Ch. Dolpho of Abbotsford in whelp to Am. & Can. Ch. Suntory Affirmative Action. Mrs. Hubert kept the two bitches from this litter and they became Can. Ch. Krishankara of Abbotsford and Can. Ch. Mi Shankara La of Abbotsford. The brother was Am. Ch. Gyantse of Abbotsford.

According to Mrs. Hubert, this is the only litter in the history of Abbotsford that had another kennel name incorporated in the dog's name along with the Abbotsford suffix, because the Roberts did not believe in co-owning or co-breeding.

Mrs. Hubert perpetuated the line with this last Abbotsford litter. Both bitches were bred to Can. Ch. Glenmist Shankara Samsson (Can. & Am. Ch. Sa Mar of Abbotsford★ x Glenmist Persephone). Bred by Marlene Chisholm, Samsson was Sa Mar's last son. Mi Shankara La produced four champions with Samsson, and Krishankara produced two, one of which was Can. Ch. Shankara's Check Me Out, who when bred to BIS Can. & Am. Ch. Tru Blu's Stop The Press produced multiple Group-winning Can. & Am. Ch. Shankara's Tru Blu Quiet Riot and Can. Ch. Tru Blu Shankara Swizzle Stick.

Dr. Ellen Brown, BALRENE, who graduated from the University of Toronto in 1951 as a veterinarian, was given a Lhasa Apso in 1944, but it was not until 1962 that she became seriously interested in breeding and showing. Dr. Brown, from Ontario, obtained from Margaret Carroll-Vienot, CARROLL, one of Canada's earliest breeders and owner of a Canadian Register of Merit kennel, the male that became Can. Ch. Carroll Panda (Ramblersholt Ro-Pon x Can. Ch. Lotus Blossom of Abbotsford). Dr. Brown also bought a bitch, Can. Ch. Licos Yarto La (Am. Ch. Licos Chulung La ROM★ x Am. Ch. Licos Tangte La), who when bred to Panda produced among others Can. Ch. Balrene Red and the most well known, BIS Can. & Am. Ch. Balrene Chia Pao, the Best of Breed winner of the 1971 Eastern American Lhasa Apso Club Specialty.

Robyn McCarthy with Can. Am. Ch. Norbulingka Khyber and Sheila Hall with Can. Ch. Dorje's Dechin Beausous and Can. Ch. Balrene Vajradhara representing Lhasa Apso Canada in a costume parade in Montreal in 1987. *Paw Prints, Inc.*

Canadian BIS Am., Can. Ch. Teako of Abbotsford, a son of Brackenbury Kandron and Kalula of Abbotsford, was owned, bred and handled by Mrs. James Roberts of Canada. Teako's Canadian record is seven Bests in Show and 36 Group firsts, but according to Mrs. Roberts her biggest thrill was winning Best of Breed at the first Western ALAC Specialty in 1969.

Can. BIS Can. Am. Ch. SaMar of Abbotsford*, bred, owned and handled by Mrs. James Roberts, Abbotsford.

Hodges & Associates

Can. Ch. Glenmist Shankara Samsson, owned by Bonnie Hubert. *Bobbi*

Japanese and Canadian Ch. Shankara's Domino, bred by Mrs. Bonnie Hubert.

Other significant Balrene-bred Lhasa Apsos were Group-winning Can. Ch. Balrene Nicola (Dunklehaven Nicky x Kokonor's Kala) and Ch. Balrene Katmandu (Nicky x Balrene Mermaid, a Chia Pao daughter).

Dr. Brown also owned Can. Ch. Treepine Chumbi, who was sired by Nicky out of Can. Ch. Balrene Talli. Balrene is a Canadian Register of Merit kennel.

NONSUCH Lhasa Apsos of Quebec was started by Anne-Marie Adderley in 1968. Her foundation bitch was Can. & Am. Ch. Crestwood's Babycham (Carroll Ko Ko San x Simba d'Al Tiro), who when bred to Chia Pao produced Can. & Am. Ch. Nonsuch Amne Machin and Can. Ch. Nonsuch Ashanda Devi.

Additionally, Ms. Adderley acquired Group-winning Can. Ch. Yojimbo Renegade (Am. Ch. Dolsa Yojimbo ROM★ x Dolsa Black Magic), that when bred to Can. Ch. Nonsuch Katmandu produced Can. Ch. Nonsuch Lhotse Nag. When Lhotse Nag was bred to Can. Ch. Nonsuch Himalaya, she produced Can. Ch. Nonsuch Mokhimal Nag. Nonsuch is a Canadian ROM kennel.

Barbara Chevalier, LADY W Lhasa Apsos, of Quebec is a Canadian Register of Merit breeder. The foundation female for this kennel was Can. Ch. Lady W's Miss Sadie Woo (Chia Pao x Can. Ch. Yu Ching of Pitzu). Sadie was twice bred to Am. & Can. Ch. Potala Keke's Golden Gatsby ROM★ to produce Can. & Am. Ch. Lady W's Limehouse Blues, Can. Ch. Lady W's Ms Celia Blackwell, Can. Ch. Lady W's Riva Rose, Can. Ch. Lady W's Dear Mr. Gable, Can. & Am. Ch. Lady W's Becky Sharpe and Can. & Am. Ch. Lady W's Sunshine Gal.

Barbara Ratledge, LAS-A-RAB, from Alberta bought her first Lhasa Apsos in 1959 from Lui Gi kennels. Lui Gi's Cevap bred to Lui Gi's Lokum produced Al Tabu of Lhasarab, the sire of three Lui Gi champions.

Mrs. Ratledge bred the Lui Gi line until 1967 when she obtained Sumchen of Abbotsford (Brackenbury Kandron x Can. Ch. Panga of Abbotsford) from the Roberts and continued from this point to breed mostly the Abbotsford line. Sumchen was shown to multiple Best in Show wins. He and his daughter, Can. Ch. Las-A-Rab Pappa San, were the only two Lhasa Apsos to win a Best in Show out of both the Terrier Group and the Non-Sporting Group. Another Sumchen daughter, Ch. Las-A-Rab Tzena, won many Best Puppy in Show awards and many Groups. Las-A-Rab is a Canadian Register of Merit kennel.

George and Arlene Miller were living in what is now called Thunder Bay, Ontario, just fifty miles north of Minnesota, when they got a Lhasa Apso puppy for their family in 1969. She was named Kyi Nanga Punzee and was from the Carroll line, a blending of Ramblersholt from England, Glenns Pines from the United States and Abbotsford.

Punzee became a champion, earned a CD degree and was the foundation bitch for the Millers' DESIDERATA breeding program.

Punzee was bred to Mrs. Ratledge's Sumchen to produce the female Can. Ch. Desiderata Lochen Dzasa, CD. Dzasa was bred back to her sire to produce Can. Ch. Desiderata Dochen La, that when bred to BIS Can. & Am. Ch. Sa-Mar of Abbotsford★ produced Can. Ch. Desiderata Mata Hari.

Can. Am. Ch. Shankara's Tru Blu Quiet Riot, shown here with Bonnie Hubert, Shankara.

Canadian BIS Can. Am. Ch. Kyma of Abbotsford, bred by Mr. and Mrs. James Roberts and owned by Robert and Nancy Damberg. Pictured with Nancy Damberg, Kyma was a son of Sinbad of Abbotsford and Can. Am. Ch. Chuli of Abbotsford.

Shown winning Best of Breed at the 1984 Lhasa Apso Canada Specialty in Montreal under judge Robert Sharp is Can. Ch. Nonsuch Lhotse Nag, a daughter of Can. Ch. Yojimbo Renegade x Can. Ch. Nonsuch Katmandu. Pictured with owner-breeder, Ann-Marie Adderley.   *Purebred Photos.*

Dzasa was also bred to Las-A-Rab Shaba Gomba to produce Can. Ch. Desiderata Pingk Phloyd, and to Am. & Can. Ch. Potala Keke's Golden Gatsby ROM★ to produce Can. Ch. Desiderata Gung Ho.

Mata Hari was bred to Am. Ch. San Jo's Shindig ROM★ and produced Can. Ch. Desiderata Yum Yum and Can. Ch. Desiderata Yoko. Another Desiderata-bred Lhasa Apso of note is Can. Ch. Desiderata Karmann Ghia (Can. Ch. Desiderata Austin Sprite x Desiderata Sera), a granddaughter of Ch. San Jo's Soshome Up ROM★ and Ch. Hell's A Blazen Billy The Kid.

Yum Yum was bred to Can. Ch. Desiderata Lord Shenrab to produce Can. Ch. Rhambo. Lord Shenrab was also bred to Can. Ch. Desiderata Choma Lhari to produce Can. Ch. Desiderata Lady Deadlock. Desiderata is a Canadian ROM prefix.

The Millers moved to Montreal in 1973, where with common interests Mrs. Miller, Ms. Adderley and Mrs. Chevalier formed the Lhasa Apso Club of Quebec. Soon the club expanded, with Dr. Brown as an Honorary Member and several other Ontario exhibitors becoming associate members, as did Mrs. Ratledge of Alberta. Others followed from the Atlantic Provinces, British Columbia, Manitoba and the Northwest Territories, and by the mid 1970s the club became involved in updating the Canadian Lhasa Apso Standard, with Mrs. Ratledge as the Standard chairman.

When the Millers moved to British Columbia in 1977, Mrs. Miller was the president of the Quebec Club. The time seemed right to acknowledge the national character of this club, so the regional club evolved from the Lhasa Apso Club of Quebec to the national club Lhasa Apso Canada. Lhasa Apso Canada sponsors Register of Merit breeder awards, which are more difficult to earn than the American ROM because co-bred champions are not recognized for breeder ROM purposes.

TRU BLU, the kennel name for Neil and Hanni Graves of Alberta, was originated for Old English Sheepdogs, but became the name for Lhasa Apsos when the female Las-A-Rab Mai Lee came in 1974 and when another bitch, who became Can. Ch. Raja Ram Kumari, came in 1975. In 1976, the male that would become BIS Can. & Am. Ch. San Jo's Soshome ROM★ was added to the Tru Blu foundation. When Shome returned to the United States to acquire his American championship, the Graves entered into a co-ownership with the breeders of Am. Ch. San Jo's Raaga Looki Mei ROM★ and brought him to Canada where he was shown by the Graves to his championship and five BIS wins. Also in 1978, the first litter for Tru Blu out of Shome and Mai Lee produced seven males, among which were BIS Can. Am. & Ch. Tru Blu's Shome A Rerun, multiple Group-winning Can. Ch. Tru Blu's Shan Sou Te Chin and Puppy Group winner Ch. Tru Blu's Midnight Bandit.

Kumari was bred to Am. Ch. San Jo's Shenanigan, CD, ROM★★ to produce Can. Ch. Tru Blu's Sugar-N-Spice.

At the same time Looki Mei came to Canada, so did another foundation bitch that became Can. Ch. Hudai's Meiti Nijin (Looki Mei x Hudai Samsa Tequila, a full sister to Shome). Nijin was also bred to Shenanigan and produced BIS Can. & Am. Ch. Tru Blu's Hudai Easy Does It, Can. Ch. Tru Blu's Mr. Karalan and the only bitch in the litter, Can. Ch. Tru Blu's Hudai R and R. Next

Can. Am. Ch. Sumchen of Abbotsford ROM, bred by Mr. and Mrs. James Roberts, owned and handled by Barbara Ratledge, Las-A-Rab, was sired by Brackenbury Kandron out of Can. Ch. Panga of Abbotsford. Top Lhasa Apso in 1971 and 1974, and first to win BIS from two different Groups.

H. P. Spahr

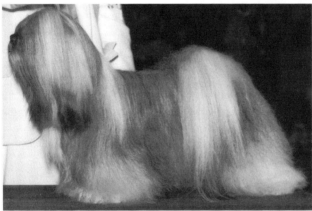

Can. Bda. BIS Can. Ch. Las-A-Rab Lhoka Mo Shun, bred by Barbara Ratledge, owned and handled by Shirley Clark. By Can. Am. BISS Can. Am. Ch. Potala Keke's Duke Wellington Can. ROM x Las-A-Rab Krishan. *Photo by Hodges*

Can. Ch. Desiderata Lochen Dzasa CD ROM was bred, owned and handled by Arlene Miller, Desiderata. This Sumchen of Abbotsford daughter is the only Lhasa Apso winner of both Eastern and Western Specialties in Canada. *Wibaut*

206

Nijin was bred to Shome and produced multiple Group-winning Can. Ch. Tru Blu's Dudly Do Rite and multiple Group-winning Can. Ch. Tru Blu's Hudai Tahna. Nijin was bred next to Zhantor the Contender, a Looki Mei son, to produce Can. Ch. Tru Blu's Ruckus at Jalco, and then to Ch. Gyantse of Abbotsford to produce BIS Can. & Am. Ch. Tru Blu Stop The Press. Tru Blu is a Canadian Register of Merit kennel.

Jan Cote, Manitoba, started JALCO Lhasa Apsos in 1976 when she purchased Exotica's Me-O-Tan, bred by Rick and Judy Weinholts, EXOTICA. Me-O-Tan was by Lyngso Sharbo Me-O-Tan of Tena out of Can. Ch. Lyngso Tshun-Tsu of Exotica. The second bitch, Toling's Takhara, was obtained shortly after Me-O-Tan. Both bitches trace back to American breeding and completed their Canadian championships owner-handled. Takara finished her American championship in 1979.

The next acquisition was the male that became BIS Can. & Am. Ch. Tru Blu's Shome A Rerun, that when bred to the BIS Can. & Am. Ch. Sharbo Top Guy daughter produced a litter of three champions, including Ch. Jalco's A Taste of Honey. When Honey was bred to Dudly Do Rite, she produced Group-winning Can. Ch. Jalco's Sneak Preview. Sneak Preview was bred to another Rerun daughter to produce the Group-winning bitch Can. Ch. Jalco's I'm Not Cute.

Honey's last litter, out of Can. Ch. Tru Blu's Hudai Tahna, produced another Group-winning bitch, Can. Ch. Jalco's Goody Two Shoes.

Bob and Sheila Pike of Ontario started ZARALINGA in the early 1970s when they purchased Can. Ch. Potala Ching Tu of Zaralinga (Am. Ch. Ruffway Marpa ROM★ x Am. Ch. Kinderland's Sang Po ROM★★) and Taglha Rana (BIS Ch. Chen Korum TI ROM★★ x Ch. Taglha Dum Cho). Bred together Ching and Rana produced Can. Ch. Tarah Shan of Zaralinga, Can. Braz. & Am. Ch. Zaralinga's Lord Raffles, Can. Ch. Zaralinga's Krissi Shan, Can. Ch. Zaralinga's How Sweet She Is, Can. Ch. Te-Di B'Ar of Zaralinga and Can. Ch. Zaralinga's Sugar Bear.

How Sweet She Is was bred to BIS Ch. Windsong's Gusto of Innsbrook ROM★★ and produced Can. Ch. Zaralinga's Wait 'N See, Can. Ch. Zaralinga's Sam The Man and Can. Ch. Zaralinga Just By Chance. A Canadian Register of Merit breeder, Zaralinga has been inactive since 1978.

TAHNA identifies the breeding program founded in Ontario in the early 1970s by Barbara Hamon-Sellwood with the acquisition of Won Ton of Zaralinga and Tarah Shan of Zaralinga. With the use of sires like Ch. Potala Keke's Tomba Tu ROM★ and Ch. Tabu's Fame and Fortune, Mrs. Hamon-Sellwood bred champions enough to qualify to be a Canadian Register of Merit breeder. Some Lhasa Apsos bred and/or owned by Mrs. Hamon-Sellwood are Can. Ch. Tahna's Tarbaby of Tebar, Tahna's Storm'n Norman, Tahna's Afternoon Delight, Tahna's Caroling Caroline, Can. Ch. Cookies N' Cream of Tahna and Can. Ch. Tru Blu's Hudai Tahna, to name only a few.

The IRLEES breeding program of Catherine Freedman-Groulx of Ontario started in the early 1970s when she purchased a female Lhasa Apso named Utsu Kushi Yuro primarily as a family dog. Kushi Yuro was sired by Balrene Bimbo

(Can. Ch. Carroll Panda x Can. Ch. Yarto La) out of MacDai Lady Kara (Balrene Hop To It x Can. Ch. Balrene Chan Keyrie).

The next purchase was the show prospect male Tahna's Wei Bham Boo (Am. Ch. Potala Keke's Tomba Tu ROM★ x Can. Ch. Tarah Shan of Zaralinga), who died before he finished his championship but not before he bred Kushi Yuro. From this litter of five, four finished as follows: Can. Ch. Irlees Song-Tsen Gam-Po, Can. Ch. Irlees Tara Ti Bet Si, Can. Ch. Irlees Nying-Ma-Pa and the female Mrs. Freedman-Groulx kept, Can. Ch. Irlees Princess Wen Chen.

Next, Mrs. Freedman-Groulx purchased the puppy bitch that became Am., Can. & Bda. Ch. Shangrelu Rainy Days O'Irlees (BIS Am. Ch. Potala Keke's Zintora x Am. Ch. Shangrelu Sneak Preview ROM★) and produced Can. Ch. Irlees Tremar By Golly By Gosh, Can. Ch. Irlees Hurricane Ja-Ma and Can. Ch. Irlees Heart of My Heart.

Princess Wen Chen produced Canadian champions Irlees Golden Dream for Karlan and Irlees Dream Cloud, CD, before she was stolen in 1979.

Irlee's foundation sire was Am., Can. & Bda. Ch. Ja Ma's Rennegade★ (Ch. Shyr Lyz Mieh Bah Bieh Tu x Ch. Lifelong Stolen Hours ROM★). Also acquired was the brood bitch Ocon Nyam Chem-Po (Ch. Chen Hy Lan Jampal x Teri Nam's Golden Chance), who produced Can. Ch. Irlees Llenroc Steppen Stone and Can. Ch. Irlees Felicity. Shangrelu Fan Dancer produced the male Can., & Am. Ch. Irlees Shangrelu Cajims Pride when bred to BIS Am., & Can. Ch. Arborhill's Rapso Dieh ROM★★.

When Cajims Black Nara for Irlees was bred to Rennegade, she produced Can. Ch. Irlees Golden Opportunity, the dam of four Irlee's champions sired by Can. & Am. Ch. MaLee's Finagle.

Ch. Cajim Irlees Mischievous produced very well for Irlees when bred to Rennegade. Irlees is a Canadian ROM kennel.

ASLAN is an Ontario-based, Canadian Register of Merit kennel and obtained its original stock from Mrs. Freedman-Groulx.

Mary and Alan Capko, TALSMA, of Ontario purchased their first Lhasa Apso from Audrey Carpenter, TREEPINE kennels, in 1974. She was Treepine Elsa (Dunklehaven Nicky x Balrene Cheri) and purchased primarily for a family companion.

When they decided to breed Elsa they went to Sheila Pike, who recommended Can. Ch. Zaralinga's Lord Raffles. A litter of eight resulted and included Can. Ch. Talsma's Oh-So-Sau-Ceih, Can. Ch. Talsma's Zaralinga's Shining Star, Can. Ch. Talsma's Sargent Pepper, Can. Ch. Talsma's W. C. Muggins and Can. Ch. Talsma's Kara Mia Myne.

Sau-Ceih was bred to Am. & Can. Ch. Sakya Hallelujah (Am. BIS Am. Ch. Windsong's Gusto of Innsbrook ROM★★ x Am. Ch. Sakya Tabriz) twice and produced among others the foundation sire Talsma's Eight Is Enough and the female Talsma's Chances R.

Elsa was also bred to Am. Ch. Sho Tru's Stardust Cowboy to produce Can. Ch. Talsma's Emprise, that when bred to Eight Is Enough produced Can. & Am. Ch. Talsma's E'Nuff Said.

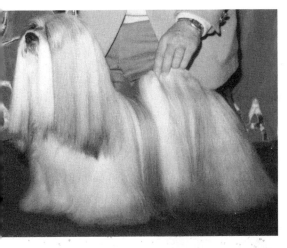

Can. BIS Can. Am. Ch. Tru Blu's Stop The Press, a Canadian ROM, owned by Neil and Johanna Graves, Tru Blu, was Best of Breed at the Fall 1988 Lhasa Apso Canada Specialty under judge Merlin Vandekinder. *Steven Ross*

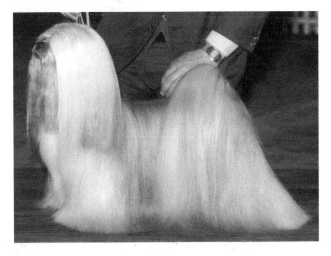

Can. BIS Can. Am. Ch. Tru Blu's Hudai Easy Does It, a Canadian ROM, owned by Neil and Hanni Graves, was the top Lhasa Apso in Canada in 1983, 1985 and 1986. *Hodges*

Am. Can. Ch. Bihar Bette Midler Potpourri, bred by Carol Strong, Bihar, and owned by Elsie Basler, Potpourri, and Mrs. Strong. *Kernan*

Two bitches, Orlane's Impact A'Talsma and Orlane's Fortunate Cookie, were acquired and both bred to E'Nuff Said to produce Talsma's Golden Tea Biskit out of Cookie and Can. Ch. Talsma Infinite Legend out of Impact.

Colin Williams's original foundation female for KIODISAN Lhasa Apsos, Can. Ch. Willie's Golden Gypsy, was whelped in December 1977, having finished her championship from the Puppy class.

Mr. Williams then obtained Can. Ch. Balrene Whiskey (Can. Ch. Balrene Hosfer x Kokonor's Kala). Also in 1978, the male that became Can. Ch. Tai Kai's King of Diamonds (Am. Ch. Tabu's King of Hearts ROM★★★ x Can. Ch. Mei Ling San From Aborah) was purchased from Elsa Lindhard.

Additional stock obtained was Can. Ch. Norbulingka's Natasha (Am. Ch. Lingkhor Bhu of Norbulingka ROM★ x Norbulingka Sangrelu); BIS Can., Am. & Bda. Ch. Krisna Hy Lan Krissi (Am. & Can. Ch. Chen Krisna Nor ROM★★ x Sen's Mop Toy); BIS Can. & Am. Ch. Excel's Ryan at Kiodisan (Am. Ch. Tra Mar's Tangleloft Cozmic Raz★ x Excel's Heidi Maya).

Krissi was bred to Whiskey to produce Can. & Am. Ch. Kiodisan's Appleseed Annie and Can. Ch. Kiodisan's Rowdyman. Krissi also was bred to Gypsy to produce Can. Ch. Kiodisan's Isn't He A Midget.

When Ryan was bred to Annie, they produced Can. Ch. Kiodisan's Q. L. Bailey.

Margaret Northey of Ontario founded VALLEYBROOK when she purchased the female that would become Can. Ch. Zaralinga's Sugar Bear. Her next acquisition was a male that would become Group-winning Can. Ch. Zaralinga Just By Chance. Ms. Northey's first litter was born in 1977 out of these two and produced Ch. Valleybrook Call Mee K-Tee and Ch. Valleybrook R. N. I. Sweet.

The next purchase for Valleybrook was the male Can. Ch. Irlees Llenroc Steppen Stone (Am. Ch. Jampo's I'm Steppen Out of Syung ROM★ x Ocon Nyam Chem-Po), that when bred to Sugar produced Can. Ch. Valleybrook Sweet Sucaryl, that is the dam of Best in Show Group Six Can. Ch. Valleybrook Jusa Minet.

Discouraged with her progress in 1987, Ms. Northey virtually started over with the acquisition of the puppy dog that became Can. Ch. Potpourri Reckless Revenge (Am. & Can. Ch. Orlane's Austin of Lorien x Am. & Can. Ch. Mastervilles Revenge Is Sweet). Ms. Northey leased Am. & Can. Ch. Bihar's Bette Midler Potpourri (BIS Am., Can. & Bda. Ch. Bihar's Revenger of Sammi Raja★ x Potpourri's Cun-Ba Bumo) and bred her to Reckless twice to produce Can. Ch. Valleybrook Ruthless Ambition.

The following is a list of the Top Lhasa Apsos in Canada
from 1962 when show data was first recorded to the present.

1962   Can. Ch. Prince Ping of Abbotsford—Roberts, Abbotsford
1963   Can. Ch. Tensing of Abbotsford—Justine Campbell, Justdean, Reg.

1964　Can. BIS Can. & Am. Ch. Teako of Abbotsford—Roberts, Abbotsford

1965　　　"　　　　　　"　　　　　　"　　　　　　"

1966　　　"　　　　　　"　　　　　　"　　　　　　"

1967　　　"　　　　　　"　　　　　　"　　　　　　"

1968　Can. BIS Can. & Am. Ch. Balrene Chia Pao—Brown, Balrene, Reg.

1969　Can. BIS Am. BIS Can. & Am. Ch. Orlane's Good As Gold—Dorothy Kendall, Orlane, USA

1970　Can. BIS Can. & Am. Ch. Balrene Chia Pao—2nd Top Dog in Canada All Breeds

1971　Can. BIS Can. & Am. Ch. Sumchen of Abbotsford—Ratledge, Las-A-Rab, Reg.

1972　Can. BIS Can. & Am. Ch. Kyma of Abbotsford—Robert and Nancy Damberg, Pawprints, USA

1973　Can. BIS Can. & Am. Ch. SaMar of Abbotsford—Roberts, Abbotsford

1974　Can. BIS Can. & Am. Ch. Sumchen of Abbotsford—Ratledge, Las-A-Rab, Reg.

1975　Can. Ch. Treepine Chumbi—Brown, Balrene

1976　Can. Ch. Tedi B'Ar of Zaralinga—Nancy Bruce, Tedi B'Ar

1977　Can. & Am. Ch. Potala Keke's Golden Gatsby—Chevalier, Lady W Reg.

1978　Can. BIS Can. & Am. Ch. San Jo's Raaga Looki Mei ROM★—Graves, Tru Blu & Nixon, San Jo USA

1979　Can. BIS Can. & Am. Ch. Tru Blu's Shome A Rerun—Cote, Jalco

1980　Can. BIS Can. & Am. Ch. San Jo's Soshome ROM★—Graves, Tru Blu

1981　　　"　　　　　　"　　　　　　"　　　　　　"

1982　Can. BIS Can. & Am. Ch. Tru Blu's Shome A Rerun—Cote, Jalco

1983　Can. BIS Can. & Am. Ch. Tru Blu's Hudai Easy Does It—Graves, Tru Blu

1984　Can. BIS Can. & Am. Ch. Suntory Affirmative Action—Graves, Tru Blu

1985　Can. BIS Can. & Am. Ch. Tru Blu's Hudai Easy Does It—Graves, Tru Blu

1986　　　"　　　　　　"　　　　　　"　　　　　　"

1987　Can. BIS Ch. Cookies N' Cream of Tahna—Hamon-Sellwood, Tahna

1988　　　"　　　　　　"　　　　　　"　　　　　　"

1989　Can. BIS Can. & Am. Ch. Tru Blu's Stop The Press—Graves, Tru Blu

The reciprocal visits to compete across the border have benefited both sides. The above list reveals such participation has stimulated the exchange of stock. Robert and Nancy Damberg, Pawprints, and Arleen Dartt, Ralda, are American breeders who have earned Canadian Register of Merit status.

Since the number of Canadian breeders and good Canadian dogs have increased so much, it was impossible to refer to as many as we would have liked. The best way to enjoy our neighboring breeders, dogs and shows is to attend some Canadian events.

Canadian shows usually are smaller than in the United States, but have a friendly atmosphere, often fostered by having two or three shows on successive days at the same location. These "clusters" were being held in Canada long before the American Kennel Club approved this practice.

Can. Ch. Zaralinga Just By Chance, bred by Sheila Pike and shown with his owner-handler Margaret Northey.

Can., Am. Ch. Lady W's Limehouse Blues shown with his breeder-owner, Barbara Chevalier. He was a son of Can. Am. Ch. Potala Keke's Golden Gatsby and Lady W's Miss Sadie Woo.

15

The Lhasa Apso in England

THE SMALL DOG we know today as the Lhasa Apso was known as early as the 1890s in England.

The Honorable Mrs. McLaren Morrison owned, bred and exhibited many of these early dogs and was an acknowledged authority on the Tibetan breeds in England.

Descriptions of the small dogs from central Asia by the canine authorities of the time and the Honorable Mrs. McLaren Morrison lead us to believe that there were several breed names for each of the dogs we know today as Lhasa Apsos, Tibetan Terriers, Tibetan Spaniels and Shih Tzu.

Names like Bhuteer Terrier, Bhutese Dogs, Lhassa Terrier, Lhasa Tibetan Terrier, Thibetan or Tibetan Terrier, Apso and the Tibetan or Chinese Lion Dogs have all been linked to the history of the Lhasa Apso.

The small Tibetan dogs were recognized as Lhasa Terriers in England and divided into ten-inch and fourteen-inch classes, with Challenge Certificates being offered from 1908. Two of the first champions are reputedly the males Ch. Rupso and Ch. Little Dargee.

Rupso was imported from Shigatse in 1907 and gained his third CC at the Ladies' Kennel Association, where he won in 1908. He also won at this show in 1909, 1910 and 1911. His height at the withers was just a fraction under ten inches.

From the Foreign Dogs column by A. Croxton Smith in the January 1913 English *Kennel Gazette*, "Champion Rupso, Mrs. Webster's Lhassa Terrier, was looking as well as ever, the last time I saw him, and the Honorable Mrs. McLaren Morrison still exhibits this variety as well as Thibet Spaniels.''

Rupso died in 1917 and his body is preserved in the dog section of the British Natural History Museum at Tring, Hertfordshire.

Little Dargee was bred by the Honorable Mrs. McLaren Morrison and registered with the Kennel Club in 1906. His sire was Terung and his dam, whelped in 1900, was Nariani. Nariani was sired by Mrs. Alan Francis's Bootles. Bootles, whelped in 1897, was out of Putima, that was also whelped in 1897. Putima's sire was Bhutan, registered in 1896 with an unknown pedigree, and her dam was also imported and recorded as unnamed.

Is the Bhutan in Little Dargee's pedigree the same Bhutan about which the Honorable Mrs. McLaren Morrison said, ''Bhutan, the terrier I imported from the Himalayas and the pioneer and only champion in the breed was a splendid dog, not only in appearance but in character''?

A memorial from the English *Kennel Gazette*, January 1899, Foreign Dogs column, written by W. R. H. Temple, ''Bhutan, the Bhutanese dog, known to his intimate friends as Boots, has also gone home. He was a quaint little chap, and said to be a perfect specimen of his breed.'' Is this the same Bhutan in the pedigree of Ch. Little Dargee that is claimed to be one of the first Lhasa Terrier champions?

By the end of World War I there were so few Lhasa Terriers they lost their right to be issued Challenge Certificates.

From the English *Kennel Gazette*, February 1923, in a column written by Robert Leighton about the 1923 Crufts dog show, he mentions that the Honorable Mrs. McLaren Morrison exhibited a team of Lhassa Terriers, all of them typical, in the Variety class for foreign dogs.

In 1928, Lieutenant Colonel and Mrs. Eric Bailey returned from service in Tibet with six small dogs from Tibet that were referred to as Apsos. In the English *Kennel Gazette*, April 1934, The Honorable Mrs. Eric Bailey states that, ''The word 'Apso' is the Tibetan name for any long-haired dog. It is a corruption of 'Rapso' which means 'goat-like.' ''

Another early theory concerning the ''Apso'' part of the breed's name is that it is a corruption of the Tibetan phrase ''Abso Seng Kye,'' which is interpreted to mean ''Bark Sentinel Dog.''

The April 11, 1970, New Delhi Tibetan judges' paper stated, ''The word 'Apso' means 'hairy one.' ''

Mr. Jigme Taring, noted Tibetan Lhasa Apso judge, states, ''Actually, Apso in Tibetan means shabby or fluffy mouth.''

From the 1934 *Kennel Gazette* article, Mrs. Bailey continues, ''Then, as regards colour, the commonest is black or iron grey, but the Tibetans prefer a golden or honey-coloured dog.'' Mrs. Bailey describes how she and her husband obtained their original stock. One of the prerequisites in their search for additional stock was the golden color of the first two, which had originally come from the Commander-in-Chief (Tsarong Shape). According to Mrs. Bailey, ''We tried very hard to get more dogs of the same kind. Similar dogs are easy to find, but

Brackenbury Lhotse owned by Miss Beryl Harding.

Eng. Ch. Brackenbury Chigi-Gyemo, bred and owned by Miss Beryl Harding.

From left to right: "Satru" (gold), "Chora" (silver), "Sonam" (gold) and "Targum" (red), circa 1934. These Apsos come directly from the dogs Mrs. Bailey brought back from Tibet. They were owned by the late Miss Marjorie Wild, Cotsvale. *Photo Courtesy of André Cuny*

215

Eng. Ch. Verles Tom-Tru bred and owned by Mr. and Mrs. F. J. Hesketh-Williams.

Eng. Ch. Brackenbury Gunga Din of Verles (left) was bred by Miss Beryl Harding and owned by Mr. and Mrs. F. J. Hesketh-Williams. His daughter Eng. Ch. Verles Keepa bred by the Hesketh-Williams, Verles Lhasas.

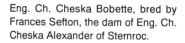

Eng. Ch. Cheska Bobette, bred by Frances Sefton, the dam of Eng. Ch. Cheska Alexander of Sternroc.

we were particular to get only the same type in all particulars, including especially colour." When the Baileys returned to England, they brought the gray-and-white dog Lhasa, because he was of the correct type and they could not find a golden male with both the required type and color to bring back.

The 1970 Tibetan judges' paper stated in regard to color, "White is considered best. . . . Next preferred is parti-coloured followed by all black. The other colours are golden, sandy, honey, dark grey, grizzle and brown. It would be wrong to say that Tibetans prefer golden colour above others."

It is the opinion of the authors that different regions in Tibet developed different colors and styles much like different kennels or areas today. We believe that the original standard preferred the golden colors because that was the color obtained by the Baileys and the Cuttings from the Tibetan hierarchy and was not the color of the Shih Tzus from which there was a desire to establish differences.

A Tibetan Breeds Association was formed in 1934, and the name Lhasa Terrier seems to have been eliminated, because the four breeds defined by the new organization were Tibetan Mastiffs, Lhasa Apsos, Tibetan Terriers and Tibetan Spaniels. The Standards for these breeds were published in November 1934, which helped eliminate the confusion between Tibetan Terriers and Lhasa Apsos, but because the Tibetan Lion Dogs from China had been accepted into the registry as Apsos there was still confusion. Although England quickly defined the Tibetan Lion Dogs as a separate breed and reregistered them as Shih Tzus, also in 1934, repercussions were felt more in other countries that did not acknowledge the definitions of breeds and the reregistrations simultaneously with England.

The breed in England continued to increase in numbers with the interest of breeders and exhibitors like Mrs. A. R. Greig; Mrs. A. C. Dudley; The Honorable Mrs. McLaren Morrison; Lt.-Col. J. Scott Cockburn and Miss B. Bingham; Mrs. E. M. Snow; Mr. H. J. Troughton; The Lady Freda Valentine; Mrs. M. K. Vernay and Miss M. Wild, who collectively exhibited twenty-six Lhasa Apsos in the 1937 Crufts show.

The future of the English Lhasa Apso seemed secure until World War II curtailed dog breeding, and their numbers were severely reduced. The only lines containing any of the early foundation dogs to survive were those of Mrs. Greig and Miss Wild. Miss Wild's dogs unfortunately died of disease in 1940, therefore the use of the Greig's Ladkok-Lamleh bloodlines by the Ramblersholt and Furzyhurst kennels are today's only remaining link to the original foundation dogs.

Because of their committment to the breed, fanciers such as Miss Marjorie Wild, Cotsvale; The Honorable Mrs. Eric Bailey; The Lady Freda Valentine; Miss Beryl Harding, Brackenbury; Mrs. Thelma Morgan; Mrs. Florence Dudman, Ramblersholt; Miss J. Hervey-Cecil, Furzyhurst; Mr. Desmonde Goode, Camvale; Mrs. Daphne Hesketh-Williams, Verles, as well as Mrs. Frances Sefton, Cheska, and Yvonne Mason, Coburg, before they relocated to Australia, built up the reduced numbers from the remaining stock supplemented by imports.

The name of the breed was changed in 1958 to Tibetan Apso.

An exceptional import was Jigmey Tharkay of Rungit, that was imported by Mrs. Jill Henderson. Mrs. Henderson was Secretary to the Himalayan Climbing Club at the time of the British Everest Expedition and brought Jigmey and a bitch back to England from Tibet in 1958. Jigmey was a very good, bright golden dog, very upstanding and fearless. According to Mrs. Thelma Morgan, these two were first registered as Shih Tzus, but when they were exhibited at the Ladies Kennel Club, fanciers from both breeds readily agreed that they were Apsos, and they were reregistered as such. Imported at a time when new blood was needed, Jigmey was very instrumental in improving the breed and has had a lasting effect on the breed in England. The bitch imported at the same time left no offspring. Unfortunately, the Hendersons left England after three years and Jigmey left with them.

Miss Beryl Harding, who obtained her first Lhasa Apso, Brackenbury Lhotse, in 1953, worked closely with Miss Wild, Cotsvale. Miss Harding reared and handled to championship status two Cotsvale Lhasa Apsos when the late Miss Wild was too old to do this for herself. Upon seeing Jigmey Tharkay of Rungit, Miss Harding immediately bred her best two brood bitches, Lhotse and her daughter, Brackenbury Min-nee, to him. Lhotse produced Eng. Ch. Brackenbury Chigi-Gyemo. Min-nee, produced the famous Eng. Ch. Brackenbury Gunga Din of Verles, who was born in December 1958 and died in May 1974.

Mrs. Daphne Hesketh-Williams of Verles chose her first Lhasa Apso, a present from her husband, at six weeks of age. This Lhasa Apso was Gunga Din. His owner describes him as being golden and white, very gay and fearless and full of fun and character. He was the first British postwar champion, gaining the first five Challenge Certificates (CCs) offered in 1965 after the breed had once again increased its numbers in order to have CCs issued. Mrs. Hesketh-Williams states that after retirement she brought him back for Crufts in 1967 where he again went Best of Breed, winning his sixth CC, after which she retired him for good. Thereafter he only appeared to lead the Champions Parade at the English Lhasa Apso Club Championship show each year until his death.

Gunga Din sired Eng. Ch. Pontac Adham Tarhib, Eng. Ch. Verles Yandup of Cheska, Eng. Ch. Cotsvale Brackenbury Kan-Ri, Eng. Ch. Verles Nying-Chem-Po, Eng. Ch. Verles Keepa, Eng. Ch. Sauchrie Mingmastering and Eng. Ch. Willowcroft Kala from Hardacre.

Eng. Ch. Verles Tom-Tru, a son of Mrs. Florence Dudman's Ramblersholt Rham and Verles Dhomtuck (a Gunga Din daughter), was the first English-bred Lhasa Apso to win Best in Show at a really large open show. That was the Sutton open show in 1967. Tom-Tru was born in December 1963, owned by Mrs. Hesketh-Williams and was retired after winning 10 CCs. He is the sire of the famous winning and excellent-producing dog Eng. Ch. Hardacre Hitchcock of Belazieth (whose dam was Eng. Ch. Tungwei of Coburg) and Eng. Ch. Hardacre Hedda.

The popularity of the breed in England continued as evidenced by Miss

The winners of the 1973 English Lhasa Apso Club Specialty judged by Monsieur André Cuny (center) are Tintavon Basieren (right), a son of Eng. Ch. Cheska Gregor and Tintavon Nyima of Showa, owned by Mrs. J. S. Luck, the Best in Show Winner and (left) Eng. Ch. Belazieth's Honey Amber, a daughter of Eng. Ch. Hardacre Hitchcock of Belazieth and Verles Jogmaya of Belazieth owned by Mr. and Mrs. R. G. Richardson, the Best of Opposite Sex winner.

Saluq Anna Purna Quapito and Saluq Quincy owned by Mrs. Valerie Stringer.

Harding's statement that, "In 1953, it was a record to get five Lhasa Apsos . . . as against 165 at our Apso show in March 1977."

In March 1969, the Lhasa Apso Club had ninety-one entries for its first open show. The judge was Monsieur André Clement-Cuny from France. The next September it held its first championship show. These two shows are now annual events in early spring and fall, respectively.

The name of the breed was changed from Tibetan Apso back to Lhasa Apso in 1970.

A milestone for the Lhasa Apso in intervariety competition came in October 1973 at the Ladies Kennel Association all-breeds show. There Eng. Ch. Cheska Alexander of Sternroc was the first Lhasa Apso ever to win Best in Show at an English all-breeds championship show. He was bred by his owner, Mrs. Frances Sefton, and co-owned and handled by Mrs. Pamela Cross-Stern, Sternroc. Alexander was born May 2, 1969 (Eng. Ch. Tayung of Coburg x Eng. Ch. Cheska Bobbette). He was the first Lhasa Apso to win Best in Group at Crufts and won a total of thirty-six CCs. As proof of his ability to produce, Alexander is the sire of the second Lhasa Apso to win Best in Show at an all-breeds championship show. This was Ch. Piplaurie Isa Silvergilt of Hardacre and the first bitch to win this title, which was in 1976. Alexander is also the sire of Ch. Clarween Rosella, the 1977 Crufts Best of Breed winner who won her tenth CC in a breed entry of seventy-nine.

About thirty Lhasa Apsos have been imported since 1969, most of them from the United States. It is the opinion of Mrs. Valerie Stringer, Saluq, that the most influential of these imports were Licos Ting La of Cheska (Am. Ch. Licos Omorfo La ROM★ x Dama's Lu Country Fair ROM★★), owned by Mrs. Frances Sefton; Saluq Annapurna Quapito (Ch. Oracles Du Chomalari x Annapurna Oxy) and Saluq Shaggy Wonder Ulan (Rohilla Sonam x Polka De Hamerhouck), owned by Mrs. Stringer; Am. & Can. Ch. Hardacre Kinderlands Bhu-Sun (Am. Ch. Larrmar De-Tsen ROM★ x Bogoda Belle of Kamachi), owned by Mrs. Anne Matthews, and English BIS and American BIS Eng. & Am. Ch. Orlane's Intrepid ROM★★ (Am. BIS Am. Ch. Windsongs Gusto of Innsbrook ROM★★ x Am. Ch. Orlane's Brandywyne★), owned by Mrs. Jean Blyth and a dog that also made a reputation in America.

A list of champions shows Intrepid the sire of at least eight English champions, among which is the top winning bitch BIS Ch. Saxonsprings Fresno, whose dam is Ch. Hardacre Not So Dusty of Saxonsprings (Hardacre Pied Piper x Ricmara Premeno). Fresno was bred by Mrs. Blyth and owned by Mr. Geoff Corish. She is the winner of eight Best in Show awards, fifteen Groups and forty-seven CCs. Fresno's grandsire is the imported Bhu-Sun and she is the dam of two champions, Danish and Int. Ch. Saxonsprings Flier and Eng. & Am. Ch. Saxonsprings Fun 'N' Games, both sired by Eng. Ch. Saxonsprings Hackensack (Intrepid x Saxonsprings Lady-B-Good).

Three kennels dominated the show scene in the last decade, either through their own homebred champions or by having bred or imported the sires or dams of champions owned or bred by others. These were Belazieth, Mr. and Mrs. R.

Mrs. Jean Blyth, Saxonsprings, pictured with her Lhasa Apsos on Ilkey Moor in West Yorkshire, England. *Photo by Anne Roslin-Williams and submitted by Dorothy Kendall*

Eng. BIS Eng. Ch.Saxonsprings Fresno, owned and handled by Geoff Corish and bred by Mrs. Jean Blyth, Saxonsprings. *Photo by Anne Roslin-Williams and submitted by Dorothy Kendall*

Best in Show at the World Show and Best of Breed at the 1983 Westminster Kennel show was Eng. Am. Dutch Ger. Belg. Ch. Saxonsprings Alamo ROM*. Alamo was bred by Mrs. Jean Blyth, Saxonsprings, and owned by Dorothy Kendall, Orlane. *Gilbert*

G. Richardson; Hardacre, Mrs. Anne Matthews and Saxonsprings, Mrs. Jean Blyth.

Some influential champions of the last decade were BIS Eng. & Can. Ch. Belazieth's Malcolm (Hitchcock x Freth Diane) and his son, BIS Ch. Belazieth's Salt-N-Pepper, out of Hardacre Gloria of Belazieth. Salt-N-Pepper, who died in December 1988, is the sire of Eng. Ch. Belazieth's Charlie Farley out of Eng. Ch. Belazieth's Honey Amber (Hitchcock x Verles Jogmaya of Belazieth); Eng. Ch. Brackenbury Kangra out of Eng. Ch. Saraya of Brackenbury (Eng. Ch. Wyrley Hermes x Brackenbury Sam Sara); Eng. Ch. Chobrang Le-Shi out of Hardacre Mother's Pride; Eng. Chs. Dewell Ali, Dewell Anouska of Belazieth, Dewell Bacarat, Dewell Chilli Pepper and Eng., Am. & Can. Ch. Dewell Tracy Belle ROM★, all out of Larkwood Anthea; Ch. Nedlik Pick-A-Pepper of Belazieth out of Nedlik Cassie and Ch. Nichann Nying Chang Po out of Belazieth's Sweet Marie of Nying.

Another champion of note was Eng. Ch. Saxonsprings Zako (Morgan of Saxonsprings x Saxonsprings Dze-Tu), the sire of Eng. Ch. Hardacre Peregrine out of Jemecs Satin Sash; Ch. Pantulf Clarrisa out of Nangso Gretel; Ch. Saxonsprings Bright Rod out of Orlane's Lightline O'Lamplite; Eng. Ch. Saxonsprings Buccaneer out of Saxonsprings Clovis and Eng. Ch. Saxonsprings Periwinkle out of Eng. Ch. Saxonsprings Chussekhan (Hardacre Pied Piper x Eng. Ch. Anakapelli of Saxonsprings).

Today the breed seems to be on firm footing, with the continued interest of those breeders and many others less famous that we have not mentioned although their importance has not been overlooked.

According to Mrs. Stringer, the Lhasa Apso Club's championship show usually attracted about 200 entries. Lhasa Apso entries at other championship shows (about twenty-four a year) are about 150 to 180, and Lhasa Apsos regularly go Best in Show at the open shows.

Mention of Crufts calls for an explanation of that annual attraction for dog enthusiasts. The show dates from a meeting in the 1870s between James Spratt, who was about to enter the dog biscuit business and Charles Cruft, who became his traveling salesman. After promoting the dog section at the 1878 Paris Exhibition and managing a number of shows for others, Cruft hired the Royal Agricultural Hall in London in 1891 and staged his own dog show. Under Cruft's management, the show snowballed in size and popularity, and when he died in 1938, the English Kennel Club took it over and has continued to run it.

That annual institution attracts thousands of spectators from all parts of the world, lasts four days and has an entry of over 20,000. A dog must qualify for entry by winning in specified classes at championship shows held during the previous year.

Making an English Champion requires the winning of three Challenge Certificates under three different judges. To win a CC a dog must be chosen best of its sex (equivalent to Winners class including champions at an American show) at a show where CCs are awarded. The number of CCs awarded per year are determined by the number of the breed being registered with the English Kennel Club per year.

After surmounting the tremendous hardships of having to reestablish the breed twice, it appears that the Lhasa Apso is on solid ground in England. This is due to the perseverance of the pioneer breeders and the more recent fanciers who are continuing to build on this now well-established foundation.

Eng. Ch. Cheska Alexander of Sternroc bred and owned by Frances Sefton and co-owned and handled by Pamela Cross-Stern.

Shown in center is Eng. Aus. Ch. Cheska Jesta (nine-and-a-half years) with her owner and breeder, Frances Sefton, and flanked by her two sons—on the left Aus. Ch. Cheska Archee and on the right is his younger brother Group winner Aus. Ch. Cheska Mister Ed.

Eng. Aus. Ch. Cheska Jesta, bred and owned by Frances Sefton is a daughter of Eng. Ch. Verles Yangdup of Cheska and Little Star of Cheska. She is pictured at ten-and-a-half years of age.

16

The Lhasa Apso in Australia and New Zealand

AUSTRALIA

The first Lhasa Apsos in the Australian show ring were the three that Mrs. Joan Beard, SOEMIRAH, imported from England in 1961. All from Mrs. Florence Dudman, Ramblersholt, they were a dog, Ramblersholt Trag Pon (Ramblersholt Chumba x Kikuli of Furzyhurst); a puppy bitch, Ramblersholt Dzom Tru (Chumba x Ramblersholt Metok) and a proven matron, Ramblersholt Da-Norbu (Gay Time of Lamleh x Brackenbury Nuptse). A dog, Ramblersholt Sing Gi, and brother to Trag Pon from a different litter was imported the next year. All four became Australian champions, Norbu being the first breed champion in Australia. The breed was first shown in the Toy Group, but later transferred to the Non-Sporting Group.

One of the first litters born in Australia was in 1962 when Trag Pon sired a litter out of Dzom Tru of three males and one female. The bitch, later Aus. & N. Z. Ch. Soemirah Pon Dzara, was bred to Aus. Ch. Soemirah Dzong Gi (Sing Gi x Dzom Tru) and sold in whelp to New Zealand.

The Asian Breeds Club was formed in 1967 and Lhasa Apsos were one of the breeds that received useful promotion through lectures and club shows.

In 1968, Mr. John Filmer Mason and his wife, Yvonne, COBERG, moved to Australia from England. They took with them a puppy bitch, Ngangpo of

Coburg, sired by Eng. Ch. Verles Tom Tru; a most influential producing bitch, Jordonian Droma, and her son sired by Brackenbury Kyi that became Aus. Ch. Tsangpo of Coburg and was the litter brother to Eng. Ch. Tungwei of Coburg, and Eng. Ch. Tayung of Coburg. The English Coburg kennel name was changed to TASAM in Australia. Tsangpo sired some useful stock, including Aus. Ch. Mangalam Tensing out of Soemirah Soroya (Trag-Pon x Da-Norbu). Tensing was bred back to his granddam, Droma, and produced Aust. Ch. Tasam Ten Tru Tao, the top winning Lhasa Apso in the late 1960s and early 1970s. Owned by Mrs. A. R. Day of Melbourne, Tao was the first Lhasa Apso to win a championship Best in Show at a semi-Specialty show, the Asian Breeds Club, having done so six times, a record that still stands.

Mrs. Ann Michaelis, SINGTUK, of New South Wales, imported Aus. Ch. Ramblersholt Sonam shortly before the two-year import ban that lasted from 1969 through 1971. In 1973, Mrs. Michaelis and her daughter, Angee, imported the dog that became Aus. Ch. Belazieth's Cream Cracker and the bitch that became Aus. Ch. Balazieth's Birdsong. Additionally, the Michaelises imported from England the dog that became Aus. Ch. Hardacre Morning Shine and from New Zealand the bitch Sengkyi Angel.

In 1970, Derek and Frances Sefton moved to New South Wales from England. Mrs. Sefton is the author of the small handbook *The Lhasa Apso*, first published in 1970. One of the first comprehensive writings on the breed, this handbook had tremendous impact upon the breed in every country where it became available.

The output of Mrs. Sefton's CHESKA kennel showed she could put her threories into successful practice. Having been a prominent competitor on the English show scene, the Cheska breeding program continued successfully in Australia.

Eng. Ch. Cheska Jesta, winner of ten CCs in England and runner-up in show at the first English Lhasa Apso Club Specialty in 1969, was exported to Australia in whelp to her half brother, Eng. Ch. Cheska Gregor (Eng. Ch. Verles Yangdup of Cheska x Cheska Ting Agnes) to join her owner in 1971. In December of that year, she whelped a litter in the Sydney Quarantine station.

Jesta, sired by Yangdup (Gunga Din x Brackenbury Kalu of Verles) out of Little Star of Cheska (Gunga Din x D'Ang of Windmere), went into the Australian show ring late in 1972 and won her championship in six shows. She was the first Lhasa Apso in Australia to win Best Exhibit in Show all-breeds. She won four Best Exhibits in Group and then at six years of age was Best of Opposite Sex at the Sydney Royal show in 1973 in an all-breeds entry of 4,283 dogs. She then retired.

Jesta was the dam of four Australian champions from two litters. Her son, sired by Gregor, Aus. Ch. Cheska Archee, was the top winning Lhasa Apso in the late 1970s, winning innumerable Groups and Bests in Show all-breeds, Best of Opposite Sex at the Adelaide Royal show in 1975, Best in Show at the Sydney Spring Fair in 1978 over an entry of 4,000 plus, and he won the Lhasa Apso Club Specialty show three times. Jesta's other champion son was Cheska Mister

Aus. BIS Aus. Ch. Hardacre Salad Days, bred by Anne Matthews. Hardacre was imported from England to Australia by Sue Wilson-Mackenzie, Granton, NSW.

Aus. BIS Aus. Ch. Amesen Sun Star, bred and owned by Jennie Longmire, Amesen, was six times Best of Breed at the Australian Lhasa Apso Club Specialty. This dog was also a major winner in all-breeds competition to nine years of age.

Ed, sired by another half brother, the 1971 English Import Aus. Ch. Rufus of Cheska (Saluq Annapurna Quapito x Little Star). Mister Ed, also a successful showman, won five all-breed Bests in Show and the Lhasa Apso Club Specialty show three times.

The Sefton connection to England resulted in the importation of Aus. Ch. Cheska Yangsun, Aus. Ch. Rufus of Cheska, Aus. Ch. Showa Dynamatic, Aus. Ch. Sternroc Eisenhower and, imported with Peter Warby, Brackenbury Tong of Cheska. The Seftons also imported, in addition to Jesta, the bitch Cheska Ting Blazey.

Mrs. Jenny Longmire, AMESEN, of New South Wales, owned the bitch Aus. Ch. Waldenstein Yira Ka Tru, that was the first Lhasa Apso to win a Group in Australia. Mrs. Longmire also imported the bitch Aus. Ch. Ramblersholt Ral Loo from England and the dog Aus. Ch. Surabaya Raj Marco Polo from New Zealand.

Dynamatic was sired by Saluq Shaggy Wonder Ulan out of Eng. Ch. Cheska Bobbette. Handled and co-owned by Jennie Longmire, Dynamatic won four Bests in Show all-breeds and one Best in Show at the Asian Breeds Club. Dynamatic was a notable producer as well with eighteen champion offspring to his credit, among which was his daughter, Aus. Ch. Amesen Opal Moon, bred and owned by Mrs. Longmire. Opal was a record producer of eleven champions.

Miss Diane Lemaire of Victoria imported from France the Aus. Ch. Io Kai de la Franche Pierre and later imported from the United States the dog Zangstag of Everglo and the bitch Everglo Orange Blossom.

Sue Wilson-Mackenzie, GRANTON, from New South Wales, imported the bitch BIS Aus. Ch. Hardacre Salad Days and the dog Hardacre Fezzywig from England and later the three American imports, bitches Everglo Mayflower and Everglo Pocahontas along with the dog Aus. Ch. Everglo Carol of California.

Rod and Ronnie Bennetts, BOVAIS, of South Australia, imported English-bred Aus. Ch. Jonters Jered in 1976, a dog that won three Bests in Show all-breeds. In the mid-1980s, the Bennetts successfully showed the dog Aus. Ch. Shaya the Avenger, that was bred by Shirley Hansen from Victoria. Mrs. Hansen imported the English dogs from which Avenger descended. These imports were the dogs Aus. Ch. Saxonsprings Beaver and Hardacre Isa Sensation at Piplaurie and the bitches Saxonsprings Kitting and Himwarri Charity of Hardacre. Beaver, Avenger's sire, was also a Best in Show winner and was Best in Group at the Sydney Royal.

Mrs. Sheila Warwick, SHELAURIE, moved from England to Western Australia in 1978 and with her came the dog Hardacre Pied Piper and the bitches Belazieth's Sa Tru, Aus. Ch. Shelaurie Paradise Lost and Shelaurie Lucy Locket.

Aus. Ch. Deanfield Geronimo at Saxonsprings was imported from England by Arnold Townson into North Queensland, where he became a Best in Show winner.

Also from England came a dog, Saxonsprings Flashback, and a bitch, Saxonsprings Flair, both out of Hackensack and Fresno, along with another bitch, Saxonsprings Peni Pitstop. Flair was imported by Louise Christie, New

Aus. BIS Aus. Ch. Hale Alii Bit of Gusto Am. ROM*, bred by Valiene Weathers-Heckart, Hale Alii, an American Group winner imported by Pat Davis, Udelwar, NSW, Australia.

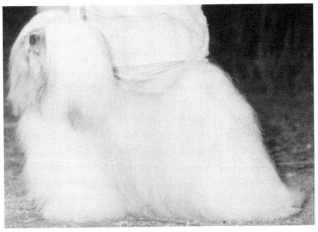

Aus. BIS Aus. N. Z. Am. Ch. Hale Alii G Watta Grouch, bred by Valiene Weathers-Heckart, Hale Alii, and owned by Pat Davis.

Aus. BIS Aus. Ch. Amesen Time Traveller, bred by Jennie Longmire, Amesen, and co-owned by Mrs. Longmire and Mrs. L. Mitchell, won the Australian Lhasa Apso Club Specialty five times.

South Wales, and Flashback and Peni were imported by Eddie and Helen Gillette, New South Wales. All three became champions, and Flashback won the Group at Sydney Royal and he and Flair won the Challenges there for three years.

The most dramatic American influence was in the late 1980s via stock from the Hale Alii kennels imported by Mrs. Pat Davis, UDELEWAR, New South Wales. The black-and-white dog Hale Alii Bit of Gusto had a successful show career, easily gaining his Australian title, but his greatest influence was as a sire. When he was bred to a variety of strong Australian bitch lines, the combination produced several BIS champions, including the dog Aus. Ch. Amesen Time Traveller, that won the Lhasa Apso Club Specialty five times, including under overseas breeder judges.

Mrs. Davis also imported a son of Gusto, Australian BIS Aus., N. Z. & Am. Ch. Hale Alii G Watta Grouch, that was a top winner in the breed, having won over thirty Best in Show all-breeds awards.

Another dog with some American breeding, although from England, was Aus. Ch. Parlu Champers. Imported by Old English Sheepdog breeders Ian and Ann Berry, RIMPOCHE, of Victoria, he was used successfully first in Victoria and then in Queensland.

Many of these imports were top show winners and produced top show winners. Many others produced progeny with qualities that contributed to the continual improvement of the breed in Australia.

The Lhasa Apso Club, which was formed in 1975, held its first championship show in 1976. From 1976 to 1990, winners of the Specialty were equally divided between males and females. The winning males were the gray Aus. Ch. Cheska Archee, that won three times; the gold Aus. Ch. Cheska Mister Ed, that was also a three-time winner; the black Aus. Ch. Amesen Time Traveller, that won five times; the gray Aus. Ch. Ladakh Marmaduke and the gold American import Aus. Ch. Hale Alii G Watta Grouch, each having won once. The winning bitches were the brindle Aus. Ch. Udelewar Tongi Kia, the black English import Aus. Ch. Hardacre Salad Days and the black-and-white English import Aus. Ch. Nedlik Peppers Pick, each a two-time winner; the silver Aus. Ch. Udelewar Moka Kara, a one-time winner, and the grizzle Aus. Ch. Amesen Sun Star, that won six times.

Australia is isolated by distance and quarantine regulations from the international dog world and the inevitable is that line and family breeding have established a genetically strong breeding base. New blood from time to time is essential and has been imported at great expense. The imports, mainly from England and America, have been successfully blended in by Australian breeders to produce a remarkably consistent population of Lhasa Apsos without extremes.

NEW ZEALAND

Both the North and South Islands of New Zealand have seen a slow but steady increase in the number of Lhasa Apsos since 1963, when Miss Jean

Marlow, SURABAYA, a Poodle breeder, imported Aus. Ch. Lelo Tehran and Aus. Ch. Lelo Ting a Ling from Australia. Next, Miss Marlow imported from Australia two bitches, the Aus. Ch. Soemirah Pon Dzara in whelp to Soemirah Dzong Gi and the English import Aus. Ch. Ramblersholt Dzom Tru, along with the dog English import Aus. & N. Z. Ch. Ramblersholt Trag Pon, all previously owned by Joan Beard. Miss Marlow imported in 1971 from Mrs. Florence Dudman in England the dogs Ramblersholt Ranadzong (Saluq Annapurna Quapito x Ramblersholt Rin Poo) and Ramblersholt Dzons (Ramblersholt Tih Tsong x Ramblersholt Da Ab Tru). Sadly, a previous import, Ramblersholt Rama La, never arrived, as the dog was lost overboard during the six-week sea voyage to New Zealand; importing by air was not allowed at that time.

Another Poodle breeder, Iris Wilson, MONTELLE, imported one of the next two males to arrive from England, both having been bred by Anne Matthews, Hardacre. BIS N. Z. Ch. Hardacre How's That, a parti-color, sired by Eng. Ch. Verles Tom Tru out of Eng. Ch. Tungwei of Coburg, became an influential sire, as did N. Z. Ch. Hardacre Holdfast of Fortstones, also a parti-color. Owned by Mrs. Elizabeth Luck, FORTSTONES, Holdfast was sired by Hardacre Pied Piper out of Eng. Ch. Hardacre Hedda and was the first Lhasa Apso in New Zealand to win Best in Show at a championship show. Holdfast was the sire of eight champions.

Ms. Wilson imported Singtuk breeding from Australia to establish the bitch foundation for her breeding program, while Mrs. Luck imported N. Z. Ch. Halley's Min-Kum of Fortstones (Eng. Ch. Hardacre Hitchcock of Belazieth x Ricmara Kalahari of Halley's) from England. Min-Kum, a bitch, was bred especially for Mrs. Luck by her mother.

The next import was the dog N. Z. Ch. Belazieth's Marksman (Bangers-N-Mash from Belazieth x Belazieth's Gay Glad), with a line back to BIS Am. Ch. Everglo Spark of Gold ROM★★★★ and owned by Dave and Fran Hill, ROMIEREZ. He won Reserve Non-Sporting Group at the NZKC national show in 1981, as well as having made other major wins. The Hills returned to the Richardsons' Belazieth kennels in England for the bitch N. Z. Ch. Belazieth Cheeky Girl (Eng. Ch. Belazieth's Malcolm x Eng. Ch. Belazieth's Saucy) and the dog Eng. Ch. Belazieth's Tom Thum (Eng. Ch. Nedlik Pick A Pepper of Belazieth x Belazieth's Shine On).

Margaret Walker, SHENGA LA, owned the English import N. Z. Ch. Hardacre Dandy Lion (Hardacre Kassis Kid x Hardacre Shady Lady).

Several other early breeders that came into the breed from an Old English Sheepdog background were Margaret Youngman, DAVYHULME, Dave and Pam Woodhous, EAST ANGLA, and Sue Fielder, WAIOTAPU, who all showed regularly to promote interest in the breed.

Richard Schmitzerle, CANRITH, used Fortstones stock to produce N. Z. Ch. Canrith Jo Kang and N. Z. & Aus. Ch. Canrith Stop Makin' Sense, both Specialty and Group winners.

Wanda Kent, NORBU KURI, imported N. Z. Ch. Halley's Squiff, a bitch that won many top awards. Her litter brother, N. Z. Ch. Halley's Squirrel of

Triple Grand N. Z. Ch. Halley's Quip of Fortstones is the top winning Lhasa Apso in New Zealand. She was imported and owned by Elizabeth Luck, Fortstones, from South Canterbury, New Zealand.

Diane Pearce

N. Z. BIS Ch. Gorvic Cotton Chops, bred and owned by Gordon Paterson and Vicky Lee.

Multiple BIS Ch. Misti's Play It Again Sam ROM**, shown winning Best of Breed at the 1989 National Capital Area Lhasa Apso Club Specialty under the Australian breeder-judge, Frances Sefton, Cheska. Sam is handled by his breeder and owner, Beverly Drake, Misti Acres. The trophy presenter is Edmund Sledzik, President of NCALAC.

Fortstones, has also had a strong influence as a sire. Although Squiff and Squirrel were sired by the international champion Saxonsprings Alamo, Elizabeth Luck's Saxonsprings Quango (Intrepid x Ducal Demelza) was New Zealand's first Saxonsprings import.

Beginning her career with a Best Puppy in Show, the top winning Lhasa Apso to date is Mrs. Luck's English-imported bitch Triple Grand N. Z. Ch. Halley's Quip of Fortstones (Hardacre Pied Piper x Ricmara Kalahari of Halleys). The title "Grand Champion" is awarded when fifty challenges and three BIS awards have been won under three different judges. Quip has won nine all-breed Bests in Show, one Non-Sporting and six Reserve Bests in Show as well as many other Group and in Show wins.

The ILLANA kennel of Bill Stanley used as its main sires N. Z. & Aus. Ch. Amesen Gold Joker (Cheska Nicodemus x Aus. Ch. Amesen Opal Moon) and N. Z. Ch. Illana Winning Toss (N. Z. Ch. Hardacres How's That x N. Z. Ch. Illana Dandyspark). In the late 1980s, Mr. Stanley imported his first English dog, N. Z. Ch. Deelayne Ruff Diamond, a combination of Belazieth and Hardacre, plus Orlane, Kinderland and Annapurna.

The kennel of Margaret Herlihy, EURIDYCE, originally a breeder of Shetland Sheepdogs, along with her colleague Arnold Townson in Queensland, Australia, has combined the available native lines with the Saxonspring imports to Australia and New Zealand, including Aus. & N. Z. Ch. Deanfield Geronimo at Saxonsprings (Alamo x Saxonsprings Bayberry of Bearstakes), N. Z. Ch. Saxonsprings Clotmilde (Sealaw Sneak Preview at Saxonsprings x Saxonsprings Good As Gold) and N. Z. Ch. Saxonsprings Shine On (Hickory of Saxonsprings x Saxonsprings Lady Be Good), as well as the Australian import Arlani Country Kricket (Aus. Ch. Brackenbury Saxa x Aus. Ch. Cheska Pritikit).

The BAO SHI kennels of Christine Mune, with an interest in color breeding, had among others the Australian import Aus. Ch. Arlani Everbody's Talkin', sired by Aus. Ch. Hale Alii Bit of Gusto out of Aus. Ch. Arlani Ain't I Sumthin. Sumthin, campaigned by Margaret Herlihy, and a successful winner in both Australia and New Zealand, is a combination of Cheska and Orlane bloodlines.

Newer breeding programs that are expected to make positive impressions on New Zealand Lhasa Apsos are AMAHL of Christine Burt and GORVIC of Gordon Patterson and Vicky Lee.

In a very strong Non-Sporting Group, where the Lhasa Apso competes with twenty-eight other breeds, the breed has consistently been considered for, or awarded, Group and in Show awards over the past twenty years.

Foundation bitch of Dr. F. P. Clement's de Gandamak
Kennel is Jo Wa de l'Annapurna bred by Miss V. Dupont.

Int. Ch. French Ch. Vivien de Cambales, bred by Mme. Courroux, Cambales, is believed to
be the only French-bred French champion in the last decade. He is a cross of Saxonsprings
and Dolsa. His owner is Mlle Liard. *Compliments of André Cuny*

17

The Lhasa Apso in Continental Europe

FRANCE

France was one of the first countries to recognize and perpetuate the Lhasa Apso in Europe. Monsieur André Cuny, a well-known breeder, provided the following story of the origin of Lhasa Apsos in France:

In 1949, Mademoiselle Dupont was traveling in Flanders. Quite by accident while strolling through the town square in Lille she was taken aback, quite literally, by a rare specimen of dog with long hair, a Lhasa Apso. Following a hasty inquiry as to the origin of this sparky little dog she learned that he was there 'thanks to the English.'. . .

In effect, she learned that two English subjects succeeded in bringing from India, by boat, two Lhasa Apsos. Faced with the possibility of paying, themselves, the "quarantine charges" the Englishmen were forced to relinquish the dogs to some people living in Antwerp, Belgium. So it was then, in Antwerp, that a young lady, not recognizing nor appreciating the value of her gift, promptly handed him over to a pet shop owner in Lille for resale. And Mademoiselle Dupont made her way to that shop.

So that the breed might continue and, more importantly *multiply*, Mademoiselle Dupont was pressed to find a "foundation bitch" who could carry on her shoulders the entire future of the Lhasa Apso in France. After a tremendous volume of correspondence with the United States, Mademoiselle Dupont succeeded in obtaining a female from Mrs. Cutting.

This female carried the registration number "one" in the *Livre des Origines*

Francaises (French Kennel Club registration book of purebred dogs and bitches) for Lhasa Apsos. This bitch was named Hamilton Kangmar, her origins were prestigious—a daughter of Ch. Hamilton Tatsienlu★. She was the queen of the ring at dog shows and soon became champion of both France and Switzerland and International champion. Her greatest glory rested on her many descendants, notably the marvelous champion Fo de l'Annapurna, who was a fantastic and prolific stud for the ANNAPURNA kennel and others.

Mlle. Violette Dupont died in 1984.

The first kennel to produce champions after Mlle. Dupont's Annapurna was DE GANDAMAK, the kennel of the late Dr. F. P. Clement and André Cuny. The foundation bitch Jo Wa de l'Annapurna, a Fo daughter, produced in two litters three famous females. Mani de Gandamak was an International champion and the top winning European Lhasa Apso of that time. Dr. Clement also imported from the United States Int. Ch. Licos Djesi La, a superb sire. Mr. Cuny is retired from breeding but continues to be active in the breed as an international judge.

Madam Tikhobrazoff, DE BODH GAYA, became the owner of both Fr. Ch. Noctuelle de Gandamak and Int. Ch. Mumtaz de Gandamak, Mani's sisters. Mumtaz bred to Djesi La produced Fr. & Int. Ch. Padme de Bodh Gaya and Int. World Ch. Po Yang de Bodh Gaya. All the de Bodh Gaya Lhasa Apsos came from this line.

Another breeder of these years was Mrs. Simone Chauvin-Daroux, DE LA NERTO. A foundation sire bred by Mr. Lajunie and owned by this kennel was Int. & Fr. Ch. Sinbad de la Nanda Devi. A more recent product of this kennel is Fr. Ch. Majao de la Nerto, bred and owned by Mrs. Chauvin-Daroux.

About the French show scene during the last ten years, Mr. Cuny has this to say:

> If you look at the French show results you can see that all the big events were won by Lhasas coming principally from Holland. The only real breeder to continue to work hard is Mrs. Corroux (kennel DE CAMBALES). In fact, she is the only one to have produced in Ch. Vivien de Cambales a French champion since a decade. . . . He is linebred on Ch. Dolsa Marlo Matador.

A dog or bitch needs four National Certificates (CAC) under three different judges to become a French champion, but because the Paris show is a championship event, one French champion is made in each breed and sex each year. Similarily, a dog or bitch requires four International Certificates (CACIB) under three different judges with a full year between the first and last certificate in order to become an International champion.

BELGIUM

Belgium was one of the first countries in continental Europe to have Lhasa Apsos. Mrs. Mewis Van Der Ryck's kennel prefix, SHAGGY WONDER, was well known because her early acquisition of the breed made her a popular source for foundation stock by other European breeders.

We know very little about the origin of this kennel but after pedigree study it appears that the foundation for this kennel was the English Brackenbury line, the American Hamilton line through Americal and the Swiss Rohilla (Americal and Annapurna) line. In 1965, Mrs. Van Der Ryck imported from America Orlane's Golden Puppet, the dog that, already an American champion, became a champion in Austria, France, Holland, Germany and won the title of West German Bundessieger.

By combining these foundation lines Mrs. Van Der Ryck produced numerous important Shaggy Wonder dogs.

SWITZERLAND

Mrs. Stoeklin-Pobe's Swiss kennel prefix, ROHILLA, can be found behind many successful European Lhasa Apsos. The basis for the Rohilla breeding program appears to be American through the use of Americal's Tiki and French through the Annapurna line. Rohilla and Shaggy Wonder were somewhat contemporary, although Rohilla was not so prolific.

SWEDEN

Lhasa Apsos are firmly established in Sweden, although not a numerically large breed. They have a band of enthusiastic followers and the breed holds its own in the Group.

The breed first came to Sweden in 1965 when Mrs. Marianne Baurne, KRYSANT, imported from England the dog that became Swed. Ch. Dryhill Tansi and in 1966 the bitch that became Int. Ch. Brackenbury Lhamo. She later imported a Lhasa Apso from the Shaggy Wonder kennel in Belgium and Montsweag Chumulary Chumbi, a bitch, from America. Other imports to Sweden were Swed. Ch. Brackenbury Yama, Nord. Ch. Hamista Yu-Lin, Nord. Ch. Cheska Ting Anthony, Eng. & Nord. Ch. Namista Yarsi and Nord. Ch. Camvale Jason, all arriving in 1968 and 1969.

Although Lhasa Apsos were a comparatively new breed, three had won the Group by 1972. One was Mrs. Gunilla Anderson's Nord. Ch. Namista Yu-Lin. The other two represented one of the influential early Swedish breeders, Mrs. Greta Lindevall, TING E LING. They were Swed. Ch. Ting E Ling's Geisha and Swed. Ch. Ting E Ling's Bagatelle. Mrs. Lindevall imported and owned the American-bred dog Int. & Nord. Ch. Sharbo Ka-Zur Khan (BIS Am. Ch. Sharbo Zijuh Zer Khan ROM★ x Am. Ch. Everglo Flair ROM★), that when bred to Krysant Chen Dremna produced Ting E Ling's Alladin.

Swedish dogs have National, Nordic and International championships available to them. A National championship requires three CCs won after a dog

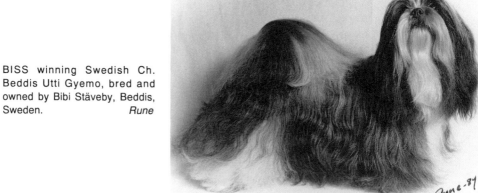

BISS winning Swedish Ch. Beddis Utti Gyemo, bred and owned by Bibi Stäveby, Beddis, Sweden. *Rune*

Eng. Ch. Int. Nord. Ch. Right On Cue From Viento, a top winner in both Sweden and Norway.

Multiple BIS BISS Int. Nord. Ch. Tintavon Sa-Skya, the top winner in Sweden. *Photo by Foto Pax*

becomes eight months old. A Nordic championship requires a CC after that age from each of the countries Finland, Norway and Sweden. Requirements for an International championship are given in the section on Lhasa Apsos in France.

In 1976, the American import Int. Nord. Ch. Dolsa Tsamten Tu (Am. Ch. Zijuh Don-Na Tsamten ROM★ x Am. Ch. Dolsa Vita de Maru) was the first Lhasa Apso to win Best in Show in Sweden, which he did twice in one year.

Only a few of the older breeders are still active. Tintavon and Beddis have been breeding over twenty years.

TINTAVON was originated in 1969 in England by Paul Stanton and Terry Young with the aquisition of the foundation bitch Tintavon Nyima of Showa (Eng. Ch. Tayung of Coburg x Chi-Ri of Cacique) and the dog Eng. Ch. Cheska Gregor (Eng. Ch. Verles Yangdup of Cheska x Cheska Ting Agnes).

Imported from England, the top winner in the history of the breed in Sweden was the bitch Int. & Nord. Ch. Tintavon Sa-Skya. She was sired by Gregor out of Eng. Ch. Wicherty Thea of Tintavon (Camvale Tomu Singtuk x Ramos Sephone) and bred by Paul Stanton. Owned by Marina Reutersward, Sa-Skya was the winner of six all-breed Best in Show awards and was the number one Lhasa Apso from 1976 to 1979. Ms. Reutersward also imported the Group-winning Int. & Nord. Ch. Tintavon Burundai (Gregor x Nyima). Mr. Stanton moved Tintavon to Sweden in 1976 and handled Sa-Skya and Burundai to their many prestigious wins. Two other Lhasa Apsos have won Swedish all-breed BIS awards and were both owned by Mr. Stanton and Torbjorn Skaar, Tintavon. They were the German import German Youth, Int. & Nord. Ch. Traschi Deleg Kunga and English import Int., Eng. & Nord. Ch. Ffrith Smoke Signal (Eng. Ch. Sternroc Jaunty Hoagey x Dynamic Dinah). Kunga is also a Best in Show winner in Norway, a multiple Group winner in Finland and the dam of at least seven champions. Smoke Signal, bred by Glenys Dolpin, was the number one Lhasa Apso in 1988 and is a multiple Group winner. Another important import owned by the Tintavon kennel is English import Int., Eng. & Nord. Ch. Right On Cue From Viento (Hurricane Higgins of Viento x Nellow's Cream). Bred by Mr. J. J. B. and Mrs. S. M. Wadham, Right On Cue is a multiple Group winner in Sweden and Norway and was the number one Lhasa Apso in 1986 and 1987 in Sweden. Tintavon has produced more than thirty Scandinavian champions, including thirteen Group winners that have been bred and/or owned by them.

The BEDDIS kennel is owned by Bibi and Tove Staveby and is well known for black-and-white parti-colors. The Stavebys established their breeding program with the early imports but in recent years have linebred on Eng. & Am. Ch. Orlane's Intrepid and have also imported a male from Orlane.

The kennels OF AKERFJALLEN, owned by Harrine Damasdi-Cederholm, KAMIRAS, owned by Marianne Nordell, and SATRUS, owned by Halldis Jidebrink, are three of the older successful kennels that continue on a smaller scale.

Some of the more successful breeders in recent years are Jane Wallstrom, INPERIES (Tintavon and Beddis); Isobell Boman, DREAMBRIDGE (Tintavon and Tabu); Rona Wanne, WARONA (Beddis and Nichann); Jean Persson, KRA-

KULLEN (Tintavon and Ting E Ling); Inger Wikstrom, NITROS (Tintavon), and Britt Nyman, MITELLAS.

The Swedish Standard is similar to the original English and current American Standard. Lhasa Apsos compete in the Toy Group, which consists of twenty-six breeds and is essentially a combination of the American Non-Sporting and Toy Groups.

FINLAND

The breed has been in Finland for many years but it is only recently that the breed has gained in popularity.

Anna-Liisa Passio, MILLAN, is the oldest breeder and has done the most for the breed. She still breeds but no longer shows. The kennel name Millan is very well known in Finland, having produced numerous champions. Most other breeders obtained their foundation stock from Millan.

Kirsi Paunio, LHAMOIN, and Eila Junnolala, SHABANOUN, have both imported several Lhasa Apsos from Tintavon in Sweden. Tintavon Thalia and Tintavon Tamarisk are multiple Group winners. The combination of Tintavon with Millan has proved to be a successful start for these two kennels.

Eva Resko imported from the Norwegian kennel Tanacs the top winning Tanacs Dancing in the Dark and has also imported from the American kennel Orlane.

Since rabies came to Finland in 1988, the boundaries have been closed to dogs from Norway and Sweden, which has also put a stop to the loaning of stud dogs. Before 1988, it was popular to travel across the border to shows. Only time will tell how this restriction will affect the breed in Finland.

HOLLAND

In 1966, Mrs. Annie Schneider-Louter imported the first Lhasa Apsos to Holland. A male Shaggy Wonder Orrin came from Belgium, and females Pilt-down Droma and Verles Nang Wa both came from England and were from the English lines Brackenbury and Verles. Nang Wa became a champion as well as the Bundessieger, Winter 1969, and was the first Lhasa Apso to win Best of all Tibetan breeds in Frankfurt, Germany, in June of 1969.

Probably one of the most significant importations made by Mrs. Schneider-Louter for her WARWINCKEL kennel was the American-bred dog that became Int. Ch. Dolsa Marlo Matador (Am. Ch. Zijuh Don Na Tsamten ROM★ x Cameo's Densa Dobra). Although Matador was a very successful show dog, being the first Lhasa Apso to win BIS in the Netherlands, it is as a producer that he left his mark. A dog of the seventies, Matador's influence is still seen,

Finnish Ch. Tintavon Tamarisk was bred in Sweden and is owned by Finnish breeder, Eila Junnola, Shabanon.

Holland Ch. Misty Mistery Des Coquins (Ch. Kai La Sha Tom Tru x Ch. Cessna des Coquins).

Holland Ch. Chakpori's Demion (Ch. Shaggy Wonder Dede x Chakpori's Fame).

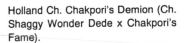

not only in Holland but in many of the dogs in other European countries as well.

The next significant imports by the Warwinckel kennel were that of Am. & Eng. Ch. Saxonsprings Alamo and in 1988 the American BIS dog Am., Can. & Mex. Ch. Marlo Rocky Road, a dog that has also been very successful in the European show ring.

The RAMATSCHE kennel of Mrs. Busser was the second Lhasa Apso kennel in Holland. Mrs. Busser's first imports also came from Shaggy Wonder in Belgium but were different from the Warwinckel imports because the Ramatsche imports were based on the United States Americal line and the French Annapurna line through the Rohilla bloodlines that were also used by Shaggy Wonder. The Ramatsche Lhasa Apsos were more elegant than many others to that time in Holland and can be found behind many of the current champions. The last Ramatsche litter was born in 1982.

In the beginning, there was a division of bloodlines, with one group of breeders using the Warwinckel line. Two of these breeders were de Kleine Oosterling and, still actively breeding, Ebbink's Hoeve.

The other group perpetuated the Shaggy Wonder–Ramatsche line. One such breeder was Mrs. Knulst-van Wel, SWANANDA, who bred Int. Ch. Swananda Do' Rhe Chambra (Int. Ch. Ramatsche Crheza Khan x Ramatsche B'Dorpa-San) that was twice World Champion. This kennel is still breeding albeit sparingly.

Mrs. de Wijs established the CHAKPORI kennel with Shaggy Wonder and Ramatsche lines. She bred Int. Ch. Chakpori's Dots (Int. Ch. Shaggy Wonder Dede x Ramatsche E'Rdo-Rje Milarepa) and Int. Ch. Chakpori's Kira (Int. Ch. Ramatsche E'Rdo-Rje Panschen-Lama x Milarepa). Kira was the 1983 Top Dog All Breeds in Holland. Mrs. de Wijs also imported from England Eng. & Int. Ch. Saxonsprings Cascade and Int. Ch. Saxonsprings Pasadena, both sired by Intrepid, and from the United States Int. Ch. Orlane's Windflower and Am. & Int. Ch. Juell's Lord of the Rings.

Mrs. G. M. I. van Tintelen-Zylmans, DES COQUINS, based her breeding program on Ramatsche, English and German imports that go back to the American lines Licos, Americal and Everglo. Especially important to this program was the German import Int. Ch. Traschi Deleg Seng-Tru (Tsarong x Amrita), and to perpetuate these lines Int. Ch. Kai La Sha Tom Tru (Am. Ch. Ja Ma's Infra Red x Am. Ch. Kai La Sha's Kha Char) was imported from America. Tom Tru not only was an excellent sire for the des Coquins kennel but left his mark on the European Lhasa Apso in general. Int. Ch. Misty Mistery des Coquins, the top winning Lhasa Apso in 1987, was sired by Tom Tru. Misty's dam was Int. Ch. Cessna des Coquins (Int. Ch. Hardacre Last Word x Ramatsche Rdo-Rje La-Yana). Cessna was out of Mrs. van Tintelen-Zylmans's first litter and was the first des Coquins champion.

Although the breeders are few in Holland, the quality Lhasa Apso produced in this small country is recognized throughout Europe.

1982 Danish Dog of the Year Int. Dk. Ch. Nang-Wa Rai.

Jorgen Bak Rasmussen

1984 #1 Danish Lhasa Apso Int. Dk. Ch. BDSG To Ken Ja's Bonnie shown here at ten years of age. Bonnie was owned by Karen Olesen, Fu-Kao.

1986 Danish Dog of the Year Int. Dk. Ch. El Gunga Din's Anjin Sama.

243

DENMARK

In 1968, the two-year-old male that became Int. & Nord. Ch. Shaggy Wonder Pongyi (Am. Ch. Orlane's Golden Puppet x Pedon) was imported. He was followed the next year by a bitch, Shaggy Wonder Ssi Ssi (Americal's Kyi Rong x Petty v.d. Lancelot). The first Lhasa Apsos in Denmark, they came from the Shaggy Wonder kennel of Mrs. Mewis Van Der Ryck in Belgium.

Ssi Ssi bred to Pongyi produced the dog Int., Dk. & Cs. Ch. Jolly Bear's Ching and the bitch Jolly Bear's Bittewitt, that can be found in the background of most Danish Lhasa Apsos.

Two present-day breeding programs originated with full siblings to Bittewitt. They are the EL GUNGA DIN kennel of Lis Davidsen and the NANG-WA kennel of Britta Kristensen. Anne Lise Wolf, TO KEN JA, got a daughter of Bittewitt as her first Lhasa Apso in 1972.

Early in the 1970s, the Lhasa Apso breeders, along with the Tibetan Spaniel and Tibetan Terrier breeders, formed the Tibetan Club, which published a magazine and arranged shows. The shows were small because the quarantine regulations limited outside entries to the other Scandinavian countries, and in turn Danish breeders could only show their dogs in Sweden, Norway and Finland.

In 1975, because rabies was found in Denmark, the rabies border was moved to between Denmark and Sweden, opening up the opportunity for Danish breeders to exhibit in Germany, Holland, France and other European countries. The freedom from restrictive quarantine regulations encouraged importation beyond Scandinavia. Pe Don v.d. Warwinckel, Rag Pa v.d. Warwinckel and Adam v.d. Warwinckel, all bred by Annie Schneider-Louter and out of the Dolsa Marlo Matador line, were imported from Holland. From the United States came Dolsa Black Sabbath, Yojimbo Tomboi, Am. Ch. On Stage Jenny Lee (Am. Ch. Donicia's Chim Zu El Torro x Am. Ch. Tabu's Firebird ROM★), Int. Ch. Kyilee Cash and Carry (Am. Ch. Tabu's Very Short Tale x Kyilee Repeat Rendezvous), Everglo California Puppy and Everglo Red Wednesday. Also imported during this increase of popularity were the English-bred Belazieth Miss Clare, Belazieth Rose and Hardacre Patience.

Some Danish breeders who established their programs with these imports were Jytte and Bent Klitgaard, KLITGAARD; Birgit Madsen, THORII; Lis Hansen, TIBERIA, and Asta and Jorgen Hinlov, BAN-ZAI, and who all, except the Hinlovs, are still actively breeding.

In 1977, the Lhasa Apso breeders seceded from the Tibetan Club and formed the Lhasa Apso Club.

The first fourteen years were developmental, and in 1982 the breed received national recognition with the Top Dog All Breeds in Denmark being the Lhasa Apso Dk. & Int. Ch. Nang-Wa Rai (Chin-Wun x Belazieth's Rose). Rai, bred by Britta Kristensen and owned by Lis Davidsen, was also the top Lhasa Apso in 1982. Through his sire, Chin Wun, Rai's pedigree can be traced back to the first Lhasa Apsos to come to Denmark.

Also in 1982, Am. & Eng. Ch. Saxonsprings Alamo (Intrepid x Saxonsprings Coula), a visitor in Holland, came to Denmark and won Best in Show at the Show of Winners, giving him the title Winner of Winners. For the Lhasa Apso to win the two most desirable titles in Denmark for all breeds certainly is a credit to the Danish breeders.

In 1983, number one Lhasa Apso was Dk. Ch. Chenga, owned by Jyette and Bent Klitgaard, and the next year the top spot was held by Dk. D, VDH & Int. Ch. To Ken Ja's Bonnie, owned by Karen Olesen, FU-KAO. The 1986 top Lhasa Apso was Int. & Dk. Ch. El Gunga Din's Anjin Sama, owned and bred by Lis Davidsen.

The increased popularity drew new breeders. One who has been very successful is Tove Staunskjaer, PALOMINO, who imported as a puppy Dk & Int. Ch. Saxonsprings Famous Flier (Eng. Ch. Saxonsprings Hackensack x Eng. Ch. Saxonsprings Fresno) from England in 1983. Flier was the Top Lhasa Apso and Top Dog All Breeds in 1985 and 1987 and won the title Winner of Winners in 1986. Staunskjaer also owned the 1988 number one Lhasa Apso Dk. & Int. Ch. Wanda v.d. Warwinckel, sired by Alamo as is Dk. & Int. Ch. Adam v.d. Warwinckel, the sire of the 1986 winner Anjin Sama.

The 1989 top Lhasa Apso was Dk. & Int. Ch. Palominos Criss Cross, bred by Tove Staunskjaer and owned by Hanne Beer.

Another successful modern Danish kennel is SCHEEL, the prefix for Kresten and Birte Scheel, who have imported several Lhasa Apsos from the American kennel Orlane. A combination of Intrepid and Inimitable, these imports are Orlane's Peppermint Pattie, Irresistible, Impetuous and Intimate.

Other American Lhasa Apsos that have influenced the Danish breeding program are Dolsa Kai Teba T'Bisquit; Dolsa Diplomat; Lysis Story Book Ending (Am. Ch. Tabu's Cover Story ROM★ x Am. Ch. Lysis Touch of Class); Kai La Sha Indian Summer; Am. Int. Ch. Kai La Sha Honest Injun and Am. Ch. Suntory Superfudge.

Additionally, German imports Ja Ma Jigme Traschi Deleg, Traschi Deleg Tsonga and Traschi Deleg Ani and Holland imports Migou de Coquin, Excuse Me de Coquin and Chakpori's Mahatma have been positive influences on the breeding programs for which they were imported.

In a comparatively short time the Danish breeders have experienced successful results from their breeding programs. Danish Lhasa Apsos are known all over Europe for their high quality.

THE FEDERAL REPUBLIC OF GERMANY

In 1965, Dr. Mary Tauber, VOM POTALA, an all-Tibetan breeds authority, imported the bitch Krysant's Lendzema from Sweden and the dog Verles Norbu from England. She bred Norbu to another English import, Ting Ambrosia of Cheska, a Licos Ting La daughter. This mating produced Ting-La v. Boliba, the first German-bred Lhasa Apso to earn the title German Bundessieger, which was in 1972. Ting-La v. Boliba became Dr. Tauber's foundation sire and pro-

BISS Ger. Ch. VDH-Ch. Bundessieger
Traschi Deleg Sang-Mo.

German, Dutch BIS Ch. Traschi Deleg Seng-Tru, bred by
Gerti Bracksieck and owned by J. van Tintelen.

Dom Melskens

Ger. Ch. Ta Ma Shing v. Potala, bred by Dr. Mary Tauber, Vom
Potala, with her daughter, Ger. Ch. Cashila v. Kalung, bred by Gitta
Haberle, Von Kalung.

duced the bitch Dschomo v. Potala when bred to Lendzema. Dschomo was bred back to her father to produce Tschiri v. Potala, to Int. Ch. Dolsa Marlo Matador to produce the European winner Nal-Du v. Potala and to Int. & Ger. Ch. Pag-Mo v.d. Warwinckel, a Matador son, to produce Ger. Ch. Tamashing v. Potala. Tamashing was still competitive at age thirteen having won Best of Breeds in 1988. Dr. Tauber died in 1979 but will always be present in the hearts of those who were fortunate enough to know her and who still follow her ideals.

In 1969, Gerti Bracksieck, TRASCHI DELEG, acquired her first Lhasa Apso, a black Krysant's Lendzema daughter that was sired by an imported regis-tered male that was brought to Germany from a Tibetan refugee camp in Nepal. The next acquisition was the inbred bitch Tschiri vom Potala, followed by the Holland import that became Int. & Ger. Ch. Pag-Mo v.d. Warwinckel, the foun-dation sire for Traschi Deleg. Pag-Mo was the first Lhasa Apso to win an all-breed Best in Show in Germany. A successful show dog, Pag-Mo also sired twelve champions, including Germ. Ch. Traschi Deleg Gyalpo out of Tschiri, multiple BIS Int. Ch. Traschi Deleg Kunga out of Germ. Ch. Lha Gje Lo Amrita, and bred to the American import Everglo Dolma, he produced among others Ger. Ch. Traschi Deleg Tschonga and Multiple Ch. Traschi Deleg Tarka-La.

Mrs. Bracksieck imported the American-bred bitch that became Ger. BIS Ch. Dolsa Red Alert by Dolsa Tsin Ah Mhun (Am. Ch. Zijuh Don-Na Tsamten ROM★ x Cordova Sin-Sa ROM★★★★) out of Am. Ch. Chamdo's Tsering Dolma (Am. Ch. Chamdo's Sir Lancelot x Americal's Moma). Red Alert, when bred to Pag-Mo, produced a bigger, more elegant style Lhasa Apso than the German breeders had been accustomed to. From this combination came Ger. Ch. Traschi Deleg Tsarong, a successful show dog in Germany and owned by the Ciciors.

Mrs. Bracksieck made her first import from the American breeder Dr. Catherine Marley, Kai La Sha, when she acquired the bitch Kai La Sha Pema-La (Am. Ch. Everglo Eager Beaver x Am. Ch. Kai La Sha Dolma★).

Tsarong was bred to Ger. Ch. Lha Gje Lo Amrita (Gyalpo x Pema-La) to produce Ger. & Dutch BIS Ch. Traschi Deleg Seng-Tru and BISS Ger. Ch. Traschi Deleg Sang-Mo. He ws also bred to Amrita's sister Aranja, and produced Ger. Ch. Lha Gje Lo Karma for Ingrid Krenner, LHA GJE LO, a breeding and showing kennel. Ms. Krenner obtained Pema-La and was successful for several years by combining the Traschi Deleg line with the American Kai La Sha line. This kennel is no longer actively breeding.

The American-bred Ger. Ch. Ja Ma's Dschigme Traschi Deleg (Am. & Can. Ch. Kai La Sha Rahula x Mor Knoll K K Puka Puka) was imported from Janet Whitman, Ja Ma, and contributed type and deep colors to his offspring.

On one of her visits to Germany, Dr. Marley brought Kai La Sha Tom Tru (Am. Ch. Ja Ma's Infra Red x Am. Ch. Kai La Sha Kha-Char) to Mrs. Brack-sieck, and when he was bred to the superb producing bitch Amrita, produced five puppies; four are being shown and three already have titles from the Junior classes. In 1989, the American-bred Am. & Can. Ch. Sharil Joymarc Patent Pending spent a three-month vacation in Germany and produced two promising litters, one with Amrita and one with the Amrita daughter Bundesjugendsieger 1989 Traschi Deleg Guliang.

Elisabeth Deger, PADME MANI, was a well-known breeder in the mid-1980s, having started with a Pag Mo daughter. She later imported the American-bred dog that became Ger. Ch. Chen Kris-Tim Nor (Am. Ch. Chen Krisna Nor ROM★★ x Krisna Chen Ti Nor), that was bred to Lha Gje Lo Chi Wi to produce Padme Mani Atrung. Padme Mani is no longer active.

OF JO FYA KANG, the kennel prefix used by Mrs. Wienekamp for both Lhasa Apsos and Tibetan Spaniels, was best known for concentrating on linebreeding on Pag Mo. This kennel's most successful show dog was Nat. Ch. Nat. Ygd. Ch. Europajgds. 79 Bjgds. 79 Bhabu Of Jo Gya Kang.

Gitta Haberle's VON KALUNG kennel started with the bitch that became Ger. Ch. Ta Ma Shing v. Potala (Pag Mo x Dschomo), that when bred back to her father produced Ger. Ch. Cashila v. Kalung. The Von Kalung kennel contributed to the Lhasa Apso scene with the many imports brought to Germany from various countries. Several were from England, but Ms. Haberle is best known for the American imports Ger. Ch. Marlo White On White (Am. Ch. Suntory Four On The Floor x Am. Ch. Marlo One Of A Kind); Am. Ch. Marlo Dolsa Jazzercise (Am. Ch. Jampo's 'Tis Himself x Brimfield Dolsa Marlo Parfait); Ger. Ch. Kai La Sha Sherab (Am. Ch. Everglo Eager Beaver x Everglo Sunkist Miss) and Kai La Sha It's My Turn (Kai La Sha Sailor of Llenroc x Kai La Sha Willow The Wisp). Although Ms. Haberle is no longer active, because of the use of these imports by her Von Kalung kennel and other breeders she has strongly affected the Lhasa Apso in Germany.

Marion Tusch, SHELKAGARI, developed her breeding program with the combination of Von Kalung, Traschi Deleg and Lha Gje Lo lines. The best-known produce from her breeding program was the bitch Ger. Ch. Shelkagari Bhumi, that was shown by Ms. Haberle.

Karin Acker, VON TRI SONG, acquired and finished the half brother and sister bred by Hannelore Vick, TRADUN, who also breeds Tibetan Terriers under the same name. Ger. Ch. Tradun Bhimo, a Gyalpo son, and Ger. Ch. Tradun En Ly, a Tsarong daughter, were both out of the bitch Seng Kyi Khimo Royal (Reza Wang de Kleine Oosterling, a Matador son, x Seng Kyi Karma Royal). After breeding several litters Ms. Acker imported two bred bitches from the English Nedlik kennel of Sue Ellis, which are mostly of older English bloodlines. The Von Tri Song breeding program is based on combining the Nedlik and Traschi Deleg lines.

Jutta Wachtel, VON TSCH SCHU, established her kennel with imports from the Holland kennels Chakpori and De Coquins, which she combined with Von Kalung lines. Ms. Wachtel showed Ger. Ch. and World winner Chakpori's Likir (Dutch Ch. Chakpori's Dots x Dutch Ch. Saxonsprings Pasadena) for several years before she began breeding.

Mrs. Kramer, SHING TROU, combined Chakpori and old English lines with lines going back to Matador. Two successful dogs bred by this kennel were Ger. Ch. Shing Trou Anki Tan Po and Ger. Youth Ch. Shing Trou Maran.

Ger. Ch. Tradun En-Ly, bred by Hannelore Vick, Tradun, and owned by Karin Acker, Von Tri Song.

Bundesjugendsieger 1989 Traschi Deleg Guliang (Ch. Kai La Sha Tom Tru x Ch. Lha Gje Lo Amrita).

Traschi Deleg Yag-Po (Ch. Traschi Deleg Tsarong x Ch. Lha-Sje-Lo Amrita), owned by Kerstin Handrich, is typical of the Lhasa Apso in Germany where show dogs are also companions with the freedom to romp in their owners' gardens.

249

Under the prefix JALGA, Johanna Rothe combined dogs that were imported from Nepal with German-bred specimens. This has resulted in very typey and promising get. Most of them are black with typical temperament—full of dignity, chary of strangers in the sense it is meant to be (not chary because of fear but because of loyalty to their own people).

Most German breeders are organized in the KTR (Klub für Tibetische Rassen), which is a club founded in 1967 and is responsible for all Tibetan breeds. About 650 members are organized in this club and fifteen to twenty shows are held each year. The KTR has developed a system for establishing the number one Lhasa Apso each year. The first number one Lhasa Apso was in 1989 and was the silver-gray bitch BISS Ger. Ch. Bundessieger 1989 Tintavon Aniara (Eng., Int. & Nord. Ch. Ffrith Smoke Signal x BIS Ch. Traschi Deleg Kunga), owned by Gerti Bracksieck.

In Germany, show dogs are also house dogs, so it is imperative that they are temperamentally and structurally sound. German dogs are included in family life and must be able to participate in all kinds of activities. In Germany, all Lhasa Apsos are owner-handled and no one keeps more than five to ten dogs at a time. Lhasa Apsos must have easy-to-care-for coats because no one clips a Lhasa Apso's coat off. At the same time they would not spend hours grooming and bathing each week. Most of all the Lhasa Apsos must be little individualists, the "Little People" as they are called in their country of origin; this is what makes them so different from other breeds. Most German fanciers appreciate the breed's charisma as a very rare and special gift that must be preserved.

CZECHOSLOVAKIA

Lhasa Apso breeding in Czechoslovakia was first established in 1977. Today there are four basic lines. The oldest is from early imports from India and Bangladesh. Another well-known line is based on imports from the United States, mainly Dolsa. Another line was developed with the dogs from East Germany, Von Batang. Now imports from kennels in England like Terso and Canada like Irlee are joining the scene, giving more possibilities for breeding and showing.

In 1985, there were 22 Lhasa Apsos registered, and in 1987, there were 39 puppies whelped, with 1988 revealing 180 registered, which shows the growing popularity. Seventeen kennels are registered.

There were two international CACIB (FCI championship) shows held in 1989 along with about eight national shows.

EAST GERMANY

The first Lhasa Apsos in East Germany were the English imports Laxo of Kenstaff and Silly Billy of Kenstaff, arriving in 1978. The next imports were

East German Ch. Endro von Patan, a Swiss import, is a Best in Show winner with titles in Hungary and Czechoslovakia as well as East Germany.

Afrodite Perla Pamiru, owned by Jana Ohnoutkova in Czechoslovakia.

A group of Padmas Lhasa Apsos owned by Gerlinde Kremser in Austria. They are (from left) Freya v. Kalung, Ch. Traschi Deleg Tarka-La, Ch. Padmas Deva and Padmas Kata.

Endro von Patan and Golda von Patan, a Kai La Sha Torma daughter, that came from Switzerland. Traschi Deleg Tsi Tai and Joko of Jo Gya Kang were imported from West Germany. These imports are the basis of the Lhasa Apso in East Germany.

At this time there are about twenty breeders registered, but only a few are longtime breeders. The breed continues to progress with thirty litters producing 137 puppies being registered in 1988.

All dogs that are considered for breeding must be free from hip dysplasia. To date, no patella problems have been found in the breeding stock. A good balanced and compact Lhasa Apso is prefered. Legginess is a serious fault.

ARANKAS, ARN-BRI'S, VON BATANG, VON DER LINOWER HEIDE and QUILIAN SHAN are some of the better-known kennels in East Germany. Baishan von der Linower Heide was a well-known sire, and later Feyer von Batang (Endro v. Patan x Traschi Deleg Tsi-Tai) was a successful show dog as well as a predominant sire.

There are about ten shows for the "Eastern Breeds" each year.

Now that the Germanys are united, it will be interesting to see what effect, if any, there will be on dog breeding and showing. As the Germans are avid dog enthusiasts, there is little question that the sport will surely benefit.

HUNGARY

The breed is slowly becoming better known and more popular in Hungary. ROMANCA dogs are seen at the shows along with dogs that are down from the lines of Mrs. Baumgartner (East Germany). These dogs trace back to Von Patan and Traschi Deleg lines.

Monkia Suliok is a well-known breeder from Budapest.

AUSTRIA

As in most European countries, Lhasa Apsos are bred on a small scale in Austria.

Mrs. Gerlinde Kremser, PADMAS, is the premier breeder, having imported her foundation bitch, Traschi Deleg Tarka La (Pag Mo x Everglo Dolma Traschi Deleg) from Germany. Tarka La became Int., Austrian, Yugo. & Hung. Ch. and Austrian Bundessieger. She passed the hard rules required from the Austrian Kennel Club for excellent hips, sound stifles, PRA free and no lens-luxation. Tarka La's son is Int., Austrian, Yugo. & Germ. Ch. Austrian Bundessieger Padmas Deva. Mrs. Kremser also imported the American-bred Chen Tai Chi Razzle Dazzle from Patricia Chenoweth, Chen, and Freja von Kalung from Gitta Haberle in West Germany.

Kennels that are perpetuating the breed with litters from Mrs. Kremser's dogs, Nepal imports and an occasional dog from Germany and England are

AKASHA DWARA, SIDDHI PARK, VON NIEDERROTTNANG and LHA GYALO.

Quite a few Lhasa Apsos, imported from Nepal and other Himalayan countries, are coming to Austria with people mostly from Nepal as companions and house pets. Occasionally one of the best specimens is used for breeding.

There are several CACIB shows in Austria during the year and more recently some of the Austrian dogs are also shown in other European countries.

ITALY

The breed in Italy is still in the formative stage with different types and lines being bred and shown.

Dogs from de Warwinckel, Chakpori and Orlane have been imported during the last few years.

Guarnotta Biovanni has several dogs from Chakpori and Orlane.

Well known is Paolantoni Stefano's World champion, Harlow dell Alberico. Also well known is Vestrini Marizia's World champion, Junior dell Alberico.

NORWAY

One of the first breeders in Norway is the well-known Marit Braset, ERMINTRUDE. She imported Hale Alii One Fine Fellow, that was successful in his short stay in Norway.

The breed's undisputed number one is the English import Int. & Nord. Ch. Saxonsprings Fol De Rol, owned by Dag Linna and Svein Helgesen, TANACS, and co-owned by Grete Arnesen, LOWEBO, who has a well-established breeding program that has been successful for many years. Fol De Rol is a multiple Best in Show winner, Top Dog All Breeds in 1986 and is also top producer in the history of the breed. The Tanacs kennel concentrates mainly on the Saxonsprings lines and has imported among others Eng. Ch. Saxonsprings Jefferson (Eng. Ch. Saxonsprings Cascade x Eng. Ch. Saxonsprings Not So Dusty) and Saxonsprings Song 'N Dance. Tanacs's most recent winner is the homebred Swedish and Norwegian Ch. Tanac's Point of Vantage.

Another successful breeder is Ann-Mari Johannessen, MIAS, who is well known for the English import Int. & Nord. Ch. Hardacre Phanny, that when bred to Int. & Nord. Ch. Tintavon Baryshnikov produced Swed. Ch. Mias Phrescott. The first importation of a Lhasa Apso from Australia to Scandanavia was made by Ms. Johannessen. This was Ch. Cheska Chandigarm, a dog that is proving to be a successful sire.

The first all-breed Best in Show winner was the Swedish-owned, German-bred, German Youth Ch., Int. & Nord. Ch. Traschi Deleg Kunga in 1985 at Tonsberg. In 1986, the same owners, Paul Stanton and Torbjorn Skaar, at the same show won Best in Show with Int. & Nord. Ch. Tintavon Pandorah.

The Sherpa Tenzing and family with one of their favorites, a little bitch "Blanche Neige" as photographed many years ago.   *Courtesy of André Cuny*

Norbu clowns for the camera after winning first prize at the Apso show held at Tibet House in New Delhi.

18

The Lhasa Apso in
Other Countries

INDIA

Present-day Tibetans-in-exile in India, Nepal, Sikkim, Bhutan and other countries of the world continue to raise and treasure their dogs. Lhasa Apsos are found in all Tibetan communities.

As the economic picture of the exiled Tibetans improves, the care and attention to their dogs improves accordingly. Each year it is evident that more attention is being paid to the grooming, health and care of Lhasa Apsos owned by exiled Tibetans, though in many areas little canine veterinary help is available.

Modern genetics is not generally used by breeders in India. The hardships of maintaining a healthy kennel are great, but kennels do exist. At one time the late Tenzing Norgay, the famous Sherpa guide who climbed Mount Everest with Sir Edmund Hillary, raised Lhasa Apsos.

Mr. Jigme Taring, Taring House, was recommended by the fourteenth Dalai Lama to be an authority on Lhasa Apsos. He was born in Tibet in 1908, the son of Taring Raja, Tsota Namgyal. He is the Ex-Principal, Central School for Tibetans in Mussoorie. Taring's family, right from their early days in Tibet, were fond of the native dog breeds and have kept them all. He joined the Tibetan government service in 1932 at the time of the thirteenth Dalai Lama, and at the time of this writing is eighty-three years of age. He always appreciated all kinds of wildlife in Tibet until his escape to India in 1959.

In a letter to the authors dated December 28, 1990, Mr. Taring states,

So with my experience and after seeing numbers of books on Lhasa Apsos, I have come to notice that there are two distinct types of Apsos in foreign countries. This might perhaps be due to the change in climate, food and better care they get than in their native land or could it be a hybrid of some sort is a mystery to myself.

On the whole, I do appreciate and admire your work on Lhasa Apso, especially at the time when this breed is in danger of being diminished after the Chinese occupation of Tibet. I have heard from the recent people coming out of Tibet that there are restaurants in Lhasa where dog meat is served as delicacy. I do hope that the Lhasa Apsos will be spared for their fame in the foreign countries since many years.

The Northern India National Kennel Club includes the exhibition of Lhasa Apsos and the Tibetans sponsor their own dog show annually in Delhi. After his retirement in 1975, Mr. Taring was asked to judge at this annual show. He was associated with the Council of Judges who had attended the first championship dog show, organized by the International Lhasa Apso Association. Also, Mr. Taring was taken as a special breed judge of Tibetan breeds on the panel of FCI judges and judged at least three ILAA dog shows.

Others in Delhi and the Simla area hill stations have produced good Lhasa Apsos. Even in Ladakh, in northwest India near the western Tibetan borders, there is a small breeding program under the sponsorship of the government agriculture department.

The Lhasa Apso is still much a part of the exiled Tibetan household. Very few dogs were brought out by refugee groups because the journey was too difficult, therefore little stock remains of dogs that actually came from Tibet. Most dogs in India and neighboring Himalayan countries would be descended from dogs brought out of Tibet prior to 1959.

SOUTH AFRICA

The first Lhasa Apsos in South Africa were imported from England by Mrs. White. This was the pair Willowcroft Chela and Zangaru Tseng of Cacique that produced Tsing Ling of Cacique and S.A. Ch. Tu Tru of Cacique, which were both purchased by Dorothy Caseley from Rhodesia. Mrs. White also imported from England the male S.A. Ch. Ricmara Lancelot. When Mrs. White moved back to England, Lancelot remained in South Africa with Ms. Caseley. Lancelot and Tu Tru, along with Nang-Par of Kenstaff and Hardacre Petunia, which were imported from England in 1972 by Mrs. Diana Roby, provided the initial foundation stock for the Lhasa Apso in South Africa. Bred together, Lancelot and Tu Tru produced the bitch S.A. Ch. Shetland Isle Tasem; Nang-Par and Petunia produced S.A. Ch. Tanakpur of Roburg and S.A. Ch. Theri.

Tanakpur was bred to Tasem and produced the bitch Norbalinka Tashi of Lountanbro.

Theri was the first Lhasa Apso to place in a Group in South Africa and was the foundation bitch for the enduring FREEZELAND kennels of Mrs. Sue

South African Ch. Tabu's Heart To Heart O'Gramar, bred in the United States by Carolyn Herbel, Tabu, and Grace Vanden Heuvel, Gramar, is shown here with the late Penny Ashford, Penash, who imported him to South Africa. He later went to Jill Laylin, Simtuka.

South African Ch. Freezeland Bacchus of Salpoint, a top winner for the 1986–87 show season, he was bred by Sue MacNab, Freezeland, and is owned by Sally George-Pointon, Salpoint.

MacNab, who is also a renowned Old English Sheepdog breeder. Mrs. MacNab bred Theri first to Nang Wa Camelot to produce the bitches Ch. Freezeland Lhotse, and then in 1977 to the English dog Viento Smarti Parti to produce the bitches Freezeland Tamika, Torma and Lhama and the dog Freezeland Tompar of Zenanas. In 1983, Mrs. MacNab bred Loutanbro Amelinda of Freezeland (Tompar x Tashi) to the American import S.A. Ch. Lady W's Kid Curry to produce S.A. Ch. Freezeland Bacchus of Salpoint. A top winner for the 1986–87 show season, Bacchus is owned by Sally George-Pointon, SALPOINT.

Freezeland Lhotse was the foundation bitch for Vivienne and Cedric Mandelbaum's DE MANDELHOF kennel. The Mandelbaums are probably best known for the 1977 importation of the American Lhasa Apsos that were the half brother and sister S.A. Ch. Xanadu's Genghis Khan de Mandelhof, sired by Am. BIS Ch. Pongo's Oddi Oddi and S.A. Ch. Wolfhill's Ramblin Rose de Mandelhof, sired by Am. BIS Ch. Xanadu's Raphael. Both Genghis Khan and Ramblin Rose were out of Xanadu's Scheherazade and produced the successful S.A. Ch. de Mandelhof's Zothique. Because of the successful blending of these American imports with the English-based native South African lines, other breeders looked to America for additional stock.

After showing to her championship in 1978, S.A. Ch. Freezeland Minee, Cathy Feinstein, ZENANAS, imported the bitch that became S.A. Ch. Se Mor Zinzi of Zenanas in 1979. A successful show contender, Zinzi died in 1983, after which Ms. Feinstein imported another bitch from the United States. This was Karriads Emmy Lou of Zenanas, that when bred to S.A. Ch. Lady W's Boy Boy produced S.A. Zenanas Toran of Takarla. Ms. Feinstein also obtained the bitch S.A. Ch. Lady W's Sister Jocasta.

Another kennel to start with a Freezeland foundation was TAKARLA, the name used by Ian and Lynne Bell. Obtained in 1978, Freezeland Torma was shown until the Bells imported the dog that became Multiple S.A. BIS Ch. Lady W's Boy Boy and the most successful Lhasa Apso in the show ring from 1980 through 1983. Born on Christmas Day 1978, Boy Boy was bred by the Canadian Register of Merit breeder Mrs. Barbara Chevalier, Lady W. His sire was Am. BIS Potala Keke's Candy Bar, and his dam was Lady W's Sweet Georgia Brown. Boy Boy won eight BIS awards, twenty-seven Utility Group firsts and many other top awards in South Africa, including the Dogmor Dog of the Year award in 1983. The Bells also imported in 1980 the brood bitch Lady W's Abigail and a male that became S.A. multiple Group-winning Ch. Lady W's Kid Curry, and later Irlees Karbon Kopy of Ja Ma that had an Everglo background and Lady W's Mr. Parrish, a litter brother to Ms. Feinstein's Jocasta.

The most recent successful importation by the Bells is S.A. Am. Ch. San Jo Mor-Knoll Bugaboo (Am. Ch. San Jo's Rusty Nail ROM★★ x San Jo's Patti Waggin), that was runner-up to South Africa's Show Dog of the Year in 1987. Bugaboo was bred to Group-winning Ch. San Jo's The Weather Beater (Am. BIS Ch. SJW Waffle Stomper ROM★ x Am. Ch. San Jo's Tabatha ROM★) and produced the multiple BIS S.A. Ch. Takarla's Post No Bills, the South African number two, top winning show dog for 1989.

South African Group winner Ch. Tharalu Tung Chin of Mandelay, bred by Mr. B. Rudolph and owned by Jill Laylin, Simtuka.

S. A. Ch. Tabu's Heart of Gold O'Gramar, bred in the United States by Carolyn Herbel and Grace Vanden Heuvel and owned in South Africa by the Veldmans, Mandelay.

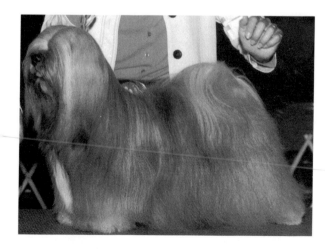

South African and American Ch. Chiyoko Nobody Doesit Better, bred by Marie Allman, Chiyoko, and owned by Mr. and Mrs. Norman Herbel, Tabu. *Petrulis*

259

The foundation for Rina Mason, CANSIEH, was the bitch S.A. Ch. Freezeland Tamika and the dog S.A. Ch. Hillendahls Gold Dust, imported from the United States. The Cansieh breeding program is responsible for, among others, these South African champions: Cansiehs Andieh, Buddieh and Abbieh.

Penny Ashford, PENASH, was very much a part of the South African Lhasa Apso scene. In 1979, she bought Freezeland Lhama, and in 1980 she brought in her first import, the American-bred bitch Potala Pandan Chiyoko's Jewel of Penash (Pandan Sin-Tsa x Potala Pandan Cherry Red). In 1981, Mrs. Ashford imported Hillridge Take Aim (Am. Ch. Tabu's Stars and Stripes x Cameo's Red Robin) and later Cameo's Diamond Rio of Penash (Am. Ch. Cameo's Acapulco Gold x Am. Ch. Cameo's Porsche). The next import was in 1982 and was the male that became S.A. Ch. Tabu's Heart To Heart O'Gramar (Stripes x Am. Ch. Tabu's Queen of Hearts ROM).

Jewel was bred to Boy Boy and produced S.A. Ch. Penash Macherie of Takarla, Penash Kaylei and Penash Zandy. Zandy was bred to Loutanbro's Mahogany of Penash (Freezeland Tompar of Zenanas x Norbalinka Yanem of Loutanbro) to produce Penash Ebony 'N Ivory, that when bred to Kaylei produced S.A. Ch. Penash Le Roi. Mrs. Ashford died in June 1989, a victim of cancer.

Another kennel that was actively breeding and exhibiting in the early 1980s was MANDELAY of the Veldmans. They imported a bitch, Wolfhill Upanishan O'Mandelay (Am. Ch. Xanadu's Ar-Jay x Woflhill's Mis-Tieh Morn) in 1981. The bitch that became S.A. Ch. Tabu's Heart of Gold O'Gramar came in 1982 with her litter brother, Mrs. Ashford's Heart to Heart. Heart of Gold died prematurely in 1985 but not before she produced several offspring. In 1983, Am. Ch. Chiyoko Nobody Doesit Better (Am., Can. & Bda. Ch. Shen Pa Ni-Khyim ROM★ x Am. Ch. Chiyoko Nik Ki of Laran) was leased from the authors for one year to be used for breeding and to be shown if feasible. Nobody Doesit Better became a South African champion as well as a multiple Group and Reserve BIS winner, but was not returned to the United States after one year. Instead he was kept in South Africa for several more years and died prematurely at an unknown time and place. He, like Heart of Gold, left offspring in South Africa.

The SIMTUKA kennel of Mrs. Jill Laylin is the haven for some of the produce of both the Penash and Mandelay breeding programs. Mrs. Laylin successfully showed the Group winner S.A. Ch. Tharalu Tung Chih of Mandelay (Nobody Doesit Better x Mandelay Misty Morn of Tharalu) and the bitch S.A. Ch. Simtuka's Nowrooz Marigold (Tung Chih x Loutanbro Mishu). Also living at Simtuka among others is Heart to Heart and his daughter, Mishu, bred by Mrs. R. A. C. Homan, LOUTRANBRO.

Philip and Elizabeth Knagg, BLOWINGSANDS, emigrated to South Africa in 1985 bringing with them the English-bred dog that became S.A. Ch. Blowingsands Rokiga. Sired by Roonsgars Dandyman, an Eng. Ch. Saxonsprings Hackensack son, Rokiga was bred by Margaret Marsh. The Knaggs also own S.A. Ch. Krystal of Blowingsands and her sister Soolin of Blowingsands, both daughters of the famous Boy Boy and S.A. Ch. Freezeland Soot'n Snow (S.A. Ch. Penash Le Roi x Freezeland Minerva). Soot'n Snow was bred to S.A. Ch. Freezeland Bacchus of Salpoint to produce Freezeland Wild Oscar of Blowingsands, and to Rokiga to produce Blowingsands Noi-Sonn.

Commitment to the breed by these breeders during the last twenty years has made the Lhasa Apso a top contender in South African all-breeds competition.

BRAZIL

Lhasa Apsos first were imported to Brazil in 1969 with the first dog becoming Group winner Braz. & Int. Ch. Judge of Sheron. Judge came from Winnie Drake's Drax kennel in Hialeah, Florida.

The pioneer kennel in Brazil was KAMAMURU, owned by Lord and Lady Duveen, who imported many dogs and established a large Lhasa Apso kennel. It was their Kyi Chu–bred bitch that produced the first litter in Brazil. They also owned the first dog to win Best in Show in South America, which was one of several that the Duveens imported from Ruth Deck's Rondelay kennel, Int. Ch. Rondelay Tootsea. The Karamuru kennel is no longer breeding Lhasa Apsos.

The top ranking dog, all breeds, for 1977 was the Canadian-bred multiple BIS Int., Can. & Braz. Ch. Zaralinga's Lord Raffles, owned by Susy and Joao Maximiliano and bred by Sheila Pike, Zaralinga. A sire force in Brazil, Raffles produced many quality Lhasa Apsos, the most famous of which was group-winning Braz. & Int. Ch. Linden do Laio, which was bred and owned by Mrs. Ceres de Oliveira, DO LAIO.

Most of the successful show dogs of the 1980s were imported from the United States as was productive breeding stock. Some of these imports were BIS Am. Ch. Ruffway Patra Dutch Treat, owned by Mr. and Mrs. Martinelli and Group-winning Braz. & S. Am. Ch. Orlane's Poltergeist, owned by Mr. and Mrs. Mario Knoll, EXCALIBUR QUEST.

Mrs. Celma Joia imported BIS Ch. Orlane's Arhat of Unnayami, Orlane's Anada, Orlane's I'm Arthur and Innsbrook's Mandy of Unnayami.

The top winning Lhasa Apso in 1988 was Braz. Ch. Peter's Kennel x'Lori (Poltergeist x Peter's Kennel Suzy).

The Excalibur Quest kennel was originated about 1984, with a Lhasa Apso intended as a pet that became Group-winning Braz. Ch. L'chart do Laio, a son of Linden. The Knolls acquired additional stock and have based their breeding program on lines from Zaralinga, Rondelay and Orlane.

The Brazilian breeders are served by the Brazil Lhasa Apso Club, which sponsors a yearly Specialty show. The 1977 Specialty featured judge Dr. Adolfo Spector of Argentina. His choice for Best of Breed was Raffles and Best of Opposite Sex was Lady Chod Chin Do Daxteri.

The numbers of breeders in Brazil is small but devoted to developing quality Lhasa Apsos.

America's Sandur, UD is believed to be the first Lhasa Apso to achieve the Utility Dog title.

The late Edward T. Jones with Ching Ching Choti, UD receiving first place in Utility at Salisbury, Maryland, November 13, 1971. The judge is Doris H. Miller. Ching continued in competition until 1973, the year Mr. Jones died.

19

The Lhasa Apso in Obedience

THE RULES of the American Kennel Club provide for the awarding of CD, CDX, UD and TD certificates to be gained in Obedience Trials and tracking tests conducted under AKC sanction.

The titles of Companion Dog (CD), Companion Dog Excellent (CDX) and Utility dog (UD) are awarded to each dog certified by three different judges to have made 50 percent of the available scores in a specified number of exercises and final scores of 170 or more in Novice, Open and Utility, respectively, at three trials in each class where at least six dogs competed.

The title of Tracking Dog (TD) is awarded after a dog is certified by two judges to have a passed a licensed or member club tracking test in which at least three dogs competed. A dog holding both UD and TD titles may use the letters UDT, signifying Utility Dog Tracking.

The key to successfully training a Lhasa Apso for Obedience is understanding the unique temperament that was developed in Tibet and has been preserved through the decades. Lhasa Apsos are independent, self-preserving, self-thinking and watchful in their attitude. When outside their home they usually prefer to be spectators rather than participants, unless they have been trained otherwise. Natural companions, they do not need formal training to make them suitable house pets; however, such training will enhance their natural traits, making them even nicer to live with.

With this in mind, keep practice sessions short to hold your dog's attention, but do work every day. Always stop on a positive note before it becomes bored.

Respect your Lhasa Apso as the other member of your team. Expect your dog to do an exercise, but only after you have shown it the exercise numerous times and the dog has had plenty of practice over an adequate amount of time. Firmness is important so that it knows it must perform its exercises during Obedience practice. Rough or extremely forceful training is unnecessary and is most likely to cause the stubborn side of your Lhasa Apso's character to appear.

Remember, a Lhasa Apso is a companion dog by heredity and works better when given the chance to make its own decision to do the exercises over a period of time, rather than being forced into quick obedience. For this reason, not all Obedience classes and trainers are suitable for the independent Lhasa Apso. Select your class and trainer very carefully. Be sure the trainer understands that different breeds need different training methods and that your Lhasa Apso is no exception.

With respect, firmness and consistent practice, your Lhasa Apso will learn to enjoy its Obedience work and the two of you will become a successful team.

Participation in Obedience by Lhasa Apsos has been significantly less than in Conformation as in comparison to many other breeds. It is believed that in addition to longer training time, the heavy head furnishings with good fall over the eyes as requested in the Standard was found to be inhibitive to Obedience work, especially when jumping in the advanced training was required.

For many years Lhasa Apso fanciers along with those of other breeds with hair over their eyes fought for allowance to have the hair tied back in Obedience. In 1971, and again in 1976 and 1977, the American Lhasa Apso Club submitted a request to the AKC to permit the hair of Lhasa Apsos to be tied back in Obedience. The requests were not granted because there was no provision for tying hair back in the Standard.

In the early 1980s, confusion arose as to whether the Lhasa Apso could be shown in Obedience with the coat cut back. Some believed the coat being cut back was altering the dog by artificial means, which was the AKC ruling that disallowed the tying back of the head fall.

To set the record straight, Mr. Frank Trujillo, American Lhasa Apso Club Obedience chairman, contacted the AKC and received the following letter, dated February 2, 1984, verifying that cut-back Lhasa Apsos were allowed to compete in Obedience:

Dear Mr. Trujillo:

As per our telephone conversations, enclosed please find a copy of changes in appearance by artificial means that require disqualification of a dog in the show ring.

Please be advised that cut back in Obedience is not a disqualification. I hope this publication is of help to you.

If I can be of further assistance, please do not hesitate to contact me.

Very truly yours,

Joyce Hogi
Show Records Department
THE AMERICAN KENNEL CLUB

This letter when presented to the American Lhasa Apso Club membership was accompanied by Mr. Trujillo's comment as follows, "Although the showing of a cut-back dog is not a disqualification in Obedience, I think that most of us are of the opinion that a Lhasa should look like a Lhasa anytime it is in the public eyes. Even though the hair is cut short, usually in an 'Executive Cut,' the dog should be clean and groomed before entering the ring. This is not only to show our pride in ownership of the dog but to also show our pride in what 'these hairy little fellows' have accomplished in getting to the Obedience Trial."

Apparently a majority of the fancy shared Mr. Trujillo's opinion because the fanciers continued to petition the AKC for acceptance to tie the hair back, thus allowing the Lhasa Apso to be shown in Obedience in full coat. In 1989, the battle was won with the following quote being inserted into the AKC's Obedience regulations:

> Any dog whose hair over its eyes interferes with its vision, may have the hair tied back with either a neutral colored rubber band or a small plain barrette. (Obedience Regulations, Amended to March 1, 1989, published by American Kennel Club, Section 16, paragraph 9, p. 8)

An additional clarification of this new regulation was published in the December 1990 issue of the American Lhasa Apso Club bi-monthly *The Lhasa Bulletin*, as follows:

> In response to a request fom an ALAC member for an interpretation and clarification of AKC Obedience Rule Ch. 1 Section 16, second paragraph from the end, regarding Hair tie back, The American Kennel Club answered:
> 'A Lhasa Apso may be shown in the Obedience ring with the hair over its eyes tied back using one rubber band such as a Poodle or Shih Tzu's hair is normally tied back in the breed ring, or with the hair parted and one rubber band used on each side of the part as a Maltese is normally shown (without the foldover topknot).
> 'Braiding the fall is not acceptable.
> 'Please do not hesitate to conctact the Performance Events Department if we may be of further assistance.
>
> Roberta L. Campbell
> Administrator of Performance Events'

It will be interesting to see how this new ruling will affect the statistics for successful participation in Obedience for the Lhasa Apso in the future.

Janine Grinta, Obedience enthusiast and owner of Watcher Under Freeflyt Objex, UD, the eleventh Lhasa Apso in history to earn a UD title, compiled much of the material that allowed us to include the following statistical information.

The first Lhasa Apso to earn an Obedience title was an unregistered dog, Segundo Verdejo, in 1949. Bred and owned by Mrs. Dorothy Sabine de Gray, Las Sa Gre Lhasa Apsos, he was sired by the unregistered Ch. Juanito Verdejo out of Ch. Las Sa Gre. Having earned the breed's first CD in 1949, he won the first CDX the next year. In 1952, an unregistered dog named Sargent earned both his CD and CDX titles. The following year, 1953, Sargent became the first

Lhasa Apso to earn the UD title. The first registered Lhasa Apso to earn the three titles was American's Sandur, having earned his CD in 1955, his CDX in 1956 and his UD in 1957. The first champion to earn a CD title was Ch. Ming Tali II, while the first champion to win a CDX was Ch. Dandi Jin Rik'i. To date, no champion has earned a UD title.

The third Lhasa Apso to win the coveted UD title was Ching Ching Choti. We are sharing with you the following letter from Caroline D. Jones, co-owner of Ching Ching and widow of his owner, handler and trainer, the late Edward T. Jones, because it is typical of the joys and trials of training a Lhasa Apso and reflects the pleasure of accomplishment.

> It was a tragic, avoidable accident to a previous Lhasa that propelled us into obedience training as soon as we acquired Ching Ching from Mrs. E. J. Bartness of Stafford, Virginia. The Fairfax County Dog Training Class was strictly for amateurs—canine and human—and we were the worst of the lot.
>
> Diploma in hand at the end of the brief training, we innocently entered Ching Ching in his first show, in Georgetown. It was, predictably, a fiasco—but it opened up to us a new and wonderful world. We resolved to train him properly, however long it took, and try again when we were ready. Lhasas are bright and eager to please; ultimately Ching Ching realized his exercises were serious business and he reveled in his work. Still, shows were crushing disasters, for the crowds delighted him. He licked judges, courted children and had a merry, feckless time.
>
> Suddenly, it all fell into place. In December, 1969, he earned his CD degree and his mistress was ready to retire, triumphant. Our mutual master decreed otherwise and forthwith started training for CDX. Ching found jumping a lark, but the five-minute down was his nemesis. When he was finally ready, he merrily batted it off in three straight shows in eight days (October 3, 4 and 10, 1970). By that time we were all totally committed and confident. Preparing for the final degree, we went to class almost weekly, let Ching work out his own break-throughs on the difficult hand signal and scenting exercises.
>
> When he achieved the coveted UD at Atlantic City, New Jersey, on December 5, 1971, it was especially gratifying that he hadn't just squeaked through his degrees; he had been on the money on numerous occasions, including first place at least three times. He was still a ham and a crowd-pleaser, but he finally made the connection; when he gave it his all he could prance into the winners' circle and eat up the applause.
>
> Throughout the effort we felt that Ching Ching was achieving something unique for the breed. But his greatest accomplishment remains this: the joy and pride and companionship he brought to his devoted master's last few years of life.

The American Lhasa Apso Club established an Obedience Register of Merit (ROM) award in 1973, which is available to all ALAC members who have achieved three Obedience titles on Lhasa Apsos they own. This can be three CDs on three different Lhasa Apsos, a CD, CDX and UD on one Lhasa Apso or any other combination equaling three AKC Obedience titles.

The fourth and sixth Lhasa Apsos to earn UD titles were Me Tu of Charmel and her daughter Ming Tu of Charmel, the only family affair among the elite fraternity of Utility Lhasa Apsos. They were owned, trained and handled by

Sheng-La's Tashi Tamina, CDX was not started in obedience training until she was past seven years old and had her CDX title by the time she was eight. "Tami", owned and trained by Florence Dickerson, proves that training success is never limited by a dog's age.

Mee-Tu of Charmel, UD clearing the bar jump for Utility obedience work.

Princess Shana, Am., Can. CD performs a long down exercise at an obedience demonstration. Shana was owned, trained and handled by Susan Gehr, Gar San Lhasas.

267

Melodye Haverly and earned for her Charmel Lhasa Apsos the first Obedience ROM awarded by ALAC, which was in 1977.

Tailsinn Lhasa Apsos of James and Joanne Lancaster also won an Obedience ROM in 1977 with Tailsinn Huli of Karo-La, CD, Tailsinn Tobo, CD, and Tailsinn Chintamini, CD.

The fifth Lhasa Apso to earn the UD title was Haywood's Alana Pansette Tu, UD. Known as Pansy, she received her CD and CDX titles in 1975 and 1976 and her UD in 1977. Her owner, trainer and handler, John Haywood, fondly tells the story of Pansy in the Utility ring when he pivoted for the directed retrieve and the judge pointed to John's feet. There was Pansy, struggling to free her coat from under John's shoe!

In 1978, the Green Pond Lhasa Apsos of Miriam Krum earned the ALAC Obedience ROM with Green Pond's A Golden Glow, CD, in 1975; Green Pond's Ani, CD, and Green Pond's Bow Bay, CD, both in 1978. Bow earned a CDX in 1981.

The seventh and eighth UD titlists were Marilyn Mele's Sesame Shing Chaa Lee, which earned her UD in 1980, and Saccone's Sasha, which earned her UD in 1981 for owners Meredith and Martin Saccone.

Joan Clarke's Habibi Lhasa Apsos earned the Obedience ROM in 1982 with Habibi's Pitachen's 1976 CDX title and Habibi's Petite Beaute's 1981 CDX title. In 1983, Linda Jarrett's Sera Mar Lhasa Apsos earned the Obedience ROM title with Jarrett's Tom-Mey Tong, CD, and Tom Mey's Junior Mop Sey, CDX.

The American Lhasa Apso Club sponsored its first Obedience Trial in conjunction with its 1983 National Specialty show. The first Lhasa Apso to receive ALAC's High in Trial (HIT) award, May 15, 1983, was Tiger Ming III, CDX, from the Open A class under judge John Wills and bred, owned, trained and handled by Brenda Schmelzel.

The 1984 HIT winner was Kasha Ann McGillicudy, CD, from the Novice A class under judge Bonnie Baker and owned, trained and handled by Irene Bishop.

In 1984, Tiger Ming III, CDX, and Honey Ming II, CD, earned the Obedience ROM for Brenda Schmelzels's Bala Lhasas.

Betty Wathe was also awarded an Obedience ROM in 1984, which was earned by Halcyon's Golden Kismet, the ninth Lhasa Apso to earn a UD title. Kismet was awarded HIT at the 1985 National under judge F. L. Henry, at the 1988 National under Charles Mulock and at the 1989 National under Doris Baster.

The 1985 recipients of the Obedience ROM were Jean Foster with Princess Suisi-Too, UD, the tenth Lhasa Apso to earn a UD, and Florence Kantor with Honey Bun's Abso Seng Kye, CD, Nik-ki's Singtuk, CD, and Nuseng Tacin My-T-Luv Bear, UD, the twelfth of the breed to earn a UD title.

Jean Foster and Princess Suisi-Too, UD, won HIT at the 1986 National trial under judge Dorothy McCauley and again in 1987 under judge Mrs. R. E. Foster.

The 1986 obedience ROM winners were Janine Grinta with Watcher Under

Tiger Ming CDX, HIT at the first ALAC Obedience Trial, is shown here with his breeder, owner, trainer and handler, Brenda Schmelzel, Bala; Frank Trujillo, ALAC Obedience Chairman and Carolyn Herbel, ALAC President.

1986 and 1987 ALAC HIT, Princess Suisi-Too UD, shown here at the 1986 Trial with her owner, trainer and handler, Jean Foster, judge Dorothy McCauley and trophy presenter, Carolyn Herbel, ALAC President.

Alexandria Dancer UD, owned, trained and handled by Diana Serlo, shown with judge, N. L. Russell. *Photo by BK and Compliments of the ALAC Obedience Album*

269

Freeflyt Objex, UD, and Deanna Maxwell with Ch. Lin Dalai's Jon-Boi of Joy, CD, and Joy's Rusty Penny, CDX.

No Obedience awards were earned in 1987 and 1988. In 1989 Susan Rich's San Sei Lhasa Apsos earned the Obedience ROM title with San Sei Sundancer, CDX, and San Sei Little Miss Chips, CD, and Diane Serlo qualified for the award in 1989 with Alexandria Dancer, the fourteenth Lhasa Apso to earn the UD title.

Pooh's Tigger, owned by Steve Winchester, is the fifteenth to earn the UD title.

The 1990 HIT at the National was Barjea Lyndy Midnite Ms Chief from the Novice B class under judge Rosalie Alvarez and owned, trained and handled by Jody Mannheimer and co-owned by Barbara Peterson.

During the forty-one years since the first Obedience title was earned, Lhasa Apsos have won 401 CDs, 71 CDXs and 15 UDs. During that time thirty-five were champion companion dogs and three of those champion CDs went on to earn CDXs. To the best of our knowledge, only one all-breed BIS winner is also an Obedience titlist; this is BIS Ch. Orlane's Span-Kieh, CD, owned, trained and handled by Jolene Cazzola, Jolee.

The first Lhasa Apso to receive the HIT award at an AKC all-breeds Obedience trial is HIT Halcyon's Golden Kismet, UD. Before the HIT award was presented by the AKC, Sargent, UD, was the highest-scoring dog at an all-breeds trial in 1953. He also tied for the highest-scoring dog at several other trials.

Brenda Schmelzel, the ALAC Obedience chairperson since 1984, supplied us with the club records that made it possible to give a statistical overview of the parent club's participation in promoting and rewarding the Obedience Lhasa Apso. In addition, Ms. Schmelzel founded an Obedience scrapbook for the club from which many of the Obedience photos for this chapter were obtained.

Photographed at the 1985 ALAC Obedience Trial are, left to right, Watcher Under Free Flyt Objex CDX (acquired UD later), owned by Janine Grinta; Habibi's Petite Beaute CDX, owned by Joan Clarke and the 1985 HIT, Halcyon's Golden Kismet UD, owned by Betty L. Wathe.

20

The American Lhasa Apso Club

T HE AMERICAN Lhasa Apso Club (ALAC) was founded on February 9, 1959, during the Westminster Kennel Club show. Fourteen members answered the roll call at that first organizational meeting and the secretary reported sixty-one members enrolled.

CHARTER OFFICERS

That secretary was the late Dorothy Benitez, who was never absent from the list of officers in the following eighteen years serving as secretary, secretary-treasurer and treasurer. Mrs. Benitez was also the true keeper of records, for it was Dorothy who answered all our questions for this book about early club information.

Another charter member who did not move from her position as first vice president for fifteen years was the great lady and foundation breeder of Lhasa Apsos, the late Grace Licos. Mrs. Licos coordinated many of the Western ALAC Specialties including the first, held in 1969.

The late Dorothy Cohen, who acquired many of the Hamilton Lhasa Apsos after the death of Mrs. Cutting, was in the first founding group as a member of the board of directors.

The late Marie Stillman, Americal, Frank T. Lloyd, Ming, and Paul Williams, Cornwallis, were also founding members and members of the first board of directors.

Mr. C. Suydam Cutting was made honorary president, a position he held until the time of his death in 1972. The late Fred Huyler was the first president and treasurer for the $590.92 that ALAC started with. Marilyn Sorci, Shangri La, was the first corresponding secretary, and the late James Anderson, who first dreamed of starting a club, was the second vice president.

EARLY GOALS

The members at this first meeting discussed the financial report and plans, along with plans for a first Specialty show and also their membership in the American Kennel Club. They declared the ALAC colors to be Tibetan turquoise and silver. The constitution and by-laws were drawn up in that first year and were not changed until the time of ALAC's incorporation in the state of Virginia in 1972.

The second meeting of ALAC, held again in conjunction with the Westminster Kennel Club show in February 1960, found twelve members present. Among them, in addition to the officers, were Dorothy Sabine de Gray, Las Sa Gre; Ann Griffing, Chig; Frank T. Lloyd, Ming; John Partanen, Rinpoche, and Paul Williams, Cornwallis.

The secretary reported a membership of eighty-one. The election of officers made no change from the previous year.

In May of 1960, the president appointed Robert and Anna Griffing, Frank Lloyd and Dorothy Benitez to serve on a committee to make plans for a match show.

FIRST SANCTIONED MATCH

The first ALAC sanctioned B match was held on September 16, 1962, on the grounds of Hamilton Farms, judged by Mr. Edward H. Goodwin, Robert Griffing presiding as match chairman. The entry fee was fifty cents per dog. An entry of thirty-eight was on hand for the historic event. Best in Match was Kham of Norbulingka and Best Adult Bitch was his dam, Karma Kosala, both owned by Phyllis Fulton (Marcy) of Washington, D.C. Best Puppy in Match was Chig Seng, owned by Robert Griffing, Mountainside, New Jersey.

The Parade of Champions included:

Ch. Linga-Drog-Po (3 yrs.), owner Robert Griffing
Ch. Hamilton Namsa (3 yrs.), owner Dorothy Benitez
Ch. Ming Thudi (4 yrs.), owner Estate of Frank T. Lloyd, Jr.
Ch. Ming Teri (5 yrs.), owner Estate of Frank T. Lloyd, Jr.
Ch. Ming Siming (6 yrs.), owner Estate of Frank T. Lloyd, Jr

The first ALAC match show held in 1959 on the grounds of Hamilton Farms.

Can. BIS Can. Am. Ch. San Jo's Soshome ROM* Can. ROM, shown winning the Stud Dog Class at the 1982 ALAC National Specialty under judge Nick Calicura, Shoshome, owned by Neil and Johanna Graves, Tru Blu, is shown here with Mr. Graves. Get are Am. Can. Ch. Zhantor Maestro, bred and owned by Don and Naomi Hansen, Zhantor, and handled by Mr. Hanson, and Can. BIS Can. Am. Ch. Tru Blu's Shome-A-Rerun, bred by Mr. and Mrs. Graves and owned by Jan Cote, Jalco.   *Photo by Roberts*

Ch. Hamilton Sandupa (7 yrs.), owner C. S. Cutting
Ch. Hamilton Kung (7 yrs.), owner C. S. Cutting
Ch. Ming Toy Nola (8 yrs.), owner Anna M. Griffing
Ch. Hamilton Tatsienlu (13 yrs.), owner C. S. Cutting
Ch. Le (14 yrs.), owner Dorothy Benitez

ALAC MOVES AHEAD

The 1963 election of officers saw a change, with Robert Griffing becoming ALAC's new president and Alfred Stillman, Marie Stillman's son, the new second vice president. Secretary and treasurer became one job and Dorothy Benitez was elected to that office. The new corresponding secretary was Anna Griffing.

The second ALAC match show was held on June 2, 1963, at the Griffing residence in Mountainside, New Jersey, with Dorothy Benitez the judge. The entry of thirty-seven included Lhasa Apsos from Georgia, Florida, Maine, Pennsylvania, New York and New Jersey. Best in Match went to Chig Seng, owned by Robert Griffing.

The 1964 election saw all officers the same as the previous year. The club approved the publication of a club pamphlet describing the history, Standard and requirements for membership. By now the club had *The Lhasa Bulletin*, which was to be sent to the membership four times a year.

On July 12, 1964, the club conducted a Plan A sanctioned match, again held at the Griffing home. There were thirty-six entries, judged by Mrs. Elbertine Campbell. Best in Match was won by Lama of Norbulingka, owned by Mrs. Phyllis Taylor (Marcy) and Best of Opposite Sex was Licos Cheti La, owned by Paul Williams.

The slate of officers for 1965 did not change, and by April 1965 *The Lhasa Bulletin* reported plans for the second Plan A match at the home of the Griffings, but the focus of this *Bulletin* was the hope for a Specialty show in 1966.

The 1965 Plan A match had a total of forty-seven entries, with some coming from as far away as Arizona, Nevada, Michigan and Florida. Frank Landgraf, who had judged at Westminster the previous year, officiated, and Mrs. Landgraf worked, as she often did, as his ring steward. Best in Match was Merda Cai, owned by Aleta D. Styers of Niles, Michigan, and Best of Opposite Sex was Rondelay's Dorje Gyalpo, owned by George H. Montgomery of New York City.

The October 1965 *Lhasa Bulletin* included the following memorandum to the members: ". . . Your club, The American Lhasa Apso Club, has decided to hold its first Specialty Show in conjunction with the Trenton Kennel Club show in Trenton, New Jersey, on May 8, 1966. . . ."

The 1966 annual election was held as usual at the time of the Westminster show and the officers again remained the same. A motion was made and passed that a committee be appointed to see if the Standard of the breed could be revised to make it more understandable not only to the members but also to the public and dog show judges.

THE FIRST SPECIALTY

Plans were made for the important first annual Specialty show, and in a membership *Bulletin*, President Griffing announced that the AKC approved the application for holding the Specialty in conjunction with the Trenton Kennel Club show. As part of this announcement Griffing wrote: "At last we have arrived! Yes, after three years of match shows, a Plan B in 1962, a Plan A in 1964 and 1965, we have finally arrived."

President Griffing's enthusiasm continued as he reported the results of the first Specialty. The successful entry of fifty-two Lhasa Apsos was, he believed, a record. Mr. James Trullinger was the judge and his choice for Best of Breed was Ch. Kham of Norbulingka, owned by Mrs. Phyllis Taylor (Marcy).

THE PACE INCREASES

*The Lhasa Bulletin*s were being sent out more frequently by President Griffing as the pace of club activity increased under his leadership. One reported a successful 1966 fun match and a new record entry of sixty-two Lhasa Apsos. The match was judged by Cyril Bernfeld, and America's Lhasa, owned by Dorothy Benitez, won Best in Match.

This same *Bulletin* announced that ALAC's second annual Specialty was approved. The *Bulletin* added that "we are still hoping to run a Specialty with the Beverly Hills Kennel Club. We are working on it and if successful will let you know at once."

By now the registrations of Lhasa Apsos with the AKC had increased from 245 in 1960 to 859 for 1965 and jumped over the thousand mark in 1966.

The annual election in 1967 provided a new president, Alfred Likewise, and the office of secretary-treasurer was again split, with Dorothy Benitez remaining as the treasurer and Patricia Gleeson as the new secretary. All other officers remained the same.

There was much discussion at this annual meeting concerning the responsiblity of ALAC to have involved members nationwide. There was also concern about the revision of the Standard, but attending members were informed by their new president that such a change could not be attempted until ALAC had been accepted by the AKC as a member club.

There was no change in officers resulting from the 1968 annual election. The club voted to sponsor a Futurity in conjunction with the 1969 Specialty show, and Robert Griffing was appointed Futurity chairman.

The highlight of this annual meeting was the presentation of the first annual Achievement Awards. The winners of Achievement Awards that first year were:

Ch. Tyba Le of Ebbtide, Ch. Tn Hi Di-Ly-Hri, Ch. Tibet of Cornwallis, Ch. Kinderland's Sang-Po, Ch. Chig Chig, Ch. Sharpa Chenga Eastcroft, Ch. Agra's Imprecious and Ch. Kyi Chu Kum Nuk.

The 1969 annual election provided only one change in the slate of officers. Mary Likewise became the new secretary. Grace Licos announced that the Western Specialty was approved to be held in conjunction with the Kennel Club of Beverly Hills and that all the preparations were made.

May 4, 1969, was the date of the fourth Eastern ALAC Specialty and the first ALAC Futurity. The judge for both events was Henry Stoecker.

The first Western ALAC Specialty was held in conjunction with the Kennel Club of Beverly Hills on June 21 and 22, 1969. The judge was Forrest Hall, who chose Ch. Teako of Abbotsford for Best of Breed. The inception of the Western Specialty insured the national complexion of the club.

ALAC INTO THE SEVENTIES

The 1970 annual election found competition from additional write-in nominations because of the enthusiasm of the increasing membership. Counting of the seventy-seven ballots resulted in a new president, Ruth Deck, Rondelay, and a new secretary, Cheryl Hueneke. All other officers remained the same.

The only change in officers after the 1971 annual election was the position of secretary, now filled by Jean Stang (Jefferson).

The 1971 Futurity judging procedure had changed, so the judge, Phyllis Marcy, was able to choose a Grand Futurity winner instead of simply a Best Puppy and Best Adult. Both Specialties were held as in years past, with the Western show highlighted by the presence of Tenzing Norgay, Sherpa, of Mount Everest fame, who presented the trophies.

President Ruth Deck wrote in the August 1971 *Lhasa Bulletin*, "It is felt that serious consideration should be given by all of our members to the proposal by Norman Herbel regarding a new *Bulletin*. As perhaps most members do not realize, the *Bulletin* at present is pretty much the result of the President's effort. . . ."

The 1972 annual election results showed Robert Sharp as the new president and Ruth Smith, Kyi Chu, as second vice president, with all other officers unchanged.

During this period Keke Blumberg (Kahn) was appointed to head the breed Standard committee, and President Sharp, working closely with Edmund Sledzik and David Goldfarb, succeeded in the incorporation of ALAC.

The annual awards program was revitalized with the establishment of the First Annual Awards Dinner, held in New York City in conjunction with the 1973 Westminister show.

Robert Sharp was reelected at the 1973 annual election, and Carolyn Herbel was elected as the new secretary. The other officers remained unchanged.

Futurity chairman Norman Herbel presented a new Futurity program to be

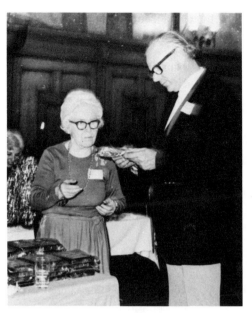

The late Anna Griffing presenting an ALAC award to Robert Sharp at the 1973 Annual Awards dinner in New York City.

Stephen Campbell, ALAC Awards Chairman, presenting an award to Barry Tompkins at the 1974 Annual Awards Dinner in New York.

The panel participating in the Forum held in conjunction with the 1974 ALAC Annual meeting. Sitting left to right; David Goldfarb, Stephen Campbell, Phyllis Marcy, David Marshall, Paula Lieberman, Dorothy Kendall, Grace Licos. Standing Edmund Sledzik, Robert Sharp and Carolyn Herbel.

277

implemented in 1974. This program called for three regional Futurities (Eastern, Midwestern and Western), thereby allowing more participation in this event throughout the country.

President Sharp appointed Stephen Campbell as the new awards chairman, and under his guidance 1973 was the first year that ALAC offered Register of Merit (ROM) recognition to outstanding producers, both individual dogs and breeders, as well as top twenty listings for these categories.

Because of the large entry of the previous year, the 1973 Eastern ALAC Specialty used two judges. Also held in conjunction with the Eastern Specialty was the 1973 Futurity. The Western Specialty was held at the Kennel Club of Beverly Hills as in the past.

The most rewarding announcement President Sharp made in 1973 was that ALAC would be first published in the 1974 March issue of *Pure-bred Dogs— American Kennel Gazette*, and if all went as expected ALAC should be accepted as an AKC member club in June of 1974. Another goal had been reached.

The 1973 awards were presented at the Second Annual Awards Dinner held at Luchow's in New York City at the time of the 1974 Westminster show. Presented were many awards, among which were twenty-eight champion plaques, two Obedience plaques and five breeder ROM awards. These presentations were to increase in number and importance over the years and become an integral part of ALAC Specialty activities.

To meet requirements for acceptance as an AKC member club, the original constitution and by-laws had been changed and the annual election was next held in May 1974, making this the 1974–75 term office. This election provided the club with a new president, Edmund Sledzik. The new constitution eliminated the offices of second vice president and corresponding secretary, but all other officers remained unchanged.

President Sledzik was very active in office and worked to stimulate a completely national club by traveling extensively. He also put much emphasis on increasing the number of regional clubs as well as stressing the need for revising the Standard.

David Goldfarb suggested having nationwide forums to be held in conjunction with other ALAC events around the country. Appointed chairman of the forum committee, Goldfarb conducted many forums and the club was truly a parent club, performing service to its members and other Lhasa Apso enthusiasts.

In compliance with President Sledzik's desire to make ALAC a truly national club, the membership voted to change what had become the permanent locations for the Specialties.

The May 1975 annual election for the 1975–76 term provided the club with still another new president, Norman Herbel. Carol Kuendel was the new secretary, and for the first time ALAC had the privlege to elect an AKC delegate, namely Stephen Campbell. There was no change in the other officers.

The 1975 Tenth Eastern ALAC Specialty was held in May in Trenton for the last time, and the 1975 Seventh Western ALAC Specialty was held in June at Beverly Hills.

The 1976 Eastern Specialty, held in February in conjunction with the Louisville Specialties, and the 1976 Western ALAC Specialty, held in conjunction with the March Texas Kennel Club show in Dallas, were both also held during the 1975–76 term.

The three 1975 Futurities were held successfully in the appropriate regions with the complete results appearing in the *Bulletin*.

The election of officers for the 1976–77 term, held in May, found Edmund Sledzik back in the president's chair after a one-year leave from the office. For the first time since ALAC's first election, a vice president other than Grace Licos was elected. This new vice president was Ellen Lonigro. The other officers remained the same.

President Sledzik promoted the concept of an annual Champion-Obedience yearbook to be published by ALAC.

The breed Standard committee continued to work toward a change in the Standard.

The fall 1976 *Bulletin*, edited by Norman Herbel, contained a full report of each of the three 1976 regional Futurities, complete with all placings first through fourth, photos of the winners and critiques by the judges. This was to be the last issue edited by Mr. Herbel. The spring 1977 *Lhasa Bulletin*, the only issue edited by James Kirk, contained a list of the 1976 awards presented at the Fifth Annual Awards Dinner. Some of the awards presented were seventy-seven for new champions, seven for new Obedience titles and four breeder ROM awards.

The 1977 ALAC roster listed over 500 members, a direct result of the leadership of the club and the skyrocketing popularity of the breed. More than 22,000 Lhasa Apsos were registered with the American Kennel Club in 1977, making it the thirteenth most popular of all breeds in the United States and second only to Poodles in the Non-Sporting Group.

Officers elected for the 1977–78 term were Edmund Sledzik, again as president; Keke Blumberg (Kahn), vice president; George Gassett, treasurer, and Janet Whitman, secretary.

In 1977, the board provided for, in addition to the three already in effect, a Southern Futurity region and a region for Hawaii.

In midterm, George Gassett resigned as treasurer, and Paul Voigt was chosen by the board to fill the vacancy.

Mr. Lynn Morgan sent out the February 1978 *Bulletin* containing a very long report by the AKC delegate Stephen Campbell, and an equally long progress report on renal disease in Lhasa Apsos, a project to which ALAC generously donated for many years.

Minutes of the February 12, 1978, general meeting reported that the three changes to the Standard had been passed by two-thirds of the 264 voting members.

During the Sledzik presidency, the first (1976) Championship–CD Yearbook was published, thus fulfilling his longtime goal.

Officers elected for the 1978–79 term were new president Keke Blumberg (Kahn), with all other officers remaining the same.

Mrs. Blumberg (Kahn), presiding at the first board meeting of her first term, announced a new committee, Local Club Liaison, chaired by Carolyn Herbel.

She also announced the proposal of one national roving Specialty to replace the two Eastern and Western Specialties.

The last *Bulletin* edited by Mr. Morgan contained a list of thirty-one local Specialty clubs submitted by the local club liaison chairperson and accompanied a request to update officers and addresses.

The December 1978 *Bulletin* introduced new editors Marie Belluscio and Sandra Dellano sharing the editorial duties of the *Bulletin*, which was similar to the previous publication in format. It contained several pages of minutes, AKC delegate's report and an announcement of the Seventh Annual Awards Dinner.

During this term, for the first time Futurities were held in four regions and Hawaii. The Eastern and Western Specialties were held as usual, with the club becoming truly national.

The 1977 yearbook was published during this term.

The 1980–81 election brought these changes: Leonard Ripley was elected president, Ann Lanterman assumed the duties of secretary and Keke Blumberg (Kahn) replaced Stephen Campbell as AKC delegate. All other officers remained the same.

The 1980 Eastern Specialty was held in Pennsylvania, and the Western Specialty was held in California. This was the last year for the two specialties.

The first Roving National Specialty was hosted in 1981 by the National Capital Area Lhasa Apso Club, which also included the Region I Futurity, the Ninth Annual Awards Dinner (which for the first time was not in New York City in February), the annual meetings and the 1981–82 election.

Carolyn Herbel was elected president, with all other officers remaining unchanged.

Committee duties and responsibilities were spelled out by the president in the summer 1981 quarterly.

The second Roving National Specialty was hosted in 1982 by the Cascade Lhasa Apso Fanciers of Greater Seattle, along with the Tenth Annual Awards Dinner, where the 1981 awards were presented.

The results of the 1982–83 election were Carolyn Herbel, president; Paul Voigt, vice president; Ann Lanterman, secretary; Stephen Campbell, treasurer, and Edmund Sledzik, AKC delegate.

The spring 1983 quarterly contained the finalists for the ALAC Logo Contest. This contest was the first activity of the newly formed logo committee, chaired by Marie Allman.

The 1983 Roving National Specialty was hosted by the Heart of America Lhasa Apso Club, and for the first time in history, ALAC was approved to host an Obedience Trial in conjunction with the National Specialty. As a result of the increased interest in Obedience, Frank Trujillo was appointed Obedience chairman.

It was at this Specialty that the yearbook editors, Marianne Nixon and

Multiple BIS Am. Bda. Can. Ch. Bihar's Revenger of Sammi Raja*, bred by Carol Strong, Bihar, and Joseph Colantonio, Sammi Raja, and shown here with Mrs. Strong winning Best of Breed at the 1989 ALAC National Specialty at almost twelve years of age from the Veteran Dog Class under judge Keke Kahn. The trophy presenter is Cassandra de la Rosa, ALAC President. *Baines*

Ch. Yuppies Klassi Sassi Kisi Bear (Group winner Ch. Light Up's Red Alert ROM* x Ch. Mi-Ling Golden Bear ROM), bred and co-owned by Frank and Barbara Trujillo, The Bear's Den, with Janet Whitman, Ja Ma, shown here at the 1989 ALAC National Specialty handled by Mrs. Whitman to Best of Opposite Sex under judge Keke Kahn. The trophy presenter is Cassandra de la Rosa, the ALAC President. *Baines*

Barbara Wood, presented the next yearbook, which was a hardback volume containing four years—1978 through 1981.

At the 1983 annual meeting, also in conjunction with the Specialty, AKC delegate Edmund Sledzik introduced for the first time the AKC III Phase Education Program. This was the pioneer program that initiated the video program and today's judges education program.

The 1983–84 officers remained the same, except for the vice president position, which was filled by Phyllis Marcy.

The cover of the 1983 summer and fall quarterly *Bulletin* was graced for the first time with the winning logo. It was not long before stationary, promotion items, decals, bumper stickers and trophies displayed ALAC's beautiful new logo, which was designed by Marianne Nixon.

The secretary, Ann Lanterman, resigned in February 1984. Carole Garrett volunteered to fill the position.

The fourth Roving National Specialty and second Obedience Trial was hosted in 1984 by the Lhasa Apso Club of Greater Houston. This was ALAC's twenty-fifth year and all the trophies were silver. The logo chairman commissioned a collectors' commemorative pin fashioned from the new logo. The 1983 ALAC Awards were presented at the Twelfth Annual Awards Dinner.

Editor Jack Haserick resigned and the spring 1984 issue was the thirteenth and last *Bulletin* he published.

Elected for 1984–85 was Carolyn Herbel, president; Dorothy Kendall, vice president; Carole Garrett, secretary; Marvin Whitman, treasurer, and Edmund Sledzik, AKC delegate.

The fifth Roving National Specialty and third Obedience Trial was held in Region I and was hosted in 1985 by the Canal Country Lhasa Apso Club. The 1984 ALAC Awards were presented at the Thirteenth Annual Awards Dinner by the new awards chairperson, Angie Taylor.

The 1985–86 slate of officers remained the same as the previous year.

The board of directors appointed Norman Herbel as chairman of the breed Standard committee, replacing Keke Blumberg (Kahn).

At the February board meeting, Sally Silva was appointed as the editor of the *Bulletin* and officer guidebooks were presented to the officers and board members, the result of efforts by Carolyn Herbel and Sondra Rogers.

The sixth National Specialty convention was held in Region II and was hosted in 1986 by the Riverside–San Bernardino Lhasa Apso Club. As usual the awards were presented at the Annual Awards Dinner. A record number of awards were given at this time.

The officers for 1986–87 all remained the same, except that Sondra Rogers was elected as secretary.

Norman Herbel, breed Standard committee chairman, was chosen as the AKC judges education coordinator.

The 1987 National Specialty convention was held in Region III and was hosted by the Twin Cities Lhasa Apso Club. This Specialty was the first to implement the board's action to have Select Honors to be presented after Best

Am. Can. Ch. Orlane's Scirocco ROM**, owned by Ellen Lonigro and Susan Giles, Kinderland Ta Sen, is shown here winning the Stud Dog Class at the 1986 ALAC National Specialty under judge Tom Stevenson, handled by Susan Giles. Trophy presenter is Carolyn Herbel, ALAC President. Scirocco's progeny in this class are littermates, Ch. Rufkins Chip Off the Ol Rock with Roberta Lombardi, Rufkins, and Ch. Rufkins Savannah Smiles with Beverly Drake, Misti Acres, both out of Ch. Ruffway Patra Tashi Tu ROM**. *Missy*

Ch. San Jo Zhantor Sugarplum, bred by Don and Naomi Hanson, Zhantor, and owned by Barbara Peterson, Barjea, and Mariane Nixon, San Jo, is shown here winning the Brood Bitch Class at the 1986 ALAC National Specialty under judge Tom Stevenson. Sugarplum, with Mrs. Peterson, is represented in this class by littermates Ch. Barjea San Jo Whip To The' Top with Leslie Engen, San Jo, and Ch. Barjea San Jo Smart N' Snappi with Marianne Nixon, San Jo, bred by Mrs. Peterson and Mrs. Nixon, they are sired by Ch. SJW Whipper Snapper. Trophy presenter is Carolyn Herbel, ALAC President.

of Breed judging to quality exhibits believed by the judge to be worthy of further recognition. It was also the first year that the Best of Breed and Best of Opposite Sex winners received the title Grand Victor and Grand Victrix. These titles were used for this year only because the membership overturned the board's action to use these titles. The Select Honors were, however, endorsed by the membership and continued to be given. The 1986 awards were presented at the fifteenth Annual Awards Dinner.

Officers elected for 1987–88 were Carolyn Herbel for a seventh term as president; Dorothy Kendall for a fourth term as vice president; Sondra Rogers for a second term as secretary; Marvin Whitman for a fourth term as treasurer and Edmund Sledzik remained as AKC delegate for the sixth year.

One of the most significant accomplishments for this term was the completion of the four-year project, the AKC video. Formed in 1984 with Stephen Campbell, chairman, the eleven-member committee first drafted dialogue for a slide show and had to readjust when the AKC program changed to video. At the AKC's request the committee was reduced to three members (Stephen Campbell, Dorothy Kendall and Carolyn Herbel) when the finalization of script and shooting was required. The actual filming/shooting was done in 1987.

The 1988 convention was held in Region IV and hosted by the Lhasa Apso Club of Central Colorado. The convention included the eighth Roving National Specialty; the sixth Obedience Trial; the annual meetings and election and the 1987 awards presentation at the Sixteenth Annual Awards Dinner.

The 1988–89 election chose for president Cassandra de la Rosa; for secretary Sally Silva; for treasurer Marvin Whitman and for AKC delegate Edmund Sledzik.

Sally Silva resigned as secretary in February 1989 and was replaced by interim secretary, Lynette Clooney.

Sally Silva also resigned as editor of the *Bulletin* after publishing eleven quarterly issues and as the yearbook editor, having completed the 1984 book.

Susan Giles was appointed editor of *The Lhasa Bulletin*, and the first issue of the new size (8 ½″ × 11″) bi-monthly with advertising and pictures was April 1989. This issue contained an ALAC roster listing 551 members.

The 1989 National Convention was hosted by the National Capital Area Lhasa Apso Club in Region I. The 1988 ALAC awards were presented at the seventeenth Annual Awards Dinner.

For 1989–90, the membership chose Cassandra de la Rosa, president; Susan Giles, vice president; Stephen Campbell, secretary; Carolyn Herbel, treasurer, and Edmund Sledzik, AKC delegate.

Susan Giles continued as editor of the *Bulletin*.

The AKC registered 15,405 Lhasa Apso litters and 30,040 individual Lhasa Apsos in 1989. The 1990 National Convention was hosted by the Northern California Lhasa Apso Club.

The 1990–91 election changed only one officer. Dorothy Kendall was elected president. The other officers remained unchanged.

The 1990 ALAC roster listed 550 members.

AMERICAN LHASA APSO CLUB FUTURITIES

Year	Place	Judge	Entry	Best Puppy	Best Adult
1969	Trenton NJ	Henry H. Stoecker	22	Kinderland's Tonka	Potala Keke's Luckee
1970	Trenton NJ	Grace Licos	10	Chen Tompar Nor	Ch. Kinderland's Nicola
1971	Trenton NJ	Phyllis Marcy	33	Potala Keke's Kal E Ko+	Chok Ke Tu
1972	Trenton NJ	Sharon Binkowski	39	Tabu's Gold Galaxy	Kinderland's L'OO-Ky+
1973	Trenton NJ	Patricia Chenoweth	41	Potala Keke's Fraser	Shyr Lyz D Ly Lah of Ritos+
1974	Western Region—Seattle WA	Onnie Martin	27	San Jo's Raaga Looki Mei+	Chen Krisna Tob Zan
	Eastern Region—Trenton NJ	Ellen Lonigro	63	Chok's Joker	Chok's Coffey+
	Midwest Region—Detroit MI	Ellen Brown	27	Taglha Sinsa of Kinderland+	Ming's Lord Cognac
1975	Western Region—Seattle WA	Carol Kuendel	13	San Jo's Orain+	Mingtree Raaga Marauder
	Eastern Region—Oxon Hill MD	Georgia Palmer	51	Shyr Lyz Fabalous Flirt+	Potala Keke's Golden Gatsby
	Midwest Region—New Orleans LA	Stephen Campbell	21	Blahapolo Topas Ghemston	Windsong Madoro's Mai Li Chin+
1976	Western Region—Pebble Beach CA	Ruth Smith		Alabastrine Girl of Clyde	San Jo's Shenanigan+
	Eastern Region—Boxford MA	Alfred Likewise	30	Kyma Yeti Copper Knight	Chok's Summa Puma+
	Midwest Region—Cincinnati OH	Marianne Nixon	53	Anbara's Abra Ka Dabra+	Bet R's Shangrelu Tuff Stuff
1977	Western Region—Beverly Hills CA	Stephen Campbell	31	San Jo's Kian Kandi Kan	Ch. San Jo's Hussel Bussel+
	Eastern Region—Queens NY	Ellen Lonigro	30	Misti's I've Got Da Spirit	Mor Knoll Rgyal Arisa Volents+
	Midwest Region—Appleton WI	Dorothy Kendall	44	Ch. Luty Diamond Lil+	Ch. Mor Knoll Enchantress
1978	Western Region—Monterey CA	Carolyn Herbel	40	Song's Tomaseta of Bud Bud La+	Marlo's An-Ne Mei
	Eastern Region—Owings Mills MD	Marianne Nixon	56	Mor Knoll Chok's Grand Slam	Potala Keke's Candy Bar+
	Midwest Region—Oak Park MI	Barbara Wood	33	Sankor Skylark	Cancelled+

Year	Place	Judge	Entry	Best Puppy	Best Adult
1979	Eastern Region—Lexington MA	Elizabeth Morgan	20	Piper's Kid Kandito	Hope-Full's Headliner[+]
	Western Region—Seattle WA	Leslie Ann Engen	15	Zhantor Songbird[+]	Zarrah's Kam-Bu
	Midwest Region—Graysdale IL	Phyllis Marcy	17	Kaleko's Fifth Aveue	Char-Ru's Roulette[+]
	Southern Region—Marietta GA	Shirley Scott	15	Misti Acres Strutter[+]	Taglha Kubo
	Hawaiian Region	Jean Kausch (Fergus)	10	Gung Ho Kaz Maz Jin Jin Beau	Galecliff Shazam[+]
1980	Eastern Region—Westminster MD	Georgia Palmer	26	Anbara Rimar's Footloose Fox	Chiz Ari Autumn[+]
	Western Region—Los Angeles CA	Annette Lurton	18	Marlo's I Love Lucy	P.A.A.R.s Red Buttons[+]
	Midwest Region—Topeka KS	Joyce Johanson	16	Donicia's Kara-Sel	Ruffway Patra Pololing[+]
	Southern Region—San Antonio TX	Norman Herbel	17	Chiyoko Love N' Special Things	London House Court Jester[+]
	Hawaiian Region	Carolyn Sledzik	5	Tin Chi Jin Lung	Hale Alii Sweet Okole[+]
1981	Eastern Region—Vienna VA	Gloria Fowler	53	Su Jo's Little Miss Muffet	Misti Acres Gin Jo's Bambi[+]
	Western Region—Portland OR	Brenda O'Donnell	21	Pawprints Coming Up Roses	Potala Wellington Pride And Joy[+]
	Midwest Region—Edina MN	Janet Whitman	27	Wellington's Deadly Niteshade	Cea La's Hustler[+]
	Southern Region—Denton TX	Sandra Nyberg	11	Chin Chin Wong of Kapewood[+]	NO COMPETITION
1982	Eastern Region—Piscataway NJ	Paul Voigt	24	Mor Knoll Kaleko's Black Jack	An-Adayre's Chevas Regal[+]
	Western Region—Seattle WA	Carolyn Herbel	31	San Jo Kian A Pretty Penny[+]	San Jo's Shindig
	Midwest Region—Detroit MI	Dorothy Kendall	39	Qua-La-Ti-s Magic Motion[+]	Gardenway's Precious Moment
1983	Region I—Wellesley MA	Emily Gunning	15	Talimer Sorceress	Kinderland Ta Sen Shogun[+]
	Region II—Long Beach CA	Don Hanson	30	Ruffway Patra Custom Built	Anbara San Jo Scal-A-Wag[+]

Year	Place	Judge	Entry	Best Puppy	Best Adult
	Region III—Wheaton IL	Lynette Clooney	21	Woodlyn's Ruff An Ready+	Joymarc's Sharil Prototype
	Region IV—Kansas City MO	Barry Tompkins	54	San Jo's Hussel Mei+	San Jo's Rusty Nail
1984	Region I—Horseheads NY	Marcia Jewell	17	San Jo's Mor Knoll Bugaboo	Kinderland Ta Sen Bizzi Buzzi+
	Region II—Daly City CA	Valiene Weathers	16	Zarrah Bearly A Flirt O'Anbara+	Anabara Rimar's Hot Ticket
	Region III—Greendale WI	Victor Cohen	26	Haltbar Puttin' On The Ritz	Dan-Ba Sharil Natural High+
	Region IV—Houston TX	Winifred Graye	45	Flo J's The Last Word of Madoros	San Jo's Fleetfire+
1985	Region I—Lockport NY	Cassandra de la Rosa	72	Wyndwood's Sundance of Mai Li	Wyndwood's Stormy Weather+
	Region II—Brush Prairie WA	Wendy Harper	27	San Jo's Quite An Olive+	Ch. Rufkin's Chip Off The Ol Rock
	Region III—Flint MI	Susan Giles	20	Northwind I Kina I Kan	Samara's Sugar Is Sweet+
	Region IV—Fort Collins CO	Barbara Steele	9	Trail's End Seng-ti Khan	NuSeng's Chan-Tilly Lace+
1986	Region I—Annapolis MD	Beverly Drake	15	Northwind The One And Only+	Chalin's Sparkling Sherry
	Region II—Torrance CA	Ellen Lonigro	54	San Jo Anabara Fancy Footwork	Tabu's Bobby Sox Via Hi-Life+
	Region III—Rivergrove IL	Carole Garrett	17	Ruffway Jack Be Nimble	Kinderland Ta Sen Coral Bells+
	Region IV—Houston TX	Roberta Richardson	27	Chiz Ari Wizard of Valhasar	Wyndwood's Ain't Misbehavin+
1987	Region I—North Branch NJ	Lynn Lowy	16	Kai Shan's Mirror Image	Northwind Mardel Chia Mouse+
	Region II—Seattle WA	Dorothy Kendall	8	Hylan Danc'in on the Ceilin+	San Jo's Lambsey D'Ivey
	Region III—Minneapolis MN	Niall Rogers	82	Anbara I Mean Business+	Wellington Exotica Kuroi-Kei
	Region IV—San Antonio TX	Patricia Cruz	22	Anbara Frisky Business+	Mardel Northwind Hot Stuff
1988	Region I—Hamlin NY	Darby McSorley	21	Westgate's Moondancer	Anbara Mor Knoll Rani Sonnet+
	Region II—Costa Mesa CA	Janet Whitman	14	Hoshira Hylan Hello Dolly+	Krisna Zarrah Kamara

Year	Place	Judge	Entry	Best Puppy	Best Adult
	Region III—Milford MI	Frank Trujillo	18	Talimer Show-Off	Rufkins Crackerjacks+
	Region IV—Thornton CO	Marion Knowlton	82	Hylan Hoshira Sweet Charity+	Kinderland Ta Sen Sure Fire
1989	Region I—Lanham MD	Patricia Chenoweth	53	Marlo Party-Time+	Barjea's Rhett Butler
	Region II—Brush Prairie WA	Cindy Butsic	16	Zhantor La De Da Pumpkin	Rufkins Katas Front Pg News+
	Region III—Racine County WI	Beverly Drake	21	Woodlyn's Rare Vintage	Marquis Dali Do Wah+
	Region IV—Houston TX	Carol Strong	20	Wyndwood Best Foot Forward+	Jeviehan Britt Hark The Angel
1990	Region I—Ambler PA	Don Hanson	19	Misti Acres Sandpiper	Tabu's Wine 'N Roses+
	Region II—Millbrae CA	Victor Cohen	49	Remarc Namaste Las Vegas+	Hyland Sho Tru Storm Bird
	Region III—St. Paul MN	Kay Hales	4	Woodlyn Spit'in Image+	NO COMPETITION
	Region IV—St. Joseph MO	Nancy Plunkett	21	Raz's On The Mark+	Kaleko's Leading Lady
1991	Region I—Annapolis MD	Richard Camacho	16	Misti Acres Penny Candy	Ch. Kasha Piper Me Too*
	Region II—Banks OR	Don Evans	16	Zhantor Cappuccino*	Barjea Martha's Liz
	Region III—Troy MI	Ann Lanterman	68	Anbara San Jo Look Who's Talkin'	Bihar Potpourri Harle-Kwin*
	Region IV—Fort Collins CO	Linda Jarrett	14	Fleetfire Timbers' Uptown Girl	Claret Anbara Raisin Denver*

+Indicates Grand Futurity Winner

288

EASTERN AMERICAN LHASA APSO CLUB SPECIALTIES

Year	Place	Judge	Entry	Best of Breed
1966	Trenton NJ	James Trullinger	52	Ch. Kham of Norbu-lingka ROM** (D)
1967	Trenton NJ	Keith Browne	50	Ch. Kyi Chu Shara ROM* (B)
1968	Trenton NJ	Harry H. Brunt	59	Ch. Kyi Chu Friar Tuck ROM* (D)
1969	Trenton NJ	Henry H. Stoecker	83	Ch. Ku Ka Boh of Pick-wick (D)
1970	Trenton NJ	Cyril Bernfeld	112	Ch. Kyi Chu Friar Tuck ROM* (D)
1971	Trenton NJ	Jay C. Shaeffer	116	Ch. Balrene Chia Pao (D)
1972	Trenton NJ	Frank Landgraf	172	Ch. Chen Korum Ti ROM** (D)
1973	Trenton NJ	David Doane (Dogs & Intersex) (Kenneth Stine Bitches)	167	Ch. BarCon's The Avenger ROM** (D)
1974	Trenton NJ	Alfred Likewise (Dogs & Intersex) (Joseph Faigel Bitches)	155	Ch. BarCon's The Avenger ROM** (D)
1975	Trenton NJ	Keke Blumberg (Kahn)	105	Ch. Daktazl Tsung (D)
1976	Louisville KY	Robert Berndt	101	Ch. Potala Keke's Yum Yum ROM* (B)
1977	Syracuse NY	Edmund R. Sledzik	113	Ch. Rimar's Rumpelstilt-skin ROM* (D)
1978	Falls Church VA	Edd Bivin	114	Ch. Rimar's Rumpelstilt-skin ROM* (D)
1979	Baltimore MD	Jack Russell	91	Ch. San Jo's Raaga Looki Mei ROM* (D)
1980	Ludwigs Corners PA	Norman Patton	80	Orlane's Intrepid ROM** (D)

WESTERN AMERICAN LHASA APSO CLUB SPECIALTIES

Year	Place	Judge	Entry	Best of Breed
1969	Beverly Hills CA	Forrest N. Hall	62	Ch. Teako of Abbotsford (D)
1970	Beverly Hills CA	Heywood Hartley	85	Ch. Everglo Zijuh Tomba ROM** (D)
1971	Beverly Hills CA	O. C. Harriman	100	Ch. Chen Korum Ti ROM** (D)
1972	Beverly Hills CA	William Bergum	124	Ch. Chen Korum Ti ROM** (D)
1973	Beverly Hills CA	Alfred Likewise	103	Ch. Sharpette's Gaylord (D)
1974	Beverly Hills CA	Keke Blumberg (Kahn)	92	Ch. Blackbay Georgana of Yin Hi I.Q. (B)
1975	Beverly Hills CA	Robert Berndt	111	Ch. Chen Korum Ti ROM** (D)

1976	Dallas TX	Onnie Martin	73	Ch. Potala Keke's Yum Yum ROM* (B)
1977	Houston TX	Jay C. Shaeffer	95	Ch. Yojimbo Orion (D)
1978	San Francisco CA	William Bergum	49	Ch. Everglo Sundance ROM (D)
1979	Seattle WA	Alfred Likewise	44	Ch. Maran's Tiger Tango (D)
1980	Stockton CA	Keke Blumberg (Kahn)	35	Ch. On Ba Jo Bo ROM* (D)

ROVING NATIONAL AMERICAN LHASA APSO CLUB SPECIALTIES

1981	Vienna VA	Joseph Gregory	133	Ch. Orlane's Intrepid ROM** (D)
1982	Seattle WA	Nick Calicura	101	Ch. Ruffway Patra Pololing (D)
1983	Kansas City MO	Stephen Campbell	151	Ch. San Jo's Hussel Bussel ROM** (B)
1984	Houston TX	Edd Bivin	120	Ch. San Jo's Hussel Bussel ROM** (B)
1985	Lockport NY	Dorothy Nickles	214	Ch. Nexus Lam Kam Chin (D)
1986	Torrance CA	Tom Stevenson	205	Ch. Tashi's Rock-A-Bye Baby-Dieh (B)
1987	Minneapolis MN	Norman Herbel	227	Suntory Superfudge (D)
1988	Thornton CO	Barbara Wood	198	Ch. Samara's Sugar Is Sweet (B)
1989	Lanham MD	Keke Kahn	217	Ch. Bihar's Revenger of Sammi Raja* (D)
1990	Millbrae CA	Joseph Gregory	160	Ch. Sho Tru Hylan Stetson (D)
1991	Troy MI	Carolyn Herbel	215	Ch. Fanfair Who Goes There (D)